UM
UM

ORNITHOGALUM
UMBELLATUM

AGROSTEMMA
GITHAGO

JN 06

Stumpwork Medieval Flora

Stumpwork Medieval Flora

JANE NICHOLAS

SALLYMILNER PUBLISHING

To my dear sister Judith
—with love

First published in 2009 by
Sally Milner Publishing Pty Ltd
734 Woodville Road
Binda NSW 2583 AUSTRALIA

© Jane Nicholas 2009

Design: Anna Warren, Warren Ventures
Editing: Anne Savage
Photography: Tim Connolly
Illustrations: Wendy Gorton

Printed in China

National Library of Australia Cataloguing-in-Publication entry

Author	Nicholas, Jane.
Title:	Stumpwork medieval flora / Jane Nicholas.
ISBN:	9781863513968
Series:	Milner craft series
Notes:	Includes index. Bibliography.
Subjects	Stumpwork Stumpwork--Patterns. Embroidery--Patterns.

Dewey Number: 746.44

Disclaimer
Information and instructions given in this book are presented in good faith, but no warranty is given nor results guaranteed, nor is freedom from any patent to be inferred. As we have no control over physical conditions surrounding application of information herein contained in this book, the author and publisher disclaim any liability for untoward results.

10 9 8 7 6 5 4 3 2 1

Contents

Introduction

I have long been fascinated by the illuminated manuscripts of the medieval era, seeking out examples in museums and galleries wherever I travel. The pages of my journals abound with cuttings gleaned from calendars, magazines and cards accumulated over many years. One of these cuttings, an image of a Bittersweet plant from an unidentified illuminated Book of Hours, was the subject of a class that I taught in New Zealand in 2004. During that visit, a friend showed me a wonderful book which she had purchased in France—*Promenade dans des Jardins Disparus* (*A Walk through the Lost Gardens*), produced by Michèle Bilimoff in 2001. I was enchanted! This book contained all of the plants from the *Grandes Heures d'Anne de Bretagne* (*Great Hours of Anne of Brittany*), a Book of Hours created by Jean Bourdichon in 1508, including the Bittersweet plant which had inspired my current project.

While I was already familiar with some of the often-published images from this Book of Hours, it was not until I turned the pages of *Promenade* that the full splendour of over three hundred different plants in as many panels and borders was revealed to me. I just had to embroider some of them. I ordered the book and after agonising over the myriad possibilities, I managed to select eight flowers. I have interpreted these in stumpwork embroidery for this book of medieval flora.

Five of the plants have been worked as botanical specimens, with the Latin name stitched beneath them— *Agrostemma githago*, *Geranium robertianum*, *Ornithogalum umbellatum*, *Tanacetum vulgare* and *Specularia hybrida*. These plants display the buds, blossoms and seed cases of the flower, and an assortment of insects nestling in the foliage. Another three plants have been presented as illuminated panels—*Solanum dulcamara*, *Galanthus nivalus* and *Lathius sylvestris*. As medieval illuminations abound with vibrant colours—red for love, blue for fidelity, green for hope and freedom, purple for majesty, yellow for understanding, white for innocence, wisdom and joy (as described by Candace Bahouth in *Medieval Needlepoint*)—I couldn't resist working richly coloured borders, embellished with gold thread and beads, around these three floral panels. The whole experience has been a joy!

What is it about medieval illuminated manuscripts that makes them so compelling?

> *... illumination is not meant for a large audience; a viewer's experience must be intimate ... Your patience will be rewarded by a new world opening before your eyes.*
> ALEXANDER STERLIGOV, *Western European Illuminated Manuscripts*, PAGES 9–10

I am reminded of my first encounter, in 2002, with the work of Keith Lo Bue, a jeweller, sculptor and assemblage artist. Keith commented that he liked to 'reward peoples' patience' when they take the time to look at and explore his work. I was spellbound by his pieces—the exquisite workmanship, the attention to fine detail and the element of 'surprise' to reward close scrutiny! The same characteristics are true of illuminated manuscripts—perhaps that is the reason for their allure.

Maybe it is similar qualities that make stumpwork so appealing—the intimate nature of the work, the considered placement of each stitch. Add to that the pleasure in taking time—to select exactly the right shade of silk, to research the botanical details of each plant, to add a 'surprise' with the choice of an insect—faithfully interpreted with fabric, wire, beads and thread. Perhaps this helps to explain the continuing passion that many of us have for this form of embroidery.

Pomegranates bordering a page from Les Grandes Heures d'Anne de Bretagne

ILLUMINATED MANUSCRIPTS AND
Les Grandes Heures d'Anne de Bretagne

The term 'illuminated manuscript' refers to the decorated or illustrated handwritten books produced throughout Europe in the Middle Ages. Commencing in the third century, with the development of parchment, or vellum (a smooth animal-skin surface for writing), the creation of illuminated manuscripts flourished until well after the advent of the printing press in the mid-fifteenth century.

Until the eleventh century, most manuscripts were produced by monks working in special rooms set aside for them in monasteries (scriptoria). The work of the scribes was embellished by the artistic and calligraphic skills of the illuminators. The word 'illuminated' comes from the Latin *illuminare*, which means 'to adorn', and the ecclesiastical passages that the monks painstakingly copied were indeed adorned, with miniature paintings, elaborate initial letters and richly ornamented border decorations. These manuscripts were mostly kept in the communal monastic library as private ownership was uncommon.

In the thirteenth century, the rise of universities in cities such as Paris, Bologna, and later Oxford, prompted a corresponding increase in demand for books, and manuscripts began to be produced by professional illuminators in commercial workshops. With the increase in individual ownership and the trade of books, the range of subject matter broadened. Wealthy patrons could choose from literary, scientific and historical texts; tales of chivalry, knights and courtly love; or sumptuously decorated books for private devotion.

The creation of manuscripts in the late Middle Ages involved a number of professional activities, from parchment maker to scribe, from illuminator to miniature painter, from binder to bookseller.[1] Using quills commonly made from goose feathers, scribes copied the texts, leaving spaces for the addition of miniatures, decorated initials and borders. These were coloured with pigments mixed from animal, vegetable and mineral substances. The colours were rich and luminous. One of the most exotic and costly colours was lapis lazuli, obtained by grinding a deep blue stone from the Orient. *Verte de flamme*, a green dye, was extracted from the wild iris; vermilion, the brightest of reds, was made from cinnabar (red mercuric oxide); a darker red came from the mineral red ochre; and violet, a precious vegetable colour, was extracted from sunflowers.[2] Burnished, fine gold leaf was often added to these vibrantly coloured illustrations as an indication of wealth and status.

In the fourteenth and fifteenth centuries, the production of beautifully crafted manuscripts flourished throughout Europe. Splendidly illuminated Books of Hours—prayer books for noblemen and noblewomen—were popular, and an extraordinarily coveted possession. The aristocracy attached the highest value to such devotional books, which were often lavishly illustrated with miniatures and illuminated in gold and expensive pigments. These works of art were prized as much for their beauty as for their textual contents. A Book of Hours typically contained a Calendar detailing the seasons and saints of the church year, along with devotional texts adapted for use by the laity. These included readings from the Gospels, the Hours of the Virgin (to be said at the eight canonical hours of the day), the Penitential Psalms, the Litany, the Hours of the Cross, the Hours of the Holy Ghost, the Office of the Dead and prayers in Latin or French.

One of the most magnificent and celebrated of all Books of Hours is *Les Grandes Heures d'Anne de Bretagne*. This extraordinary work was commissioned by Queen Anne of Brittany in 1500

---

1   Des Cowley and Clare Williamson, *The World of the Book*, page 14

2   Candace Bahouth, *Medieval Needlepoint*, page 94

Roses and lilies bordering a page from Les Grandes Heures d'Anne de Bretagne

and was completed, by court artist Jean Bourdichon, in 1508. Bourdichon produced a wide range of work, including jewellery, stained glass, paintings and portraits, but the *Grandes Heures* is considered to be the pinnacle of his achievements. Measuring 30 x 19.5 cm (11 3/4 x 7 3/4 in), it is too large for private devotion and was probably designed for the Queen's Chapel. For her daily use, Anne had smaller Books of Hours, several of which survive—a *Petites Heures*, a *Très Petite Heures*, measuring 12 x 7.7 cm (4 3/4 x 3 in), and another, even smaller *Très Petite Heures* which measures only 6.6 x 4.6 cm (2 3/4 x 1 3/4 in)! Anne was born in 1477, the heiress daughter of the Duke of Brittany, Francis II, and Marguerite de Foix. She married two successive kings of France, Charles VIII and Louis XII, and died in 1514, leaving behind her a reputation for piety, patronage of the arts and a love of luxury (characteristics all evident in her Books of Hours).

Les Grandes Heures d'Anne de Bretagne contains 49 full-page miniatures enclosed by *trompe-l'oeil* gold frames, which decorate the different areas of the liturgy and calendar, and over 300 pages of devotional texts, either fully or partially bordered by realistic renderings of plants, insects and animals. While Bourdichon's miniatures command great admiration, it is his paintings of 337 different plants in the borders and panels surrounding the text which are so awe-inspiring. The botanical accuracy with which the flowers are depicted in their gold-painted borders is the distinctive feature of this Book of Hours.

While contemporary Flemish illuminators were realistically portraying single flower heads or small sprays in their borders, Bourdichon achieved a new effect by greatly increasing the number of plants depicted, and by painting them as if for a florilegium or herbal. The rendering of realistic shadows behind each image further enhanced his work. He often showed whole plants, complete with roots or bulbs, displaying both the berries and the blossoms of the flower in a single design, and labelled each with its Latin and popular

French names. The flowers, fruits and vegetables in his borders are inhabited by a glittering array of insects and small animals, including the little monkeys that Anne of Brittany loved. Butterflies, ladybirds, flies, grasshoppers, dragonflies, snails, little lizards, tortoises, rabbits, caterpillars and worms are everywhere, all executed in perfect detail (notably, there is not a single bird). It is possible that the plants were copied from specimens grown at the royal gardens at Amboise and Blois. With the work involved in collecting, identifying, painting and labelling them all, it is no wonder that the book took eight years to complete! It is now preserved in the collection of the Bibliothèque nationale de France (BnF) (MS lat. 9474).

Star of Bethlehem illumination from Les Grandes Heures d'Anne de Bretagne, Ms Latin 9474, Folio 128, Bibliothèque nationale de France.

PART 1:
Botanical Specimens

Sixteenth century grape and snail motif

Before you begin ...

The projects described in this and the following section—five botanical specimens and three illuminated panels—are worked with surface embroidery and stumpwork techniques. Before you begin, it will be helpful to read the following information:

- The diagrams at the beginning of each project are actual size. The explanatory drawings accompanying the instructions have often been enlarged for clarity.

- Read through all the instructions before commencing work on a project. As a general rule, work all surface embroidery before applying any detached elements.

- Detailed instructions for the transferring of designs are provided in Part 3: Techniques, Equipment and Stitch Glossary.

- I have used Au Ver à Soie stranded silk, Soie d'Alger, for most of the embroidery. The Au Ver à Soie thread company have been going through a process of re-colouring their threads over the past few years. The colours I have used are from the *new* range of colours. Where possible, I have given DMC Stranded Cotton equivalents for the Soie d'Alger threads—the colours are close but *not* exactly the same.

- The embroidery is worked with one strand of thread unless otherwise stipulated.

- For general information regarding techniques and equipment, please refer to Techniques, Equipment and Stitch Glossary. If you are new to stumpwork, it is important that you read this section before undertaking any of the projects. As there is not the space here to provide detailed instructions on basic stumpwork techniques, you may like to refer to one of the stumpwork embroidery books listed in the Bibliography.

Each botanical specimen may be worked and framed individually, or work two, three, four or five of them separately, then combine them in the one frame. You may prefer to stitch all specimens on one piece of fabric, as a panel. I chose this option and worked the five plants on ivory satin, mounted in a slate frame. Having taught these pieces for several years now, I have seen a variety of interpretations, both in the number and arrangement of the various specimens and in the choice of background fabric. Instead of the more traditional ivory satin, some have chosen coloured silk for the backgrounds—cream, light blue, grey, pale gold, salmon, soft green and even black. They all looked lovely!

Fabric and Frame Requirements

TO WORK EACH PANEL SEPARATELY

If working an individual specimen you will need the following:

- background fabric of choice (satin or silk): 30 cm (12 in) square
- backing fabric (calico or quilter's muslin): 30 cm (12 in) square
- a good quality 25 cm (10 in) embroidery hoop

If you choose to work two, three, four or five specimens separately, it is important that you have enough of the same fabric to work all of the pieces.

Preparation

See the individual project for instructions on mounting fabrics and tracing the design outlines.

To Work All Panels on One Piece of Fabric

If you would like to work two, three, four or five specimens together, on the same piece of fabric, you will need the following:

- background fabric of choice (satin or silk): 44 cm x 30 cm ($17^1/_2$ x 12 in); this is enough for all five panels

- backing fabric (firm calico or muslin) sized to suit the slate (or rectangular) frame that you are using—at least 52 x 42 cm ($20^1/_2$ x $16^1/_2$ in); this allows for turnings at the edges

- a slate (or rectangular) frame—the top bars need a web length at least 48 cm (19 in) and the spacer or stretcher bars need to be long enough to allow at least 34 cm ($13^1/_2$ in) between the top (web) bars

Preparation

1. Mount the calico backing fabric and the background fabric of your choice into the slate or rectangular frame (see page 258).

2. To enable accurate placement of each specimen's traced outline, transfer a grid to the background fabric as follows (adjust the grid for two, three or four specimens):

   (a) On a large sheet of paper, draw a rectangle 35 x 16 cm ($13^3/_4$ x $6^3/_8$ in). Divide the rectangle into five smaller rectangles, each 7 x 16 cm ($2^3/_4$ in x $6^3/_8$ in). Cut out the large rectangle and use as a template.

(b) Tape the large rectangle template to the background fabric (checking that it is aligned with the straight grain of the fabric), then mark all corners of the small rectangles with fine needles or pins (twelve points in all). Remove the template. With fine silk or rayon thread in a sharps needle, make long stitches from each corner point to form five stitched rectangles on the background fabric (secure the thread at the back). This will be used as a reference grid when transferring the skeleton design outlines and the outlines for the botanical names.

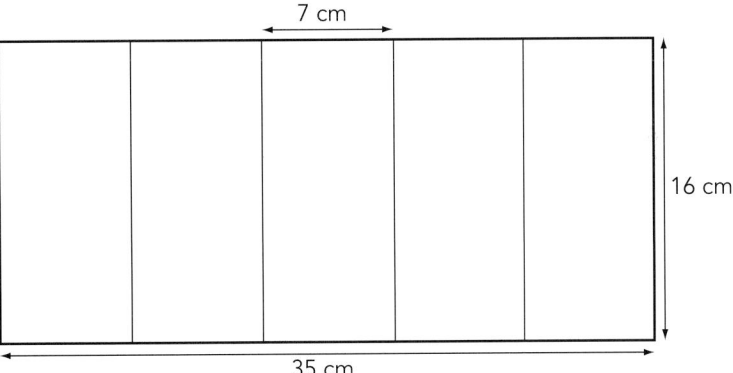

7 cm

16 cm

35 cm

3. See the individual project for instructions on tracing the design outlines within the stitched rectangle.

4. Cover all completed and unworked panels (except the specimen you are working on) with folded strips of white acid-free tissue paper, pinned to the top and the bottom of the frame, to prevent soiling and damage.

Corncockle and Dragonfly

The Corncockle, Agrostemma githago, is a summer-flowering wild flower, with dark pinkish-purple flowers and long leafy sepals. Formerly a pervasive weed, possibly the same plant as the tares of the New Testament parable, the corncockle is now very rare.

This plant was once regarded as the 'curse of medieval cornfields', a view confirmed by Gerard in his description: 'What hurt it doth among corn, the spoile of bread, as well in colour, taste and unwholesomenesse, is better known than desired'. If corncockle seeds happened to be ground up with the corn, the resulting bread was too bitter to eat. In an attempt to eliminate the presence of this weed in their harvest, an Easter custom called 'corn-showing' developed on farms in Herefordshire, the purpose of which was to weed the corncockle seedlings from the cornfields. The custom died out about 1880 with the arrival of agricultural weedkillers.

At Easter the rustics have a custom called corn-showing. Parties are made to pick out cockle from the wheat. Before they set out they take with them cake and cider, and, says my informant, a yard of toasted cheese. The first person who picks the first cockle from the wheat has the first kiss of the maid and the first slice of the cake.

T.D. Fosbroke, 1821

Worked on a background of ivory satin, this small stumpwork panel is one of a series of embroidered botanical specimens and insects inspired by the illuminated pages of medieval manuscripts. This design features the Corncockle, *Agrostemma githago*, a summer-flowering weed common in medieval cornfields, with detached dark pink petals and long leafy sepals worked with wire and needle-weaving. A Broad-bodied Dragonfly, *Libellula depressa*, with detached gauzy wings and a padded leather abdomen, a shiny blue beetle, *Plagiodera versicolora*, and a tiny Ladybird complete the design. The botanical name of the plant may be embroidered at the base of the specimen.

AGROSTEMMA
GITHAGO

*Diagrams are
actual size*

Dragonfly
abdomen outline

Blue beetle wing outline

Fore wing

Hind wing

**Dragonfly
wing outlines**

Ladybird
wing
outline

Ladybird
abdomen
outline

Circle template

Detached petal
outline

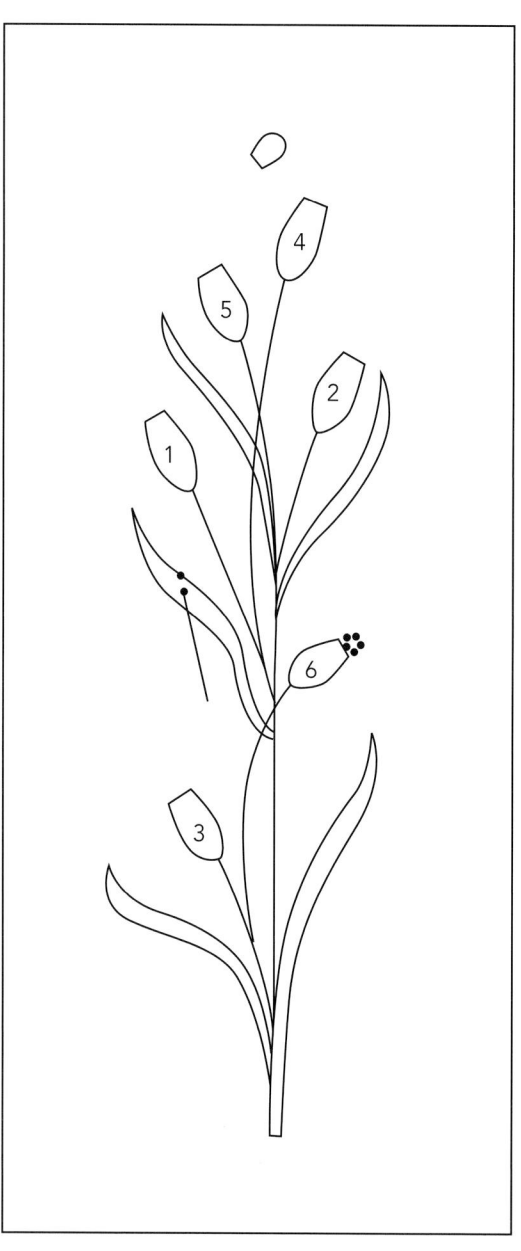

Skeleton outline

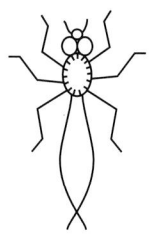

Dragonfly leg diagram

Corncockle base padding outlines

AGROSTEMMA
GITHAGO

Botanical name template

Overall Requirements

This is the *complete* list of requirements for this specimen.
For ease of use, the requirements of each individual element
are repeated under its heading—for example, Corncockle
requirements, Broad-bodied Dragonfly requirements.

- ivory satin background fabric: 30 cm (12 in) square
- quilter's muslin (or calico) backing fabric: 30 cm (12 in)
  square (*if working all panels on one piece of fabric, refer to the
  instructions on page 18*)

- quilter's muslin: three 20 cm (8 in) squares
- red cotton fabric (homespun): 15 cm (6 in) square
- bronze mottled organza: 15 cm (6 in) square
- pearl metal organdie: 15 cm (6 in) square
- copper metal organdie: 2.5 cm (1 in) square
- grey felt: 10 x 8 cm (4 x 3 in)
- paper-backed fusible web: 15 x 8 cm (6 x 3 in)
- bronze snakeskin: 5 cm (2 in) square

- 25 cm (10 in) embroidery hoop or stretcher bars (if working
  as a single panel)
- 10 cm (4 in) embroidery hoops
- needles:
  crewel/embroidery sizes 9 and 10
  milliners/straw size 9
  sharps size 12
  tapestry size 28
  sharp yarn darners sizes 14–18

- embroidery equipment (see page 266)

- dark green stranded thread (stems): Soie d'Alger 3725 *or* DMC 935
- medium green stranded thread (leaves, sepals): Soie d'Alger 2126 *or* DMC 937
- light green stranded thread (flower base): Soie d'Alger 2133 *or* DMC 3364
- maroon stranded thread (flowers): Soie d'Alger 3046 *or* DMC 3685
- dark pink stranded thread (flowers): Soie d'Alger 1034 *or* DMC 600
- pale pink stranded thread (flowers): Cifonda Art Silk 941 *or* DMC 3689
- dark purple stranded thread (beetle): Soie d'Alger 3326 *or* DMC 939
- blue fine stranded thread (beetle): Cifonda Art Silk 988 *or* DMC 825
- black stranded thread (ladybird): DMC 310
- red stranded thread (ladybird): DMC 349

- brown/black metallic thread (dragonfly, beetle): Kreinik Cord 201c
- copper/black metallic thread (dragonfly): Kreinik Cord 215c
- black soft metallic thread (dragonfly): Madeira Metallic No.40 col.70
- black metallic thread (ladybird): Kreinik Cord 005c
- variegated brown/gold chenille thread (dragonfly): col. Amber Marine
- light bronze rayon machine thread (dragonfly): Madeira Rayon 40 col. 1338

This sixteenth century image of a corncockle inspired this piece.

- grey/green rayon machine thread (botanical name): Madeira Rayon 40 col. 1062
- nylon clear thread: Madeira Monofil 60 col. 1001

- 3 mm bronze/blue bead
- Mill Hill petite beads 40374 (purple/green)
- Mill Hill petite beads 42014 (black)

- 33 gauge white covered wire (petals): nine 9 cm ($3^{1}/_{2}$ in) lengths (colour hot pink if desired, Copic RV09 Fuchsia)
- 33 gauge white covered wire (sepals): three 12 cm ($4^{3}/_{4}$ in) lengths (colour green if desired, Copic G99 Green)
- 33 gauge white covered wire (ladybird): 10 cm (4 in) length (colour red if desired, Copic R17 Lipstick Orange)
- 33 gauge white covered wire (beetle): 12 cm ($4^{3}/_{4}$ in) length (colour blue if desired, Copic B18 Lapis Lazuli)
- 28 gauge silver uncovered wire (dragonfly wings): four 12 cm ($4^{3}/_{4}$ in) lengths

---

- thin card for rectangle template and dragonfly abdomen
- heavyweight (110 gsm) tracing paper
- translucent removable tape (e.g. Scotch Removable Magic Tape)

Preparation

1. Mount the satin background fabric and the muslin backing into the 25 cm (10 in) embroidery hoop or frame. If working all panels on one piece of fabric, follow the instructions on page 258.

2. Cut a rectangle from thin card, 7 x 16 cm (2³/₄ x 6¹/₄ in). Place the rectangle template on the satin (checking that it is aligned with the straight grain of the fabric) and insert a fine needle at each corner point. Remove the template. Using rayon machine thread in a sharps needle, make long stitches from each corner point to form a stitched rectangle on the front fabric. This will be used as a reference grid when transferring the skeleton design outline and the lines for the botanical name.

3. Using a fine lead pencil, trace the skeleton outline and rectangle outline of the botanical specimen onto tracing paper. Turn the tracing paper over and draw over the skeleton outline only—not the rectangle. With the tracing paper right side up, transfer the skeleton outline to the background fabric with a stylus, lining up the traced rectangle with the stitched rectangle (it helps to have a board underneath the frame of fabric to provide a firm surface).

CORNCOCKLE

Requirements

- quilter's muslin: two 20 cm (8 in) squares
- grey felt: 10 x 8 cm (4 x 3 in)
- paper-backed fusible web: 10 x 8 cm (4 x 3 in)
- dark green stranded thread: Soie d'Alger 3725 *or* DMC 935
- medium green stranded thread: Soie d'Alger 2126 *or* DMC 937
- light green stranded thread: Soie d'Alger 2133 *or* DMC 3364
- maroon stranded thread: Soie d'Alger 3046 *or* DMC 3685
- dark pink stranded thread: Soie d'Alger 1034 *or* DMC 600
- pale pink stranded thread: Cifonda Art Silk 941 *or* DMC 3689
- 33 gauge white covered wire (petals): nine 9 cm (3$^1/_2$ in) lengths (colour hot pink if desired, Copic RV09 Fuchsia)
- 33 gauge white covered wire (sepals): three 12 cm (4$^3/_4$ in) lengths (colour green if desired, Copic G99 Green)

STEMS AND LEAVES
Follow the recommended order of work.

Stems
The stems are worked in stem stitch with two strands of thread (one each of dark green and medium green). Use a size 9 crewel needle.

Leaves

The leaves are embroidered in padded satin stitch with one strand of medium green thread in a size 10 crewel needle.

1. Outline the leaf in split stitch then work padding stitches inside the outline—either with straight stitches or chain stitches (for a more raised effect).

2. Embroider the leaf in satin stitch, enclosing the outline.

Order of Work

1. Embroider the lower right leaf.

2. To work the main stem, start at the lower left corner of the embroidered leaf and work a row of stem stitch, next to the leaf, then along the line to flower 5. Starting at the upper edge of the embroidered leaf, work a second row of stem stitch, next to the first, then continue along the line to bud 2.

3. Embroider the remaining leaves, working over the stem lines when necessary.

4. Starting at the main stem, work a row of stem stitch along the line to bud 1.

5. Work a row of stem stitch along the line to bud 4, taking the needle under the embroidered leaf then over the first stem.

6. Starting at the main stem, work a row of stem stitch along the line to flower 6, embroidering over the leaf and the stem.

7. Work a row of stem stitch along the line to bud 3.

BUDS 1 AND 2

Base

The bases of the buds and flowers are padded with grey felt (one or two layers) applied with one strand of light green thread in a size 10 crewel needle.

1. Using the base padding outlines as a guide, trace the following base shapes onto paper-backed fusible web then fuse to grey felt:
   - two shapes for bases 1, 2, 3, 4 and 5 (one is the actual size, one slightly smaller)
   - one shape only for flower base 6

   Carefully cut out the shapes.

2. Apply the felt shapes (web side up) to the background fabric with small stab stitches around the curved outside edges, applying the smallest shape first (except flower 6 which has only one layer of padding). Do not work any stitches across the top edges of the felt.

3. Work a row of buttonhole stitch around the curved outside edge (stitches about 1.5 mm apart). The base is not embroidered until the sepals are applied.

Background Sepals

Two sepals are worked on the background in needle-weaving with one strand of medium green thread. Use a size 10 crewel needle to stitch the loops and a tapestry needle for the needle-weaving.

1. Using the sepal placement diagram as a guide, trace the base 1 shape and the two dots above (which indicate the length and position of the background sepals) onto tracing paper. Transfer these dots to the background fabric with a stitch (or fine needles)—do not mark with pencil as it may show.

2. To work the loop for the first sepal, bring the needle out at A and down again at B (a scant 1 mm above the top edge of the felt), making a loop the length of the dot marked on the background. Work a second loop, exactly as the first, to make the loop double. Pass a length of scrap thread through the loop to enable it to be held under tension while working the needle-weaving.

3. Bring the needle out again at the base of the loop and change to a tapestry needle. Holding the loop under tension with the scrap thread, slide the needle through the centre of the loop, alternately from the right then the left, to fill the loop with needle-weaving, keeping the tension firm and even. Remove the scrap thread then insert the needle through the background dot, allowing the sepal to curve slightly. Secure the thread at the back. Work a second sepal in the same way, bringing the needle out at A and going down again at C.

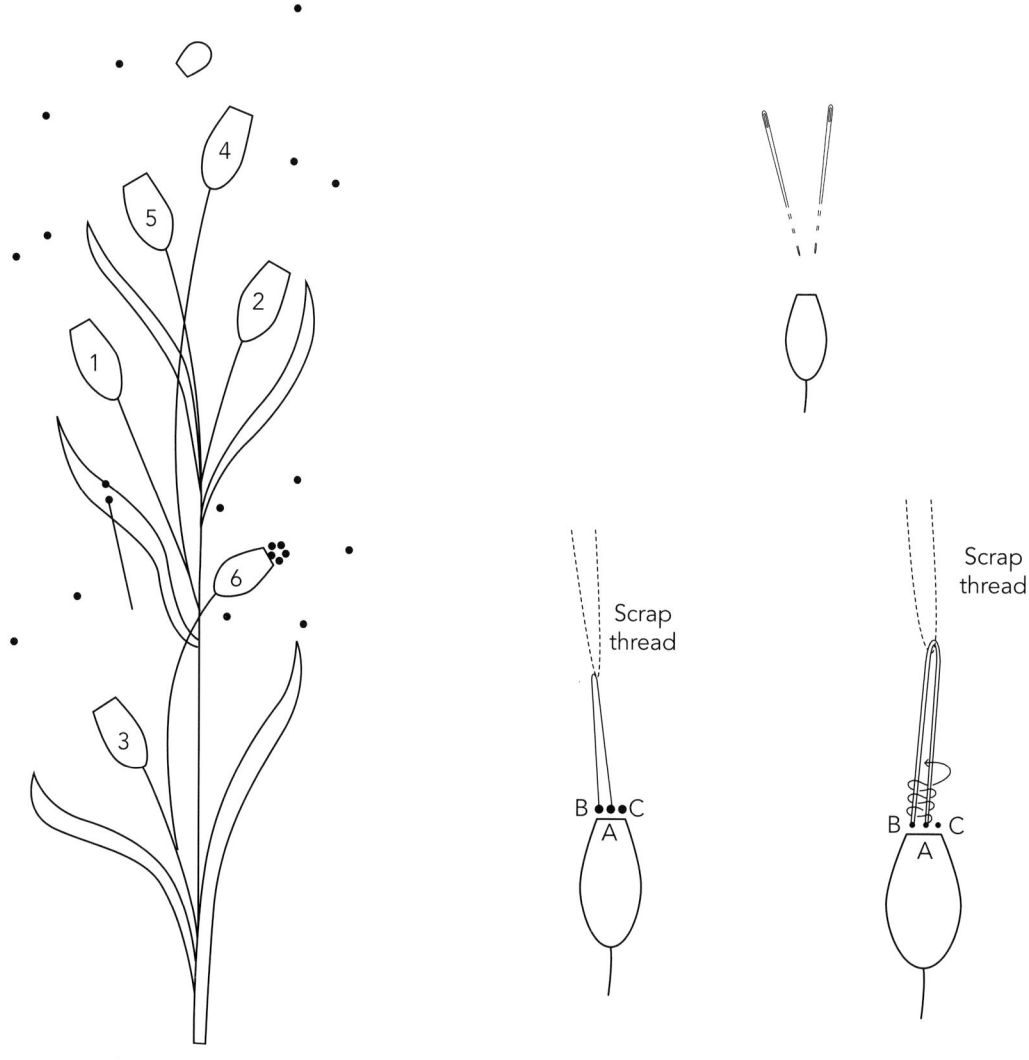

Sepal placement diagram

Detached Sepals

To work a detached sepal, bend the wire into a loop then fill with needle-weaving, using one strand of medium green thread in a tapestry needle.

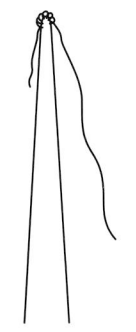

1. Starting with a short tail, wrap the centre 2–3 mm ($^1/_8$ in) of the wire with the medium green thread, leaving a long tail of thread at the end of the wrapping (this will be used for the needle-weaving). Do not secure either tail of thread at this stage. Bend the wire in half (in the centre of the wrapped section) and squeeze gently with tweezers to prevent the wrapped ends from unravelling.

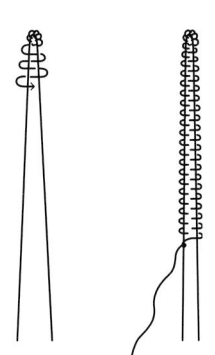

2. Adjust both tails of the wrapping thread (unwrapping if necessary) so that the bend in the wire is neatly covered. Holding the shorter tail under tension, start needle-weaving with the remaining longer tail of thread, weaving 'up' between the wires and 'down' around the outside of the wires, alternately from left to right (enclosing the shorter tail—trim after several wraps). Continue needle-weaving over the wires until the sepal measures about 1.8 cm ($^3/_4$ in). Secure the tail of thread. Work three sepals for each bud.

3. Using a yarn darner, insert the wire and thread tails of the three detached sepals (through three separate holes) in the small gap between the top of the felt and the surface sepals. Insert the side sepals first (level with the top of the felt) then the centre sepal slightly in front of them (underneath the top edge of the felt). Adjust the length of the detached sepals to correspond with the surface sepals then secure at the back of the bud with a few stitches. Do not trim the wire tails until the bud is finished.

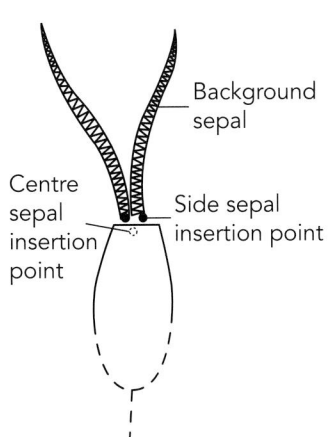

Background sepal

Centre sepal insertion point

Side sepal insertion point

To Complete the Bud

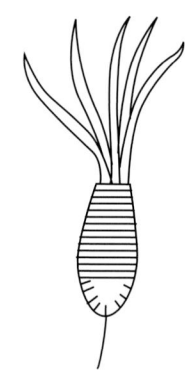

1. Using one strand of light green thread, cover the bud with satin stitch, enclosing the buttonhole outline and the tails of wire at the back. Starting at the top edge, work several stitches on top of each to cover the felt and enclose the base of the sepals, then satin stitch towards the stem, trimming the wire tails before the stem is reached.

2. With one strand of medium green thread in a sharps needle, work three wrapped stitches to form ribs over the satin-stitched base, working the two side ribs first, then the centre rib (each rib resembles a fine bullion stitch):

   - Make a stitch from the base of the bud (where the stem joins), over the satin stitch, into the base of a side sepal (carefully inserting the needle between the wires).

   - Come out again at the base of the bud and, holding the thread taut, slide the needle under and around the stitch to wrap it with thread (approximately 24 wraps; use the eye of the needle or a tapestry needle when wrapping). Insert the needle into the base of the sepal and secure the thread.

   - Work two more ribs from the base of the bud into the base of the remaining sepals.

3. Use tweezers to shape the detached sepals as desired.

Bud 3

Detached Petals

The remaining corncockle buds and flowers require nine detached petals—all the same size and worked the same way.

1. Mount muslin into a 10 cm (4 in) hoop and trace nine detached petal shapes.

2. Using one strand of dark pink thread in a size 10 crewel needle, couch wire around the petal outline, leaving two tails of wire at the base that touch but do not cross. Buttonhole stitch the wire to the muslin then work a row of split stitch around the inside edge of the wire. Work some padding stitches inside the petal.

3. Embroider the petal in satin stitch, enclosing the split stitch and working the stitches towards the base of the petal.

4. With one strand of pale pink thread in a sharps needle, work five straight stitches, over the satin stitch, towards the base of the petal. Cut out the petals.

Base and Background Sepals

Apply the padding and work the two background sepals as for bud 1, leaving a 1 mm gap between the top edge of the felt and the base of the sepals for the insertion of a detached petal and the detached sepals.

Detached Petal and Sepals

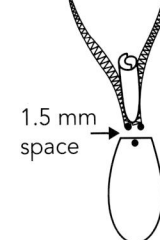

1.5 mm space

1. To shape a petal for bud 3, tightly roll one petal around the point of a fine yarn darner, starting at one side edge, to form a narrow tube. Insert the wire tails close to the base of the background sepals (A). Temporarily bend the wire tails up behind the sepals and hold with tape.

2. Work three detached sepals and insert, as for bud 1 (just below the detached petal). Now bend the petal wires down behind the base and work a few securing stitches over all wires. Do not trim the wire tails until the bud is finished.

To Complete the Bud

1. Cover the bud with satin stitch as for bud 1, trimming all the wire tails before the stem is reached.

2. Work three ribs over the satin stitched base, as for bud 1.

3. Use tweezers to shape the detached petal and sepals as desired.

FLOWER 4

Work as for bud 3, except the detached petal edges are only slightly curved under, not rolled tightly.

FLOWER 5

Work as for flower 4, except apply two detached petals at the base of the background sepals. Insert the wire tails of each petal through two separate holes (side by side), the edge of one petal overlapping the other. Shape the petals, slightly curving the side edge of each petal under towards the background.

FLOWER 6

Base

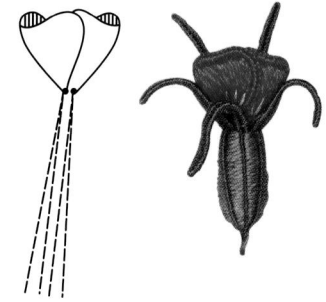

Pad the base with one layer of felt. Cover the base with satin stitch and work three ribs (as for bud 1) *before* the background sepals are worked.

Background sepals

The five background sepals are worked before the detached petals are applied.

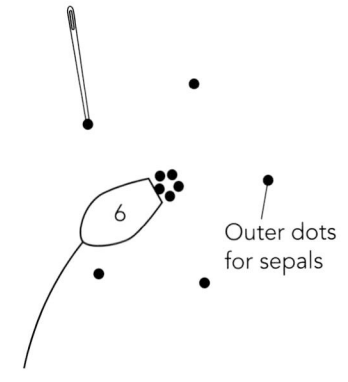

Outer dots for sepals

1. Using the sepal placement diagram as a guide, trace the base 6 shape and the five outside dots (which indicate the length and position of the background sepals) onto tracing paper. Transfer these dots to the background fabric with a stitch (or fine needles)—do not mark with pencil as it may show.

2. The sepals are worked between the inner circle of dots at the top of the base (the detached petal insertion points) and the outer circle of dots.

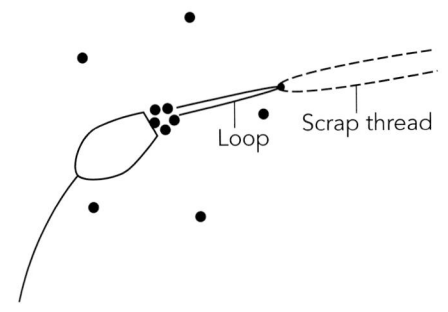

Loop   Scrap thread

To work the loop for the first sepal, bring the needle out just *outside* one of the inner dots and take it down again close by, making a loop the length of the corresponding outer dot marked on the background. Work a second loop, exactly as the first, to make the loop double. Fill the loop with needle-weaving then insert the needle through the outer dot, allowing the sepal to curve slightly. Secure the thread at the back. Work the remaining four sepals in the same way (one of the sepals overlaps the base).

To Complete the Corncockle

1. Using a yarn darner, insert the tails of the five detached petals through the inner circle of dots (five individual holes as close to each other as possible), avoiding the base of the background sepals. Bend the wires behind petals and secure to the backing fabric with small stitches. Do not cut the wires until the flower is finished.

2. Shape the petals with tweezers, pushing them gently towards the centre to make the space as small as possible. Fill the centre of the corncockle with French knots, working most of the knots with three strands of light pink thread (in a milliners needle). Add a few French knots worked with one strand of maroon thread. Trim the wires.

Broad-bodied Dragonfly

Requirements

- bronze mottled organza: 15 cm (6 in) square
- pearl metal organdie: 15 cm (6 in) square
- copper metal organdie: 2.5 cm (1 in) square
- paper-backed fusible web: 2.5 cm (1 in) square
- bronze snakeskin: 5 cm (2 in) square
- thin card for dragonfly abdomen
- brown/black metallic thread: Kreinik Cord 201c
- copper/black metallic thread: Kreinik Cord 215c
- black soft metallic thread: Madeira Metallic No. 40 col. 70
- variegated brown/gold chenille thread: col. Amber Marine
- light bronze rayon machine thread: Madeira Rayon 40 col. 1338
- nylon clear thread: Madeira Monofil 60 col. 1001
- Mill Hill Petite Beads 40374 (purple/green)
- 28 gauge silver uncovered wire (dragonfly wings): four 12 cm (4³/₄ in) lengths

The dragonfly known as the Broad-bodied Chaser, Libellula depressa, is mainly seen in summer inhabiting stagnant water and peaty ponds. The characteristic broad, flat abdomen varies in colour—the young dragonflies have an olive-brown abdomen, the older males a blue abdomen, while females are olive-brown. The wings, which have bronze-coloured wedges at the inner corners, are one of the distinctive features of this fast flying dragonfly.

Abdomen

The padded snakeskin abdomen is shaped in the hand before being couched to the background fabric.

1. Trace the abdomen outline onto paper-backed fusible web then fuse to grey felt. Cut out the shape. Also, cut an abdomen shape from thin card.

2. Using the card shape as a template, cut an abdomen shape from bronze snakeskin, 3–4 mm (¹/₈ in) larger all round than the card template.

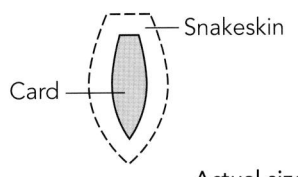

Snakeskin

Card

Actual size

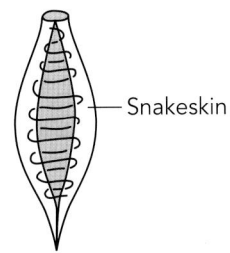

Snakeskin

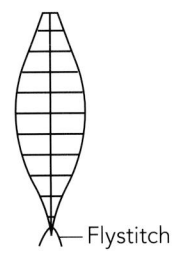

Flystitch

3. Sandwich the felt padding between the snakeskin and the card. Fold the 3 mm turning behind the card and catch the edges together with long overcast stitches, using nylon thread in a sharps needle (it is not possible to stitch right to the tail of the abdomen). Squeeze the lower edges of the snakeskin together with tweezers to form a point (this point will be held in place with couching stitches when the abdomen is applied). Manipulate the padded snakeskin into the abdomen shape with your fingers.

4. Apply the abdomen shape to the background fabric, over the abdomen placement line, with nine or ten couching stitches, using brown/black metallic thread in a milliners needle.

   - Work a couching stitch across the middle of the abdomen, angling the needle under the abdomen shape, then work four evenly spaced couching stitches on either side, making the final couching stitch at the tail of the abdomen (squeeze the tail with tweezers to form a point then couch around it to hold in place).

   - To form the centre line of the abdomen, work a long vertical stitch from the top of the abdomen (thorax) to the tail, sliding the needle gently under each couching stitch as you go (fine-tune the position of all stitches).

   - Work a fly stitch at the tail of the dragonfly.

DETACHED WINGS

This dragonfly has wedges of contrasting colour at the inner corners of the wings. This can be achieved by inserting circles of copper metal organdie between the upper and lower layers of the wing 'sandwich', then placing the wire wing outlines so that a segment of contrasting colour appears in the corner of each wing.

1. Bend uncovered wire around the wing outline templates—two fore wings and two hind wings, leaving two tails of wire at the base of each wing that touch but do not cross (these wire shapes will be used when positioning the circles of copper fabric).

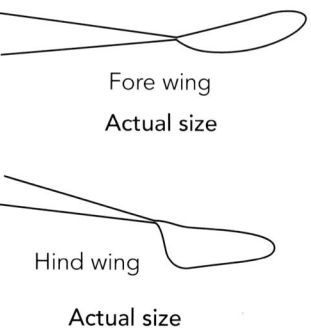

Fore wing
Actual size

Hind wing

Actual size

2. Trace four circle outlines onto a 2.5 mm (1 in) square of paper-backed fusible web and fuse to the square of copper metal organdie (between layers of baking parchment to protect the iron and the fabric). Carefully cut out the circles.

3. Mount the lower layer of wing fabric (pearl metal organdie) into a small hoop. Fuse the circles of copper organdie to the wing fabric, positioning them so that a segment of contrasting colour will appear in the inner corner of the wings (use the wire wing shapes to help with the positioning of the circles). Place a board underneath the hoop for support, and cover the organdie with baking parchment when fusing. Remove the fabric from the hoop.

4. Cover the pearl organdie (and copper circles) with the upper layer of wing fabric (bronze mottled organza), one layer of fabric rotated to be on the bias grain. Mount both fabrics into the small hoop. Place the wire shapes on the hoop of wing fabric, positioning them so that a segment of contrasting colour appears in the inner corner of each wing. Hold the wire tails in place with masking tape. Make sure you have a right and a left fore wing and a right and a left hind wing!

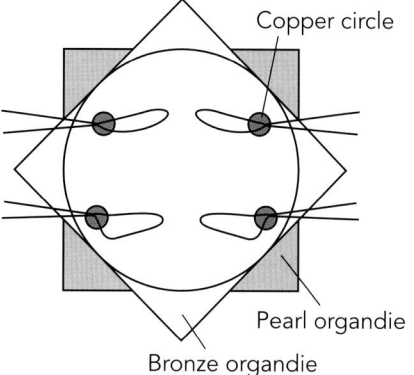

Copper circle

Pearl organdie

Bronze organdie

5. Using one strand of light bronze rayon machine thread in a sharps needle, stitch the wire to the wing fabric with small, close overcast stitches, working several stitches over both wires, at the base of the wing, to begin and end the stitching.

6. To embroider the wing marking (pterostigma) in the upper corner of each wing, work three satin stitches on top of each other, with black soft metallic thread, knotting the tails of thread together at the back.

7. Using copper/black metallic thread in a milliners needle, work the veins in each wing with two rows of single feather stitch, using the diagram as a guide. It is safer to keep the tails of thread at the front until the wings have been cut out, then insert them through to the back. The tails of thread are secured after the wing has been applied to the main fabric. Carefully cut out the wings, retaining the tails of thread.

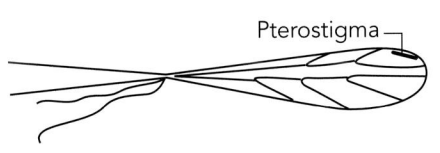

Pterostigma

8. Using a large yarn darner, apply the wings at the insertion points above the abdomen. Insert both hind wings through one hole, at the point next to the abdomen. Bend the wires under the abdomen and hold with tape. Repeat for the fore wings, inserting them at the upper point. Secure the wires and trim the tails.

THORAX

The thorax is worked with one strand of brown/gold chenille thread in the largest size yarn darner.

1. Work two straight stitches over the wing insertion points, bringing the needle out above the wings, and inserting just under the top corners of the abdomen (one stitch at each corner).

2. Bring the needle out again and wrap the straight stitches (sliding the needle under and around the stitches) with chenille thread (three or four wraps) to represent segments. Insert the needle through to the back. Take care not to twist the chenille or to pull the wraps too tight. Secure the tails of chenille at the back with a few stitches worked with stranded thread.

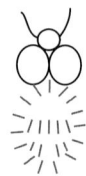

Eyes, Head and Antennae

Huge eyes make up a large proportion of a dragonfly's head. Carefully select two 3 mm bronze/blue beads for the eyes, checking that they are the same size and colour.

1. Using nylon thread in a sharps needle, apply two 3 mm beads side by side, very close to the thorax, taking the stitch through both beads. Work several more stitches, then work a stitch between the beads (across the previous stitches, towards the thorax). Push the beads together with tweezers.

2. Stitch a purple/green petite bead in front of the eyes for the mouthparts, keeping the hole in the bead parallel with the eyes.

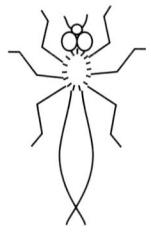

3. Using a single strand of brown/black metallic thread, work a stitch through the petite bead to form the antennae, taking the needle through the fabric in front of the bead.

Legs

With a double strand of brown/black metallic thread in a milliners needle, work each leg with three straight stitches, using the diagram as a guide to length and position. As the legs are attached to the thorax, the wings will need to be gently lifted up when stitching.

Blue Beetle

The shiny blue beetle, Plagiodera versicolora, *attracts attention by the beauty of its variable metallic colouring, with shades ranging from blue and bluish-violet, to green, greenish-gold and coppery-red. These tiny beetles abound on the pages of illuminated manuscripts.*

Requirements

- quilter's muslin: 20 cm (8 in) square
- dark purple stranded thread: Soie d'Alger 3326 *or* DMC 939
- blue fine stranded thread: Cifonda Art Silk 988 *or* DMC 825
- brown/black metallic thread: Kreinik Cord 201c
- nylon clear thread: Madeira Monofil 60 col. 1001
- Mill Hill Petite Beads 40374 (purple/green)
- 33 gauge white covered wire: 12 cm (4³/₄ in) length (colour blue if desired, Copic B18 Lapis Lazuli)

Abdomen

With one strand of dark purple thread, outline the abdomen with small back stitches, then embroider with padded satin stitch, working the stitches across the shape.

Detached Wings (Elytra)

1. Mount muslin into a small hoop and trace the wing outline, placing the straight inner edges of the wings on the straight grain of the fabric.

2. Fold the wire in half to form an inverted V shape. With one strand of blue thread, couch the wire around the wing outlines, making the first stitch at the top of the inverted V inside the wings, and leaving two tails of wire at the top that touch but do not cross. Stitch the wire to the fabric around the wing outline, using buttonhole stitch for the curved outside edges and overcast stitch for the straight inner edges of the wings. Work a row of split stitch inside the wire.

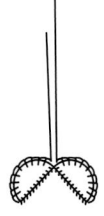

3. Embroider the wings in padded satin stitch, working the satin stitches parallel to the straight inner edge of the wings.

To Complete the Beetle

1. Cut out the wings and shape with tweezers, pushing the straight inner edges together and curving the wings into a rounded shape. Using a yarn darner, insert the wire tails through • at the top edge of the abdomen. Bend the wires towards the tail of the beetle and secure at the back of the abdomen with a few stitches. Hold remaining tails of wire with tape. Trim wire tails when the beetle is complete.

2. With one strand of dark purple thread in a crewel needle, work wide satin stitches (over and in front of the wire insertion point) to form the thorax of the beetle, then work the head with narrower satin stitches. Change to a sharps needle and stitch a purple/green petite bead on either side of the head for eyes.

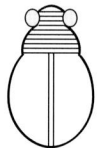

3. Using a double strand of brown/black metallic thread in a size 9 milliners needle, work three straight stitches for each leg. Work two stitches for the antennae with a single strand of thread. Gently shape the wings with tweezers. Trim wire tails.

Ladybird, ladybird! Fly away home.
Your house is on fire.
Your children do roam.

This little rhyme has interesting
origins. It started in England,
where the hop vines are burned after
harvesting is over. These vines
were usually covered with aphids
and young ladybirds feeding on the
aphids. When the hop vines were
burning the small spotted beetles
would take to the wing and their
larvae would crawl rapidly away
from their flaming homes.

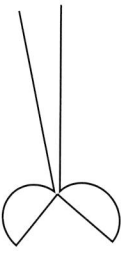

LADYBIRD

The ladybird, which features in each of the botanical specimens, may be applied wherever you wish—the abdomen outline is not included in the design. The ladybird may also be reduced in size if desired.

REQUIREMENTS

- red cotton fabric (homespun): 15 cm (6 in) square
- black stranded thread: DMC 310
- red stranded thread: DMC 349
- black metallic thread: Kreinik Cord 005c
- Mill Hill Petite Beads 42014 (black)
- 33 gauge white covered wire (ladybird): 10 cm (4 in) length (colour red if desired, Copic R17 Lipstick Orange)

ABDOMEN

With one strand of black thread, outline the abdomen with small back stitches, then embroider with padded satin stitch, working the stitches across the shape.

DETACHED WINGS (ELYTRA)

1. Mount red cotton fabric into a small hoop and trace the wing outline, placing the straight inner edges of the wings on the straight grain of the fabric.

2. Fold the wire in half to form an inverted V shape. With one strand of red thread, couch the wire around the wing outlines, making the first stitch at the top of the inverted V inside the wings, and leaving two tails of wire at the top that touch but do not cross. Overcast stitch the wire to the fabric then work a row of split stitch inside the wire.

3. Embroider the wings in padded satin stitch, working the satin stitches parallel to the straight inner edge of the wings.

4. With one strand of black thread, embroider a spot on each wing in satin stitch, working three or four stitches *across* the red satin stitches.

To Complete the Ladybird

1. Cut out the wings and shape with tweezers, pushing the straight inner edges together and curving the wings into a rounded shape. Using a yarn darner, insert the wire tails through • at the top edge of the abdomen. Bend the wires towards the tail of the ladybird and secure at the back of the abdomen with a few stitches. For extra security (especially for tiny ladybirds), bend the wires back towards the head and stitch again. Trim wire.

2. With one strand of back thread in a sharps needle, work wide satin stitches over the wire insertion point to form the head of the ladybird. Apply two petite black beads for eyes.

3. Using a double strand of black metallic thread in a size 9 milliners needle, work two straight stitches for each leg. Work two stitches for the antennae with a single strand of thread. Gently shape the wings with tweezers.

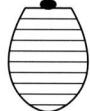  

BOTANICAL NAME

The lower edge of the stitched rectangle, around the specimen, is used to position the guidelines for stitching the botanical name AGROSTEMMA GITHAGO. (Note that if you wish to use upper and lower case letters, only the first word of a botanical name is capitalised.) The letters are stitched by eye, as traced lines would be difficult to cover.

Requirements

- grey/green rayon machine thread: Madeira Rayon 40 col. 1062
- nylon clear thread: Madeira Monofil 60 col. 001
- heavyweight (110 gsm) tracing paper
- translucent removable tape (e.g. Scotch Removable Magic Tape)

1. Cut a piece of heavy weight tracing paper 7 x 2.5 cm (2³/₄ x 1 in). Trace the guidelines and the botanical name, from the skeleton outline, onto the tracing paper, having the top guideline 5 mm (¹/₄ in) below the top edge of the tracing paper. This will be used as a template when stitching the name to the background.

2. Apply two rows of Magic Tape, 3 mm apart, to the background fabric to form the guidelines for the first word of the botanical name. Place one edge of tape above the stitched line of the rectangle and the other piece 3 mm below it. The letters will be stitched in the space between the rows of tape.

3. To start, place the tracing paper over the taped guidelines, lining up the traced lines with the taped lines. Secure the tracing paper at the left side edge with masking tape, allowing the tracing paper to be flipped up and down to help with placement of letters.

4. Using one strand of grey/green rayon thread in a sharps needle, stitch the letters, in the space between the rows of tape, with tiny back stitches, using the traced outline as a guide (aim at working five stitches for the downward stroke of the letters). A fine needle can be inserted through the tracing paper to help position the letters, if required.

5. When the first work is complete, remove the Magic Tape and reposition for the second word of the botanical name, using the traced outline as a guide (the tape above the space is applied over the word above). Position the second word as desired—it can be aligned to the right (as in the design), to the left or in the centre if preferred.

6. Finally, remove the stitched rectangle.

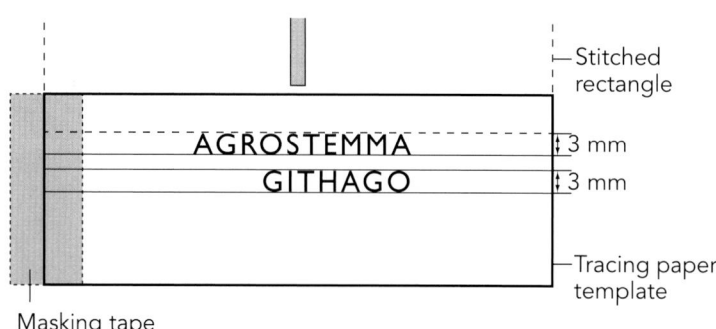

AGROSTEMMA

GITHAGO

3 mm

3 mm

Stitched rectangle

Tracing paper template

Masking tape

AGROSTEMMA
GITHAGO

Herb Robert and Caterpillar

Herb Robert, **Geranium robertianum**, *is a summer-flowering member
of the geranium family, with small pink flowers, reddish green stems and
fern-like green leaves which turn red at the end of the flowering season. The
distinctive long ridged seed cases, resembling the beaks of cranes, give the plant
its name—from the Greek geranus, meaning 'crane'. The plant is covered
with small silvery hairs which yield a peculiar odour when crushed. Herb
Robert adapts itself to a wide variety of habitats including hedgerows, damp
woodlands and rocky seashores.*

*Also known as Cranesbill, Puck, Wren Flower and Robin-i'-the-hedge, its
English name, Herb Robert, probably comes from Abbot Robert, who founded
the Cistercian order in the eleventh century. This highly regarded medieval
herb was used as a remedy for a variety of ailments. Its leaves were crushed to
make compresses for toothache, nose bleeds, bruises and wounds, having both
an antiseptic effect and the ability to control bleeding. Infusions, made from
the flowers, stems and leaves, were taken internally to treat a range of maladies
from peptic ulcers to dysentery, and applied to the hair to treat head lice. The
crushed leaves, with their fox-like smell, also made a good insect repellent.*

GERANIUM
ROBERTIANUM

The summer-flowering Herb Robert, *Geranium robertianum*, with detached bright pink petals and long ridged seed cases, is one of a series of embroidered botanical specimens and insects inspired by the illuminated pages of medieval manuscripts. Worked on a background of ivory satin, the design also features a shimmering Blue Butterfly, *Lysandra coridon*, with raised detached wings, a stripy padded caterpillar and a tiny ladybird with detached elytra. The botanical name of the flower may be stitched at the base of this plant.

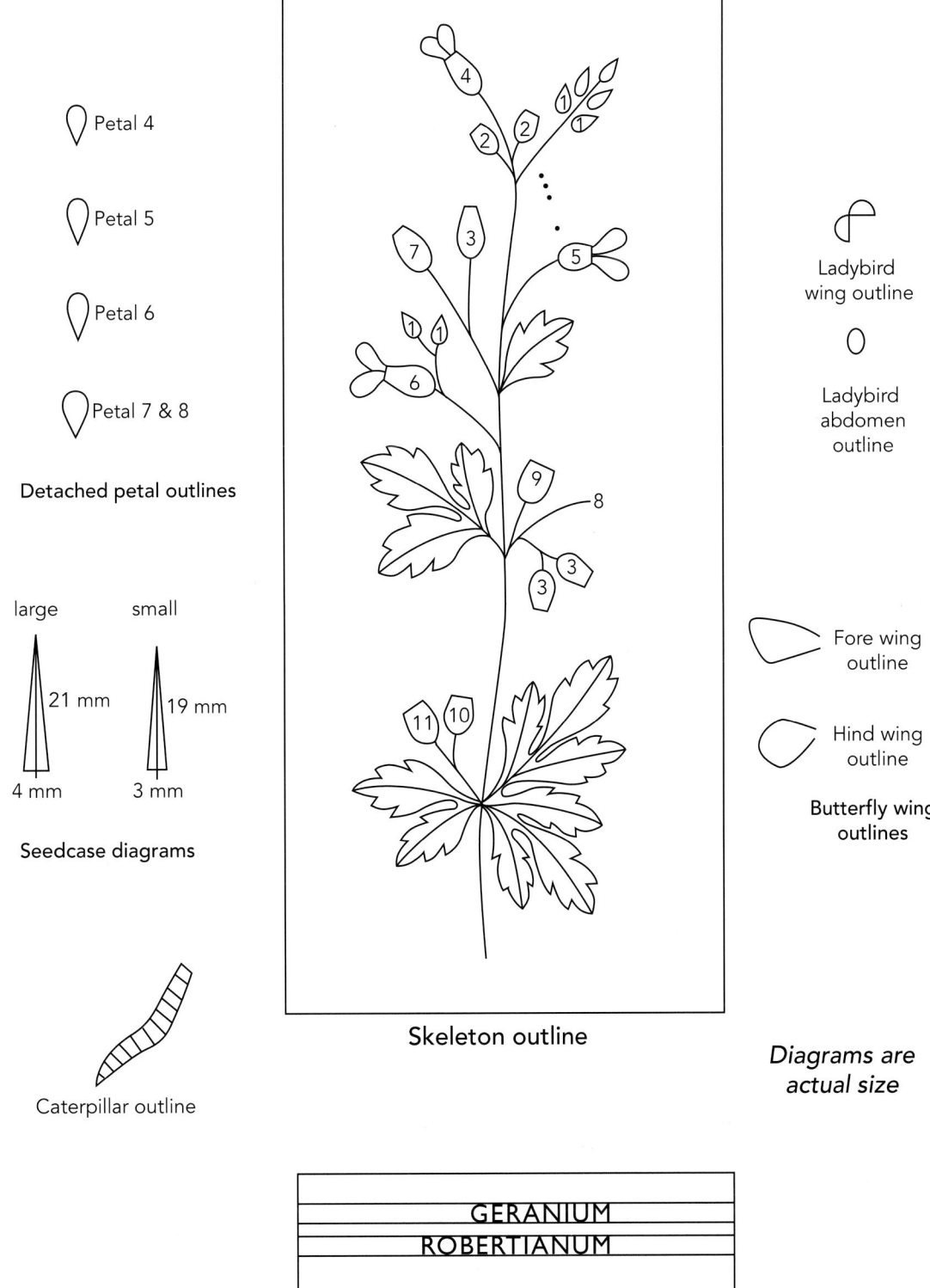

Petal 4

Petal 5

Petal 6

Petal 7 & 8

Detached petal outlines

large   small

21 mm   19 mm

4 mm   3 mm

Seedcase diagrams

Caterpillar outline

Skeleton outline

Ladybird
wing outline

Ladybird
abdomen
outline

Fore wing
outline

Hind wing
outline

**Butterfly wing
outlines**

*Diagrams are
actual size*

GERANIUM

ROBERTIANUM

Botanical name template

OVERALL REQUIREMENTS

This is the *complete* list of requirements for this embroidery. For ease of use, the requirements of each individual element are repeated under its heading—for example, Herb Robert requirements, Blue Butterfly requirements.

- ivory satin background fabric: 30 cm (12 in) square
- quilter's muslin (or calico) backing fabric: 30 cm (12 in) square (*if working all panels on one piece of fabric, refer to the instructions on page 18*)

- quilter's muslin: four 20 cm (8 in) squares
- red cotton fabric (homespun): 15 cm (6 in) square
- grey felt: 10 x 8 cm (4 x 3 in)
- paper-backed fusible web: 10 x 8 cm (4 x 3 in)

- 25 cm (10 in) embroidery hoop or stretcher bars (if working as a single panel)
- 10 cm (4 in) embroidery hoops
- needles:
  crewel/embroidery sizes 9 and 10
  milliners/straw sizes 7 and 9
  sharps size 12
  tapestry size 28
  chenille size 18
  sharp yarn darners sizes 14–18
- embroidery equipment (see page 266)

- russet stranded thread (stems): Soie d'Alger 4616 *or* DMC 3857
- dark olive stranded thread (stems): Soie d'Alger 3735 *or* DMC 936

This sixteenth century image of Herb Robert inspired my embroidery.

- dark green stranded thread (leaves): Soie d'Alger 2115 *or* DMC 3345
- medium green stranded thread (leaves): Soie d'Alger 2114 *or* DMC 3347
- light green stranded thread (seed case): Soie d'Alger 242 *or* DMC 3348
- dark red stranded thread (seed case): Soie d'Alger 4624 *or* DMC 3777
- dark pink stranded thread (flowers): Soie d'Alger 3014 *or* DMC 3831
- medium pink stranded thread (flowers): Soie d'Alger 1014 *or* DMC 3832
- dark grey stranded thread (butterfly): Cifonda Art Silk 215 *or* DMC 317
- medium grey stranded thread (butterfly): Cifonda Art Silk 213 *or* DMC 318
- light grey stranded thread (butterfly): Cifonda Art Silk 211 *or* DMC 762
- medium blue stranded thread (butterfly): Cifonda Art Silk 987 *or* DMC 334
- light blue stranded thread (butterfly): Cifonda Art Silk 986 *or* DMC 3325
- steel/grey stranded thread (butterfly): Soie d'Alger 3443 *or* DMC 414
- dark lime stranded thread (caterpillar): DMC 166
- medium lime stranded thread (caterpillar): DMC 165
- blue stranded thread (caterpillar): DMC 930
- yellow stranded thread (caterpillar): DMC 3821
- dark orange stranded thread (caterpillar): DMC 900
- black stranded thread (ladybird): DMC 310
- red stranded thread (ladybird): DMC 349

- silver metallic thread (butterfly): Madeira Metallic No.40 col.Alu
- silver/black metallic thread (butterfly): Kreinik Cord 105c
- black metallic thread (ladybird and caterpillar): Kreinik Cord 005c
- variegated grey/brown chenille thread (butterfly): col. Pecan
- soft cotton padding thread (seed case, caterpillar): DMC Soft Cotton 2142
- grey/green rayon machine thread (botanical name): Madeira Rayon 40 col. 1062
- nylon clear thread: Madeira Monofil 60 col. 1001

- 3 mm bronze/blue beads
- Mill Hill Seed Beads 374 (blue/purple)
- Mill Hill Petite Beads 42014 (black)

- 33 gauge white covered wire (petals): seventeen 9 cm ($3^1/_2$ in) lengths (colour pink if desired, Copic R37 Carmine)
- 33 gauge white covered wire (ladybird): 10 cm (4 in) length (colour red if desired, Copic R17 Lipstick Orange)
- 33 gauge white covered wire (butterfly): four 10 cm (4 in) lengths
- 28 gauge silver uncovered wire (seed cases): three 9 cm ($3^1/_2$ in) lengths and three 4 cm ($1^1/_2$ in) lengths

- thin card for rectangle template
- heavyweight (110 gsm) tracing paper
- translucent removable tape (e.g. Scotch Removable Magic Tape)

Preparation

1. Mount the satin background fabric and the muslin backing into the 25 cm (10 in) embroidery hoop or frame. If working all panels on one piece of fabric, follow the instructions on page 258.

2. Cut a rectangle from thin card, 7 x 16 cm ($2^3/_4$ x $6^1/_4$ in). Place the rectangle template on the satin (checking that it is aligned with the straight grain of the fabric) and insert a fine needle at each corner point. Remove the template. Using rayon machine thread in a sharps needle, make long stitches from each corner point, to form a stitched rectangle on the front fabric. This will be used as a reference grid when transferring the skeleton design outline and the lines for the botanical name.

3. Using a fine lead pencil, trace the skeleton outline and rectangle outline of the botanical specimen onto tracing paper. Turn the tracing paper over and draw over the skeleton outline only, not the rectangle. With the tracing paper right side up, transfer the skeleton outline to the satin with a stylus, lining up the traced rectangle with the stitched rectangle (it helps to have a board underneath the frame of fabric to provide a firm surface).

Herb Robert

Requirements

- quilter's muslin: three 20 cm (8 in) squares
- grey felt: 10 x 8 cm (4 x 3 in)
- paper-backed fusible web: 10 x 8 cm (4 x 3 in)
- russet stranded thread: Soie d'Alger 4616 *or* DMC 3857
- dark olive stranded thread: Soie d'Alger 3735 *or* DMC 936
- dark green stranded thread: Soie d'Alger 2115 *or* DMC 3345
- medium green stranded thread: Soie d'Alger 2114 *or* DMC 3347
- light green stranded thread: Soie d'Alger 242 *or* DMC 3348
- dark red stranded thread: Soie d'Alger 4624 *or* DMC 3777
- dark pink stranded thread: Soie d'Alger 3014 *or* DMC 3831
- medium pink stranded thread: Soie d'Alger 1014 *or* DMC 3832
- soft cotton padding thread: DMC Soft Cotton 2142
- nylon clear thread: Madeira Monofil 60 col. 1001
- 33 gauge white covered wire (petals): seventeen 9 cm (3^1/$_2$ in) lengths (colour pink if desired, Copic R37 Carmine)
- 28 gauge silver uncovered wire (seed cases): three 9 cm (3^1/$_2$ in) lengths and three 4 cm (1^1/$_2$ in) lengths

STEMS

The stems are embroidered in stem stitch with dark olive and russet threads. Work all rows of stem stitch with two strands of thread in a size 9 crewel needle.

1. Starting at the base, with one strand each of dark olive and russet thread, work a row of stem stitch along the main stem line to the top fork in the stem (V), then work the side stem to the upper buds 1.

2. Using two strands of dark olive thread, work a second row of stem stitch (on the left side of the first row) along the main stem line to the fork (V), then work the side stems to bases 2 and 4.

3. Using one strand each of dark olive and russet thread, work the stems to flower 7 and seed cases 9, 10 and 11, starting at the main stem.

4. All remaining side stems are stitched with two strands of dark olive thread.

LEAVES

The leaves are worked in padded satin stitch with one strand of thread in a size 10 crewel needle.

1. Using medium green thread, work the central veins of the leaves in split stitch.

2. Changing to dark green thread, outline the leaf in split stitch then pad the leaf surface with straight stitches, parallel to the central vein.

3. Bringing the needle out at the tip of the leaf, embroider each side in satin stitch, enclosing the outline and inserting the needle slightly under the central vein (to avoid a gap). The caterpillar will be worked on top of the embroidered leaf.

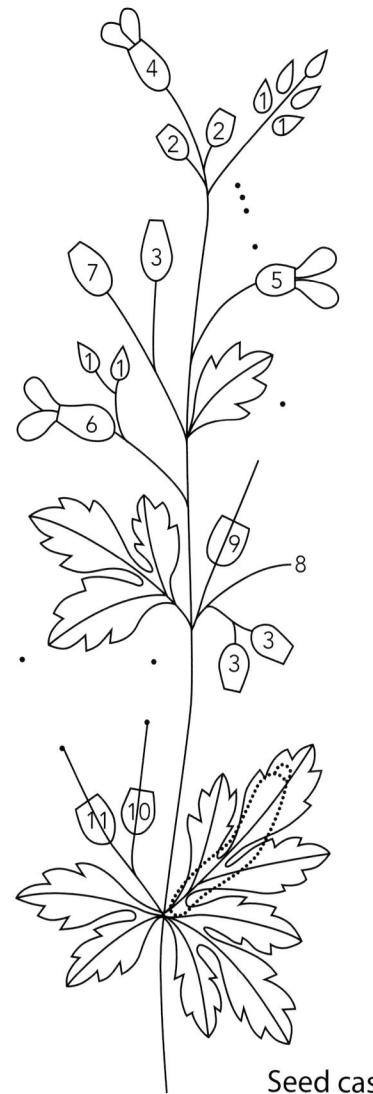

Seed case placement diagram

Buds 1

The closed buds are embroidered with one strand of medium green thread in a size 10 crewel needle. One or two buds may be worked in dark green if desired.

1. Outline the bud in split stitch. Work a chain stitch inside the outline to pad the bud.

2. Embroider the bud in satin stitch, covering the outline and working several layers of satin stitch to make the bud quite raised. Work the stitches towards the tip of the bud.

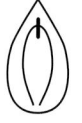

Buds 2

1. Outline the base of the bud in split stitch with medium green thread.

2. Using one strand of dark pink thread, embroider the closed petals of the flower bud in satin stitch, working the stitches from inside the base outline towards a point 2 mm (scant $^1/_8$ in) above the top edge.

3. With medium green thread, work five detached chain stitches over the base of the bud to form sepals, starting each stitch at the stem end of the base and allowing a little pink to show at the tip.

4. Using dark green thread in a sharps needle, work three straight stitches, over the chain stitches, to represent ridges on the base.

Buds 3

The bases of buds 3 and 4, flowers 5, 6 and 7 and seed cases 9, 10 and 11 are padded with a layer of grey felt applied with one strand of thread in a size 10 crewel needle.

1. Using the base outlines as a guide, trace base shapes 3 (x three), 4, 5, 6, 7, 9, 10 and 11 onto paper-backed fusible web, then fuse to grey felt. Carefully cut out the shapes and put aside until required (it helps to number them).

2. For each bud 3, apply the felt padding (web side up) to the background fabric with small stab stitches using medium green thread. Work a row of split stitch around the curved outside edge of the padded base (working the stitches on the background fabric right at the edge of the felt) to provide a green outline to the shape.

3. Embroider the lower two thirds of the padded base, within the green outline, with long and short stitch.

4. With dark pink thread, embroider the closed petals of the flower bud in satin stitch, working from the green long and short stitches towards a point 3 mm (¹/8 in) above the top edge of the padding.

5. With medium green thread, work five or six detached chain stitches over the base of the bud to form sepals, starting each stitch at the stem end of the base. Make each stitch the length of the padding, allowing the closed pink petals to show at the tip.

6. Using dark green thread in a sharps needle, work three straight stitches, over the chain stitches, to represent ridges on the base.

Detached Petals

The remaining buds and flowers require seventeen detached petals which, while varying a little in size and colour, are worked the same way. Work all the petals, on two hoops of fabric, and keep aside until required.

1. Mount muslin into a small hoop and trace seven detached petal outlines—one petal 4 outline, three petal 5 outlines, and three petal 6 outlines (number each petal to avoid confusion).

2. Trace ten petal 7 and 8 outlines on the remaining hoop of muslin.

Bud 4 Detached Petal

1. Using one strand of dark pink thread in a size 10 crewel needle, couch wire around the petal outline, leaving two tails of wire at the base that touch but do not cross. Overcast stitch the wire to the muslin.

2. Work a row of split stitch around the inside edge of the wire then a few padding stitches. Embroider the petal in satin stitch (enclosing the split stitch), working the stitches towards the base of the petal.

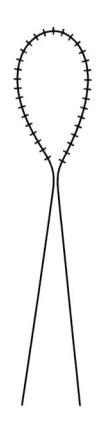

Flower 5 *Detached Petals*

1. Using medium pink thread, couch wire around the petal outline, leaving two tails of wire at the base that touch but do not cross. Overcast stitch the wire to the muslin.

2. With dark pink thread, work a row of split stitch around the inside edge of the wire, then a few padding stitches. Embroider the petal in satin stitch. Work three petals.

Flower 6 *Detached Petals*

1. Using medium pink thread, couch wire around the petal outline, leaving two tails of wire at the base that touch but do not cross. Overcast stitch the wire to the muslin.

2. With dark pink thread, work a row of split stitch around the inside edge of the wire, then a few padding stitches. Embroider the petal in satin stitch, working a few stitches in medium pink at the base of the petal. Work three petals.

Flowers 7 and 8 *Detached Petals*

1. Using medium pink thread, couch wire around the petal outline, leaving two tails of wire at the base that touch but do not cross. Overcast stitch the wire to the muslin.

2. With dark pink thread, work a row of split stitch around the inside edge of the wire, then a few padding stitches. Embroider the petal in satin stitch, working a few stitches in medium pink at the base of the petal. Work ten petals.

Bud 4

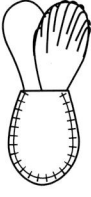

1. With one strand of dark pink thread, work a row of close, long and short buttonhole stitch to outline the top edge of each background petal (working the stitches about halfway down the petal), then embroider the remainder of the petal in long and short stitch.

2. Using dark green thread, apply base padding shape 4 (web side up) to the background fabric with small stab stitches, leaving the straight top edge open. Work a row of split stitch around the curved outside edge of the padded base.

3. Cut out detached petal 4 and shape slightly. Using a yarn darner, insert the wire tails through to the back, under the top edge of the felt, and secure behind the base with a few stitches. Do not trim the wire tails until the bud is finished.

4. With dark green thread, work a few satin stitches over the felt base, stitching from the stem towards the petal. Work five detached chain stitches over the base to form sepals, starting each stitch at the stem end of the base (work a chain stitch at each edge, one in the middle into the base of the petal, then one on each side of the middle stitch). Do not pull these stitches too tight.

5. Using dark red thread in a sharps needle, work four straight stitches, over the chain stitches, to represent ridges on the base.

Flower 5

1. With one strand of medium pink thread, work a row of close, long and short buttonhole stitch to outline the top edge of each background petal. Embroider the remainder of the petal in dark pink in long and short stitch, working up to the medium pink edge.

2. Using dark green thread, apply base padding shape 5 (web side up) to the background fabric with small stab stitches, leaving the straight top edge open. Work a row of split stitch around the curved outside edge of the padded base.

3. Cut out the three detached petals for flower 5 and shape slightly. Carefully cut off the right tail of wire from one petal and the left tail of wire from a second petal (these will become the side petals with one wire tail each). The remaining petal will be the middle petal with two wire tails.

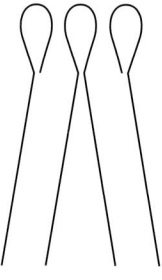

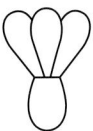

4. Using a yarn darner, insert the wire tails of the side petals through one hole to the back, under the top edge of the felt, with cut wire tail edges touching. Temporarily bend the wire tails behind the surface petals and hold with tape. Insert the middle petal wires through the same hole (this petal will be on top of the side petals). Hold all wires behind the base and secure with a few stitches. Do not trim the wire tails until the flower is finished.

5. With dark green thread, work a few satin stitches over the felt base, stitching from the stem towards the petals. Work five detached chain stitches over the base to form sepals (work a chain stitch at each edge, one in the middle into the base of the centre petal, then one on each side of the middle stitch). Do not pull these stitches too tight.

6. Using dark red thread in a sharps needle, work four straight stitches, over the chain stitches, to represent ridges on the base.

Flower 6

1. With one strand of medium pink thread, work a row of close, long and short buttonhole stitch to outline the top edge of each background petal. Embroider the petal in dark pink in long and short stitch, working up to the medium pink edge. Work a few stitches in medium pink at the base of the petal.

2. Using dark green thread, apply base padding shape 6 to the background fabric with small stab stitches, leaving the straight top edge open. Work a row of split stitch around the curved outside edge of the padded base.

3. Cut out the three detached petals for flower 6 and shape slightly. Carefully cut off the right tail of wire from one petal and the left tail of wire from a second petal (these will become the side petals with one wire tail each). The remaining petal will be the middle petal with two wire tails.

4. As these detached petals will be bent back over the base (after it is embroidered), apply them right side down. Using a yarn darner, insert the wire tails of the side petals through one hole to the back, under the top edge of the felt, petals right side down with the uncut wire tails touching. Hold the wire tails behind the base with tape. Temporarily bend the petals back over the padded base. Insert the middle petal wires through the same hole (this petal will be slightly on top of the side petals) and secure all wire tails behind the base with a few stitches. Do not trim the wire tails until the flower is finished.

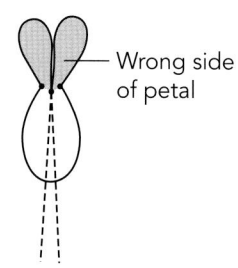

Wrong side of petal

5. Carefully bend the detached petals forward (right side down) to enable the base to be embroidered. With dark green thread, work a few satin stitches over the felt base. Work five detached chain stitches over the base to form sepals. Do not pull these stitches too tight.

6. Using dark red thread in a sharps needle, work four straight stitches, over the chain stitches, to represent ridges on the base. Now carefully bend the detached petals back over the base, adjusting the shape and position with tweezers.

7. To form the centre of the flower, work a French knot at the base of each petal, with two strands of medium green thread in a size 9 milliners needle.

8. The flower stigma is worked with one strand of dark red thread in a sharps needle (the tails of thread even to make the thread double). Insert the needle behind the centre knot, leaving two tails of thread at the front (long enough to hold). Secure the thread at the back then trim the tails of thread to form a short tuft (1.5 mm). Trim the wires.

Flower 7

1. Using dark green thread, apply base padding shape 7 to the background fabric with small stab stitches. Work a row of split stitch around the outside edge of the base.

2. With dark green thread, work a few satin stitches over the felt base, then work five detached chain stitches over the base to form sepals. *Do not pull these stitches too tight.* Using dark red thread in a sharps needle, work four straight stitches over the chain stitches, to represent ridges on the base.

3. Cut out five detached petals for flower 7 and shape slightly before applying.

4. Draw a circle of five dots (the wire insertion points), very close together, at the end of the embroidered base. Insert the wire tails of the detached petals through five individual holes (as close to each other as possible), using a large yarn darner. Bend the wire tails under each petal and secure with small stitches. Do not cut the wire tails until the flower is complete.

5. Using tweezers, gently push each petal towards the centre to make the space as small as possible. Using 2 strands of medium green thread in a size 9 milliners needle, work a circle of five French knots (in between the wire insertion points) to form the centre of the flower.

6. The flower stigma is worked with one strand of dark red thread in a sharps needle (the tails of thread even to make the thread double). Insert the needle through the centre of the circle of French knots, leaving two tails of thread at the front (long enough to hold). Secure the thread at the back then trim the tails of thread to form a short tuft (1.5 mm). Shape the petals then trim the wires.

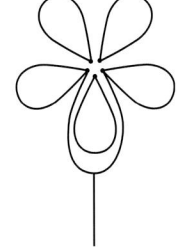

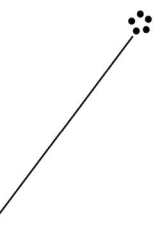

Flower 8

Cut out the five detached petals for flower 8 and work as for flower 7, applying the petals through a circle of five dots at the end of stem 8.

Seed Cases 9, 10 and 11

The seed case consists of a base (carpel) and a pointed beak. The pointed, detached beak is worked on muslin with uncovered wire using one strand of thread.

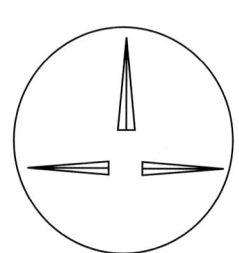

1. Mount muslin into a small hoop and draw the outlines for one large beak and two smaller beaks on the straight grain of the fabric, using the measurements provided (place a small board underneath the hoop for support).

2. Bend a 9 cm ($3^1/_2$ in) length of wire in half to make an inverted V. Using light green thread in a size 10 crewel needle, couch around the beak outline (starting at the base line and working a firm stitch at the point), leaving two tails of wire of similar length at the base. Stitch the wire to the muslin with overcast stitch.

3. Place a 4 cm ($1^1/_2$ in) length of wire along the centre line of the beak. Starting at the base line, couch then overcast stitch the wire to the muslin, working the stitches as close to the point as possible (change to a sharps needle near the tip). Take the tail of thread through to the back, inside the point of the wire, and retain. Cut off the short tail of wire at the base of the centre line.

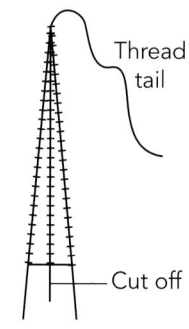

Thread tail

Cut off

4. Thread a sharps needle with a long length of medium green thread. Working towards the point, fill one side of the beak (between the wires) with rows of split stitch, taking the tail of thread through to the back near the tip. Retain the tail of thread. Repeat for the other side of the beak (there should now be three tails of thread behind the tip of the beak, which will be used for securing the tip of the beak to the background fabric).

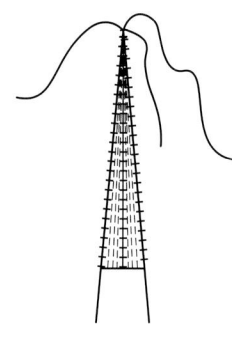

5. Work the remaining two beaks. Carefully cut out each beak, taking care not to cut the retained tails of thread.

To Apply Beak and Work Base

The beak is padded with a stitch worked with a length of soft cotton thread (or fourteen strands of light green thread if soft cotton is not available).

• — Mark with stitch or needle

— Padding stitch

1. Using the seed case placement diagram on page 56 as a guide, trace the base 9 shape, the centre line and the dot above the base (which indicates the direction of the beak) onto tracing paper. Transfer the upper dot to the background fabric with a stitch (or fine needle)—do not mark with pencil as it may show (the upper dot may be marked with pencil on the back). To pad the beak, make a stitch along the base centre line with Soft Cotton thread in a chenille needle (hold the thread tails near the stem at the back with tape).

2. To shape the beak before applying, place a chenille needle along the back of the beak (the point of the needle near point of the beak), and gently curve the sides around the needle (pull on the three retained tails of threads to help control the point).

3. Check the size of the beaks before applying—the smaller beaks are applied to seed cases 9 and 10, the longer beak to seed case 11.

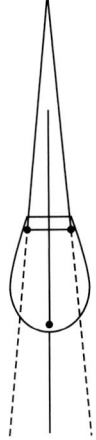

   Using the two smallest yarn darners, insert the wire tails of the beak through two separate holes inside the base outline, 1 mm below the top edge (keep the wire tails free until the tip of the beak is secured). Thread the three retained tails of thread into a fine needle. Using the padding stitch and the upper dot as a guide to direction (*not* length—the beak should be longer), insert the needle through to the back, directly *under* the tip of the beak. Pull the threads firmly then secure with tiny stitches behind the beak. Secure the lower wire tails to the back of the base with a few stitches. Do not cut the wires until the seed case is finished.

4. Using dark olive thread, apply base padding shape 9 to the background (over the base of the beak and the padding stitch) with small stab stitches, leaving the top edge unstitched. Work a row of split stitch around the curved outside edge of the base.

5. Work a few satin stitches over the felt base, stitching from the base just up to the edge of the beak. Work five detached chain stitches over the base to form sepals, starting each stitch at the stem end of the base and inserting the needle carefully *into* the beak, 1 mm up from the edge of the felt. Make the stitches quite loose (to avoid an indentation at the base of the beak).

6. Using dark red thread in a sharps needle, work four straight stitches, over the chain stitches, to represent ridges on the base.

7. With one strand of dark red thread in a sharps needle, make a stitch from the background *into* the tip of the beak for the stigma (make sure that it is long enough to be seen). The beak may be further shaped around the padding with tweezers (with a board underneath for support).

Seed cases 10 and 11 are worked in the same way.

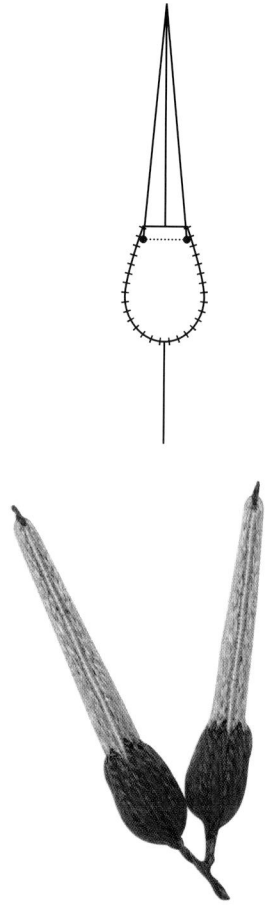

Like many of the Blues, the male Chalk-hill Blue Butterfly, Lysandra coridon, is brightly coloured to attract females. The pale silvery-blue wings have white edges with dark markings and a row of spots on the hind wings. The butterflies feed on nectar from many wild flowers, and are also attracted to dung which provides essential salts. The Chalk-hill Blue used to be seen in great numbers on chalk and limestone downlands in England, France and central Europe, but their numbers are now in decline due to the depletion of their food supply.

BLUE BUTTERFLY

Requirements

- quilter's muslin: 20 cm (8 in) square
- dark grey stranded thread: Cifonda Art Silk 215 *or* DMC 317
- medium grey stranded thread: Cifonda Art Silk 213 *or* DMC 318
- light grey stranded thread: Cifonda Art Silk 211 *or* DMC 762
- medium blue stranded thread: Cifonda Art Silk 987 *or* DMC 334
- light blue stranded thread: Cifonda Art Silk 986 *or* DMC 3325
- steel/grey stranded thread: Soie d'Alger 3443 *or* DMC 414
- silver metallic thread: Madeira Metallic No.40 col. Alu
- silver/black metallic thread: Kreinik Cord 105c
- variegated grey/brown chenille thread: col. Pecan
- nylon clear thread: Madeira Monofil 60 col. 1001
- Mill Hill Seed Bead 374 (blue/purple)
- 33 gauge white covered wire: four 10 cm (4 in) lengths

Preparation

Mount muslin into a small hoop and trace four wing outlines—a right and left fore wing and a right and left hind wing.

FORE WINGS

1. Using light blue thread in a sharps needle, couch wire around the wing outline, leaving two tails of wire at the base of the wing. Buttonhole stitch the wire to the muslin, working the sides of the wing in light blue and the corners and outer edge in light grey.

2. To form the markings on the outer edge of the wing, work 5 straight stitches over the wire (inside the buttonhole ridge) with medium grey thread.

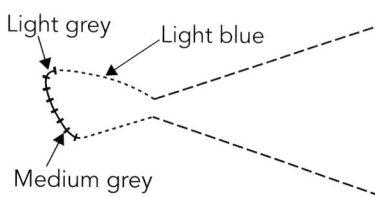

3. The wings are embroidered, inside the wire outline, with rows of buttonhole stitch and encroaching satin stitch. To provide guidelines for these rows, lightly pencil in four lines as shown. With medium grey thread, work the row at the wing edge first with close, long buttonhole stitches.

4. Work the remainder of the wing with four rows of straight stitches blending into each other (encroaching satin stitch), blending the first row into the long buttonhole stitches (leaving a narrow strip of medium grey inside the wire). Refer to the diagram for row colours.

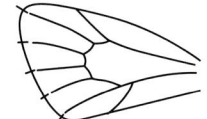

5. With silver metallic thread in a size 9 milliners needle, work the veins with fly and buttonhole stitches, using the diagram and the wing edge markings as a guide to placement.

Hind Wings

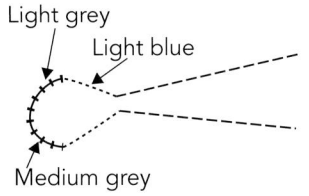

1. Using light blue thread, couch wire around the wing outline, leaving two tails of wire at the base of the wing. Buttonhole stitch the wire to the muslin, working the sides of the wing in light blue and the corners and outer edge in light grey.

2. To form the markings on the outer edge of the wing, work seven straight stitches over the wire (inside the buttonhole ridge) with medium grey thread.

3. The wings are embroidered, inside the wire outline, with rows of buttonhole stitch and encroaching satin stitch. To provide guidelines for these rows, lightly pencil in three lines as shown. With medium grey thread, work the row at the wing edge first with close, long buttonhole stitches (the ridge of the buttonhole is next to the wire).

4. Work the remainder of the wing with three rows of straight stitches blending into each other (encroaching satin stitch), blending the first row into the long buttonhole stitches (leaving a narrow strip of medium grey inside the wire). Refer to the diagram for row colours:

5. With silver metallic thread in a size 9 milliners needle, work the veins with fly and buttonhole stitches, using the diagram and the wing edge markings as a guide.

6. Using one strand of dark grey thread in a size 9 milliners needle, work 6 French knots, between the veins, to form a row of spots on the edge of the wing.

To Complete the Butterfly

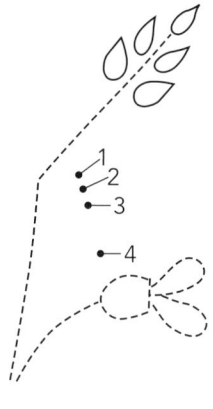

1. Carefully cut out the wings and apply by inserting the wire tails through the three upper dots as shown, using large yarn darners. Apply the hind wings first, inserting the wire tails through 2 and 3, then the fore wings through dots 1 and 2 (the wings share hole 2). Bend the wire tails under the wings and secure to the muslin backing with tiny stitches, making sure that the stitches do not protrude outside the wing span. Trim the wire tails when the butterfly is finished.

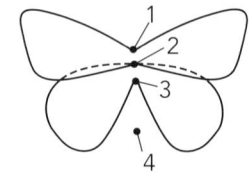

2. Work the thorax with one straight stitch across the centre of the wings (from 1 to 3), using chenille thread in the largest yarn darner. Make sure the chenille does not twist, and adjust the tension of the stitch as desired. Use stranded thread to stitch the chenille tails to the backing fabric.

3. The abdomen is worked with a bullion knot (five or six wraps), using seven strands of steel/grey thread in the chenille needle.

4. With one strand of steel/grey thread, apply a blue/purple seed bead for the head, working the stitches from side to side at the top of the thorax.

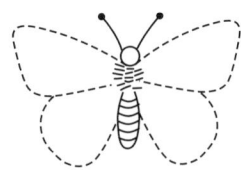

5. Using silver/black metallic thread in a size 9 milliners needle, make a stitch from one antennae 'dot', through the head bead then to the other antennae 'dot' (refer to the diagram for placement). Work a French knot, with two wraps, at the end of each antenna.

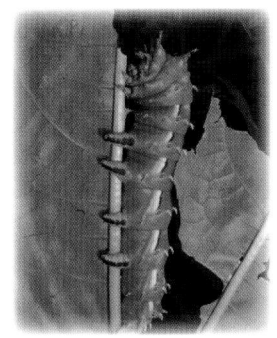

The vulnerable caterpillar often disguises itself on leaves and stems, using both shape and colour as a form of camouflage. However, some caterpillars are brightly coloured, warning birds that they are poisonous.

The caterpillar of moths and butterflies (the larva), is made up of a head and thirteen segments of which only twelve are discernable, as the final two are fused together. The three segments behind the head form the thorax. Each bears a pair of short, jointed legs, or 'true' legs, ending in a single claw, which will become the six legs of the adult butterfly or moth. The remaining nine segments make up the abdomen, on which, in most caterpillars, can be found five pairs of legs, with the claspers occurring on the last segment. The head is a hardened round capsule bearing small black simple eyes on each side, a prominent pair of toothed jaws (mandibles) and cells of hairs around the caterpillar's face to help identify the correct food plant.

CATERPILLAR

As the caterpillar is worked over an embroidered leaf, the outline is transferred to the leaf by means of a paper template.

Requirements

- dark lime stranded thread: DMC 166
- medium lime stranded thread: DMC 165
- blue stranded thread: DMC 930
- yellow stranded thread: DMC 3821
- dark orange stranded thread: DMC 900
- soft cotton padding t thread: DMC Soft Cotton 2142
- back metallic thread: Kreinik Cord 005c
- 3 mm bronze/blue bead

1. A caterpillar has twelve discernible body segments behind the head (these segments will be referred to when embroidering the caterpillar). Trace the caterpillar outline (including the eleven internal segment lines) onto paper (or a Post-it note), and cut out the shape to use as a template. Using the dotted caterpillar outline on the sepal placement diagram as a guide, position the template on the lower right leaf. Using one strand of dark lime thread in a size 10 crewel needle, outline the caterpillar shape in back stitch, working one back stitch per segment (using the lines on the template as a guide) and one stitch across the head end. Remove the template.

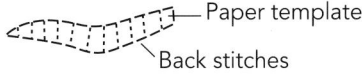

Paper template
Back stitches

2. The caterpillar is padded with soft cotton thread (or fourteen strands of dark lime thread if soft cotton is not available).

With soft cotton thread in a chenille needle, work three straight stitches, inside the back-stitched outline, to pad the caterpillar (the stitches need to be loose to follow the curve of the caterpillar body). With one strand of dark lime thread, work eleven couching stitches over the padding, using the back stitches as a guide to placement (these are the lines between the twelve segments of the body). The caterpillar will be embroidered in raised stem stitch over these couching stitches so they need to be snug but not too tight.

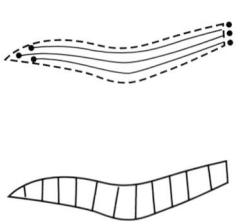

3. Using one strand of blue thread, stitch a 3 mm bead at the end of the caterpillar for the head (keeping the hole in the bead at right angles to the end of the caterpillar).

4. With one strand of yellow thread in a tapestry needle, work a row of raised stem stitch along the lower edge of the caterpillar, starting at the tail and inserting the needle at the edge of the head bead (take some rows through the bead if desired). Referring to the colour list below, work consecutive rows of raised stem stitch to cover the caterpillar, working some short rows (starting the row one or two 'segments' from the tail) to allow for the tapered tail:

- Work three rows in yellow (the third row short)

- Work one row in blue

- Work three rows in medium lime (the second row short)

- Work one row in blue

- Work three or more rows in dark lime to fill the caterpillar

5. Using one strand of dark orange thread in a size 9 milliners needle, work a row of French knots along the middle of the band of medium lime, one in each segment except the first and the last (ten knots). Work the knots across the middle row of raised stem stitch (so that they don't fall into the padding). Don't pull the stitches too tight.

6. Using 3 strands of dark lime thread in a size 7 milliners needle, work eight French knots (below the appropriate segments) to represent the eight pairs of legs:

   - Work a French knot below the first three segments behind the head.

   - Miss two segments, then work a French knot below the next four segments.

   - Miss two segments, then work a French knot below the tail segment.

7. To work the hairs at the front of the head, thread a length of black metallic thread into a sharps needle (the tails even to make the thread double). Insert the needle through the head bead, leaving two tails of thread at the front (long enough to hold). Secure the thread at the back. Trim tails of thread on the front to desired length. Using tweezers, gently squeeze the caterpillar's body and legs to define the shapes.

LADYBIRD

The ladybird, which features in each of the botanical specimens, may be applied wherever you wish—the abdomen outline is not included in the design. The ladybird may also be reduced in size if desired.

The instructions for embroidering the ladybird are on page 43.

BOTANICAL NAME

The lower edge of the stitched rectangle, around the specimen, is used to position the guidelines for stitching the botanical name GERANIUM ROBERTIANUM. (Note that if you wish to use upper and lower case letters, only the first word of a botanical name is capitalised.) The letters are stitched by eye as traced lines would be difficult to cover.

The instructions for working the botanical name are on page 45.

GERANIUM
ROBERTIANUM

Star of Bethlehem and Grasshopper

The Star of Bethlehem, **Ornithogalum umbellatum**, is a spring-flowering member of the lily family, with white star-shaped flowers and shiny green leaves with a distinct white midrib. Also known as Starflower, this wild flower is sometimes regarded as a weed of landscapes and pastures.

The name Star of Bethlehem is mainly in allusion to the six-pointed white blooms, but may also have come about because it was used as famine food by medieval pilgrims to the Holy Land, where it was found growing wild on the slopes and plains around Bethlehem. It was known in Europe in an earlier time as Dog's Onion, as the bulbs are edible if they are well-cooked, but by the fifteenth century it became associated with pilgrims and so came to be called Star of Bethlehem.

ORNITHOGALUM
UMBELLATUM

This design, inspired by the illuminated pages of a medieval manuscript, features the Star of Bethlehem, *Ornithogalum umbellatum*, a spring-flowering member of the lily family, with white, star-shaped flowers worked with detached petals. This small stumpwork panel, one of a series of embroidered botanical specimens and insects, also contains a Great Green Grasshopper, *Tettigonia viridissima*, with detached wings and raised wired legs, a small Mining Bee, *Andrena haemorrhoa*, and a tiny ladybird, both with detached wings. The botanical name of the specimen may be stitched at the base of the plant.

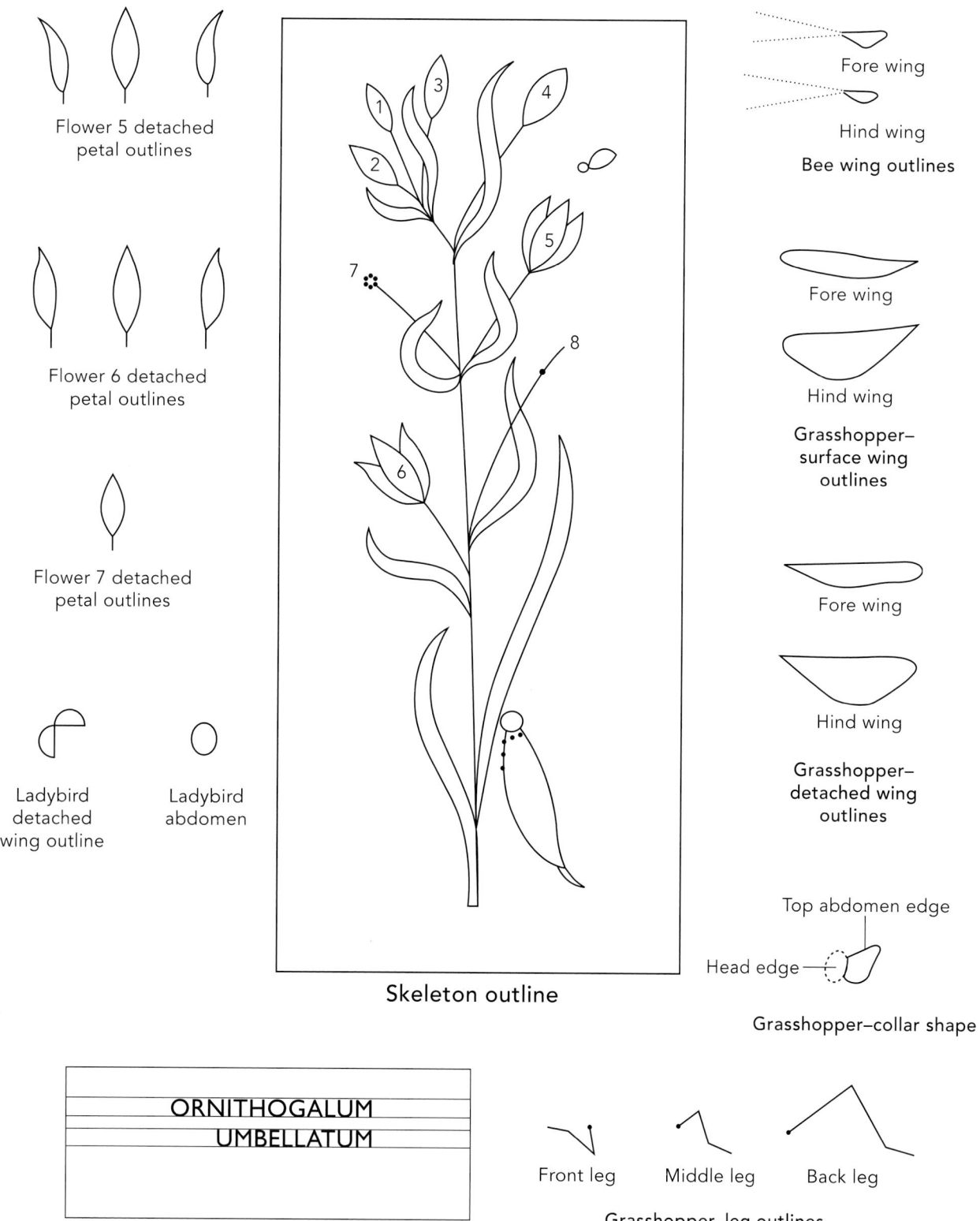

Flower 5 detached
petal outlines

Flower 6 detached
petal outlines

Flower 7 detached
petal outlines

Ladybird
detached
wing outline

Ladybird
abdomen

Skeleton outline

Fore wing

Hind wing

Bee wing outlines

Fore wing

Hind wing

Grasshopper–
surface wing
outlines

Fore wing

Hind wing

Grasshopper–
detached wing
outlines

Top abdomen edge

Head edge

Grasshopper–collar shape

ORNITHOGALUM
UMBELLATUM

Botanical name template

Front leg

Middle leg

Back leg

Grasshopper–leg outlines

Diagrams are actual size

Overall Requirements

This is the *complete* list of requirements for this embroidery. For ease of use, the requirements of each individual element are repeated under its heading—for example, Star of Bethlehem requirements, Mining Bee requirements.

- ivory satin background fabric: 30 cm (12 in) square
- quilter's muslin (or calico) backing fabric: 30 cm (12 in) square (*if working all panels on one piece of fabric, refer to the instructions on page 18*)

- quilter's muslin: two 20 cm (8 in) squares
- red cotton fabric (homespun): 15 cm (6 in) square
- orange silk organza: 15 cm (6 in) square
- honey mottled organza: 15 cm (6 in) square
- pearl metal organdie: 15 cm (6 in) square
- gold metal organdie: 5 x 8 cm (2 x 3 in)
- white felt: 5 x 8 cm (2 x 3 in)
- paper-backed fusible web: 15 x 8 cm (6 x 3 in)
- bronze snakeskin: 2.5 cm (1 in) square

- 25 cm (10 in) embroidery hoop or stretcher bars (if working as a single panel)
- 10 cm (4 in) embroidery hoop
- needles:
  crewel/embroidery sizes 7–10
  milliners/straw sizes 8 and 9
  sharps size 12
  tapestry size 28
  sharp yarn darners sizes 14–18
- embroidery equipment (see page 266)

The charming sixteenth century rendition of the Star of Bethlehem which inspired my embroidery.

- dark green stranded thread (stems, leaves): Soie d'Alger 1835 or DMC 895
- medium green stranded thread (stems, leaves): Soie d'Alger 1844 or DMC 520
- light green stranded thread (sepals): Soie d'Alger 1843 or DMC 522
- very pale green stranded thread (leaves, flowers): Soie d'Alger 3422 or DMC 524
- white stranded thread (flowers): Soie d'Alger Blanc or DMC Blanc
- yellow stranded thread (flowers): Soie d'Alger 623 or DMC 742
- olive stranded thread (grasshopper): Soie d'Alger 2145 or DMC 730
- dark lime stranded thread (grasshopper): Soie d'Alger 2144 or DMC 733
- lime stranded thread (grasshopper): Soie d'Alger 2143 or DMC 166
- gold stranded thread (bee): DMC 783
- black stranded thread (bee, ladybird): DMC 310
- red stranded thread (ladybird): DMC 349

- gold/black metallic thread (bee): Kreinik Cord 205c
- black metallic thread (ladybird): Kreinik Cord 005c
- orange rayon machine thread (grasshopper): Madeira Rayon 40 col. 1021
- gold rayon machine thread (bee): Madeira Rayon 40 col. 1055
- grey/green rayon machine thread (botanical name): Madeira Rayon 40 col. 1062
- nylon clear thread: Madeira Monofil 60 col. 1001

- Mill Hill Seed Beads 2053 (green)
- Mill Hill Seed Beads 374 (purple/green)
- Mill Hill Petite Beads 42014 (black)

- 33 gauge white covered wire (petals): twelve 9 cm ($3^1/_2$ in) lengths
- 33 gauge white covered wire (ladybird): 10 cm (4 in) length (colour red if desired, Copic R17 Lipstick Orange)
- 30 gauge green covered wire (grasshopper legs): three 12 cm ($4^3/_4$ in) lengths
- 28 gauge silver uncovered wire (wings): five 10 cm (4 in) lengths
- 32–34 gauge brass wire (grasshopper antennae): 10 cm (4 in) length

---

- thin card for rectangle template
- heavyweight (110 gsm) tracing paper
- translucent removable tape (e.g. Scotch Removable Magic Tape)

Preparation

1. Mount the satin background fabric and the muslin backing into the 25 cm (10 in) embroidery hoop or frame. If working all panels on one piece of fabric, follow the instructions on page 258.

2. Cut a rectangle from thin card, 7 x 16 cm (2³/₄ in x 6¹/₄ in). Place the rectangle template on the satin (checking that it is aligned with the straight grain of the fabric) and insert a fine needle at each corner point. Remove the template. Using rayon machine thread in a sharps needle, make long stitches from each corner point to form a stitched rectangle on the front fabric. This will be used as a reference grid when transferring the skeleton design outline and the lines for the botanical name.

3. Using a fine lead pencil, trace the skeleton outline and rectangle outline of the botanical specimen onto tracing paper. Turn the tracing paper over and draw over the skeleton outline only, not the rectangle. With the tracing paper right side up, transfer the skeleton outline to the satin with a stylus, lining up the traced rectangle with the stitched rectangle (it helps to have a board underneath the frame of fabric to provide a firm surface).

STAR OF BETHLEHEM

Requirements

- quilter's muslin: two 20 cm (8 in) squares
- orange silk organza: 15 cm (6 in) square
- gold metal organdie: 5 x 8 cm (2 x 3 in)
- white felt: 5 x 8 cm (2 x 3 in)
- paper-backed fusible web: 10 x 8 cm (4 x 3 in)
- dark green stranded thread: Soie d'Alger 1835 *or* DMC 895
- medium green stranded thread: Soie d'Alger 1844 *or* DMC 520
- light green stranded thread: Soie d'Alger 1843 *or* DMC 522
- very pale green stranded thread: Soie d'Alger 3422 *or* DMC 524
- white stranded thread: Soie d'Alger Blanc *or* DMC Blanc
- yellow stranded thread: Soie d'Alger 623 *or* DMC 742
- nylon clear thread: Madeira Monofil 60 col. 1001
- Mill Hill seed beads 2053 (green)
- 33 gauge white covered wire: twelve 9 cm (3^1/$_2$ in) lengths

STEMS AND LEAVES

Follow the recommended order of work when embroidering the stems and leaves.

Stems

The stems are worked in whipped chain stitch with dark and medium green thread, the main stem with three strands (two dark green and one medium green) and the side stems with two strands of thread (one of each green). Use a size 7 crewel needle. Whip with the same number of threads as used to work the chain stitches.

Leaves

The leaves are filled with consecutive rows of stem stitch (or outline stitch) worked with one strand of thread in a size 10 crewel needle. Work each row towards the tip of the leaf, staggering the ends of the rows to shape the leaves and form the point.

- Using dark green thread, work the first row of stem stitch along the lower outline of the leaf (the dark side), then work two or three rows with medium green until the central vein line is reached.

- Work a row of very pale green along the central vein line, then rows of medium green to fill the leaf, working the final row along the upper line.

Order of Work

1. Work the main stem in chain stitch with three strands of thread, working from the base of the stem (at the lower corner of the leaf) to the top fork in the stem (V). Change to two strands of thread and work the side stems to buds 1 and 2. Whip stems.

2. Embroider all the leaves, working over the stem lines when necessary.

3. Work the remaining side stems with two strands of thread, stitching over the leaves, or taking the needle under the leaves, as required. Work stem 8 (the seed pod stem) up to the seed pod placement mark, 6 mm ($^1/_4$ in) from the end. Whip all stems *except* the side flower stems 5 and 6. These are whipped *after* the detached petals are applied.

Seed Pod

The seed pod is worked with two rows of green seed beads, applied over the end of the stitched stem. Take care to select beads of the same size.

1. With one strand of medium green thread, stitch four green beads (on one stitch) across the stem, directly below the seed pod placement mark. Work another three stitches through these beads. Directly below this row of beads, apply three beads in the same way to form the base of the seed pod.

2. To complete the seed pod, work three or four straight stitches, from the beads, to form a point at the end of the stem.

Buds 1, 2, 3 and 4

The buds are padded with white felt (one, two or three layers), then embroidered using one strand of white thread in a size 10 crewel needle.

1. Using the skeleton outline as a guide, trace the following padding shapes on to paper-backed fusible web then fuse to white felt:

   - one shape for bud 1 (trace actual size)
   - two shapes for bud 2 and bud 3 (trace one actual size and one slightly smaller)
   - three shapes for bud 4 (trace one actual size, one slightly smaller and one slightly larger than the skeleton outline)

   Carefully cut out the shapes.

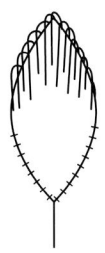

2. Apply the felt shapes (web side up) to the background fabric with small stab stitches around the outside edges, applying the smallest shape first.

3. To form an outline at the top edge of each bud, work a row of close, long and short buttonhole stitch, working the stitches over about a third of the shape, then embroider the remainder of the bud in long and short stitch.

Bud Sepals

Using one strand of light green thread, work sepals over the buds in needle-weaving (two for bud 1 and three for each of the larger buds). Work the side sepals first then the centre sepal. Use a small crewel needle to stitch the loops and a tapestry needle to work the needle-weaving. To work a sepal:

—Scrap thread

1. Bring the needle out at the base of the bud then insert again close by, making a loop slightly shorter in length than the bud. Work a second loop, exactly as the first, to make the loop double (work a tiny securing stitch at the back if required). Pass a length of scrap thread through the loop to enable it to be held under tension while working the needle-weaving.

2. Bring the needle out again at the base of the loop and change to a tapestry needle. Holding the loop under tension with the scrap thread, slide the needle through the centre of the loop, alternately from the right then the left, to fill the loop with needle-weaving, keeping the tension firm and even. Remove the scrap thread then insert the needle near the top of the bud, allowing the sepal to curve around the bud. Secure the thread at the back. Repeat for the remaining sepals.

FLOWERS 5 AND 6

The open flower buds on each side of the stem comprise
three petals embroidered on the background fabric and three
detached petals. Work the petals with one strand of white
thread in a size 10 crewel needle.

Background Petals

1. To form an outline at the top edge of each petal, work a
   row of close, long and short buttonhole stitch, working the
   stitches over about a third of the petal. Work the centre
   petal first, then the side petals. Embroider the petals in
   long and short stitch.

2. Using one strand of very pale green thread, work the centre
   vein of each petal in split stitch, starting at the base of the
   petal and ending 1.5–2 mm from the tip. Work a blush of
   very pale green at the base of the petals with a few straight
   stitches.

3. With two strands of yellow thread in a size 8 milliners
   needle, work five French knots, half way up the petals, for
   the stamen.

Detached Petals

1. Mount muslin into a small hoop and trace the three
   detached petals for flower 5 and for flower 6. As the petals
   are worked in white, take care to use the minimum amount
   of lead when tracing.

2. Using one strand of white thread, couch wire around the
   centre petal outline, leaving two tails of wire at the base
   that touch but do not cross. Buttonhole stitch the wire
   to the muslin, then embroider the petal in long and short
   stitch. With one strand of very pale green work a few
   straight stitches at the base of the petal.

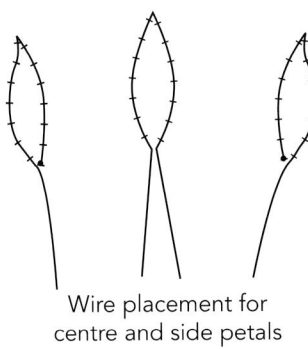

Wire placement for centre and side petals

3. Using white thread, couch wire around a side petal outline, leaving one tail of wire at the base of the petal (cutting the other tail of wire off at the base of the petal). Buttonhole stitch the wire to the muslin, then embroider as for the centre petal.

Sepals on Detached Petals

Using one strand of light green thread, work a sepal on each detached centre petal while muslin is still in the hoop. Work a sepal on each detached side petal after it has been cut out to minimise the risk of cutting the sepal thread.

1. Using a sharps needle, secure the thread at the back of the centre petal then bring the needle out at the base of the centre bud petal, *inside* the buttonhole stitch edge close to one wire tail. Insert the needle close to the other wire tail, inside the buttonhole stitch edge, making a loop slightly shorter in length than the petal. Work a second loop, exactly as the first, to make the loop double (work a tiny securing stitch at the back of the petal if required). Pass a length of scrap thread through the loop to enable it to be held under tension while working the needle-weaving.

2. Bring the needle out again at the base of the loop and change to a tapestry needle. Holding the loop under tension with the scrap thread, slide the needle through the centre of the loop, alternately from the right then the left, to fill the loop with needle-weaving, keeping the tension firm and even. Remove the scrap thread then insert the needle slightly below the tip of the petal. Secure the thread at the back of the petal.

3. Work the sepals on both centre petals, then cut out all six detached petals.

4. Work a sepal on each detached side petal *after* it has been cut out. Start the sepals as close to the base of the petal as possible to avoid seeing a white edge. Using a sharps needle, secure the light green thread at the back of the petal then bring the needle out at the base, *inside* the buttonhole stitch edge close to the wire tail. Insert the needle nearby, making a loop slightly shorter in length than the petal. Work a second loop, exactly as the first, to make the loop double (work a tiny securing stitch at the back of the petal if required). Pass a length of scrap thread through the loop to enable it to be held under tension while working the needle-weaving.

5. Bring the needle out again at the base of the loop and change to a tapestry needle. Work the sepal in needle-weaving as for the centre petal (it helps to hold the wire tail on a firm surface with masking tape).

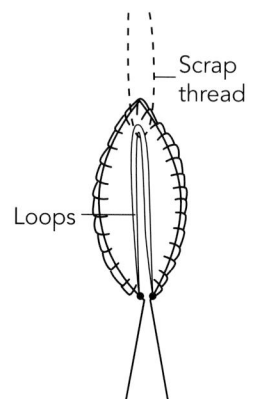

To Complete Flowers 5 and 6

1. Using a large yarn darner, insert the detached side petal wire tails through one hole, at the base of the embroidered background petals. Bend the tails up under the petals and hold with masking tape.

2. Apply centre petal through the same hole (below the side petal wires) and bend the wire tails up behind petal. Secure all wires. Trim tails after step 3.

3. Now whip the flower stems (one strand each of dark and medium green), working from the main stem towards the flower. With one strand of medium green in a sharps needle, work a few tiny stitches from the end of the stem into the base of the petals, if necessary, to camouflage the wire insertion points.

Flower 7

Detached Petals

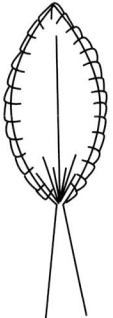

1. Mount muslin into a small hoop and trace six detached petals for flower 7. As the petals are worked in white, take care to use the minimum amount of lead when tracing.

2. Using one strand of white thread, couch wire around the petal outline, leaving two tails of wire at the base that touch but do not cross. Buttonhole stitch the wire to the muslin, then embroider the petal in long and short stitch.

3. Using one strand of very pale green thread, work the centre vein of each petal in split stitch, starting at the base of the petal and ending 1.5–2 mm from the tip. Work a blush of very pale green at the base of the petals with a few straight stitches. Cut out the petals.

To Complete Flower 7

1. Draw a circle of six dots, very close together, at the end of the flower stem. The wire tails of the petals will be inserted through these six individual holes (as close to each other as possible), using a large yarn darner. As the petals will slightly overlap each other, insert the three back petals first, through three alternate holes, then the three front petals. Bend the wire tails under each petal and secure with small stitches. Do not cut the wire tails until the flower is complete.

2. Gently push the petals towards the centre (to make the centre space as small as possible). Using nylon thread, stitch three green seed beads in the centre of the flower, stitching the beads *over* the small space in the centre of the petals.

3. Using two strands of yellow thread in a size 8 milliners
    needle, work a French knot at the base of every petal, 1 mm
    away from the centre, taking the needle through the petal
    and the background to the back (avoiding the wire tails).
    Take care not to pull the stitches between the petal and
    the background too tight (allow for the lifting of the petals
    when shaping). After a final shaping of the petals, trim the
    wire tails (shorter than the span of the flower).

The Mining Bee, Andrena haemorrhoa, is a solitary bee similar to the honey-bee in shape and colour but smaller. Solitary bees are so named because they construct individual nests, in soil, hollow stems or mortar, rather than living in organised colonies like honey-bees and bumblebees. In summer, the female Mining Bee gathers nectar and pollen which she deposits in holes dug in dry, sandy banks. She lays an egg in each hole, then seals up the entrance. The young bees develop in the nests over winter and emerge the following spring.

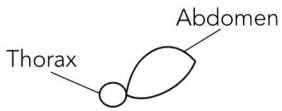

Mining Bee

Requirements

- honey mottled organza: 15 cm (6 in) square
- pearl metal organdie: 15 cm (6 in) square
- gold stranded thread: DMC 783
- black stranded thread: DMC 310
- gold/black metallic thread: Kreinik Cord 205c
- gold rayon machine thread: Madeira Rayon 40 col. 1055
- nylon clear thread: Madeira Monofil 60 col. 1001
- Mill Hill seed beads 374 (purple/green)
- 28 gauge silver uncovered wire (wings): three 10 cm (4 in) lengths

Abdomen

1. Outline the abdomen and the small circle next to it (the thorax) in small back stitches using one strand of black thread.

2. The abdomen is filled with consecutive rows of Turkey knots, worked with two strands of either black or gold thread in a size 9 crewel needle. Starting at the 'thorax end' of the abdomen, work two rows of Turkey knots in black, then two rows in gold. Repeat to form two more stripes, then finish with one or two rows of black at the tail (adjust the number of rows for each stripe, if necessary, to end up with a black tail).

3. Cut and comb the Turkey knots until a small, rounded abdomen is formed.

WINGS

1. Mount the honey mottled organza and the pearl metal organdie (as a backing) into a small hoop, one layer of fabric rotated to be on the bias grain (the wing fabrics are not fused together).

2. Bend uncovered wire around the wing outline templates— two fore wings (both the same) and one smaller hind wing—leaving two tails of wire at the base of the wing that touch but do not cross. Attach the wire tails to the organza with masking tape (do not couch the wings to the fabric as it may show). Using gold rayon thread in a sharps needle, overcast stitch the wire to the wing fabric, working several stitches over both wires, at the base of the wing, to begin and end the stitching.

3. Using one strand of gold/black metallic thread in a size 9 milliners needle, work a fly stitch for the veins in the hind wing and one of the fore wings, retaining the tails of thread at the corners of the wings (do not work a fly stitch in the remaining fore wing until later). Cut out all wings, taking care not to cut the tails of metallic thread.

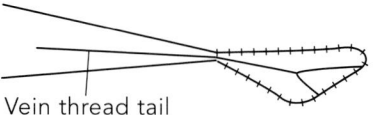

Vein thread tail

TO COMPLETE BEE

1. Using a yarn darner, insert the wire tails of the fore wing *without* veins inside the top edge of the stitched thorax, holding the wires in the direction of the head with tape (do not trim wire until the bee is finished). Position the wing close to the upper edge of abdomen, then work a fly stitch, in gold/black metallic thread, through both the wing and the background fabric (to hold the wing flat against the satin). Secure the thread.

2. Using a large yarn darner, insert the remaining fore and hind wings (and thread tails) through one hole, below the first wing. Bend the wires and thread tails under the abdomen and secure to the back (do not trim wires until the bee is finished).

3. Using two strands of black thread, work 5 or 6 Turkey knots *inside* the stitched circle (next to the wire insertion points) to work the thorax. Cut and comb into shape.

4. With one strand of black thread, stitch one purple/green seed bead next to the thorax for the head/eye, securing the tails of wire underneath as you stitch.

5. Using two strands of gold/black metallic thread in a size 9 milliners needle, stitch three legs, working three back stitches for each leg. With one strand of thread, work a fly stitch, above the bead, for the antennae.

GREAT GREEN GRASSHOPPER

Requirements

- orange silk organza: 15 cm (6 in) square
- gold metal organdie: 5 x 8 cm (2 x 3 in)
- paper-backed fusible web: 5 x 8 cm (2 x 3 in)
- bronze snakeskin: 2.5 cm (1 in) square
- olive stranded thread: Soie d'Alger 2145 *or* DMC 730
- dark lime stranded thread: Soie d'Alger 2144 *or* DMC 733
- lime stranded thread: Soie d'Alger 2143 *or* DMC 166
- orange rayon machine thread: Madeira Rayon 40 col. 1021
- nylon clear thread: Madeira Monofil 60 col. 1001
- Mill Hill seed bead 374 (purple/green)
- 30 gauge green covered wire (grasshopper legs): three 12 cm (4³/₄ in) lengths
- 28 gauge silver uncovered wire (wings): two 10 cm (4 in) lengths
- 32–34 gauge brass wire (grasshopper antennae): 10 cm (4 in) length

DETACHED WINGS

1. Using paper-backed fusible web, fuse the gold metal organdie to the orange silk organza, placing one long edge of the gold fabric along the 'centre line' of the organza (use baking parchment to protect the iron and the ironing board). Mount into a small hoop, organza side uppermost.

The Great Green Grasshopper, *Tettigonia viridissima*, is also known as the Long-horned Grasshopper or the Great Green Bush Cricket. Usually bright green in colour, they possess very long, thread-like antennae and have well-developed hind legs. They are predators, feeding on other insects with their biting mouthparts and powerful jaws.

The Great Green Grasshopper has well-developed wings which are held in a tent-like fashion when at rest. The narrower fore wings are leathery in texture while the hind wings are broad and fan-like. The males produce the familiar summer rasping sound by rubbing the front pair of wings together. The female grasshopper possesses a long, slender ovipositor at the tip of the abdomen, laying her eggs in the soil in autumn, to hatch the following spring.

2. Bend uncovered wire around the 'detached wing outlines' templates—one fore wing and one larger hind wing—leaving two tails of wire at the base of the wing that touch but do not cross. Attach the wire tails to the organza with masking tape, positioning the smaller fore wing over the 'gold backed' section of the organza, and the larger hind wing over the single layer of organza. Check that the wings are the right way up. Using orange rayon thread in a sharps needle, overcast stitch the wire to the wing fabric, working several stitches over both wires, at the base of the wing, to begin and end the stitching. Carefully cut out the wings, saving the remaining wing fabric for the surface wings.

Surface Wings

1. Place a piece of paper-backed fusible web over the 'surface wing outlines' diagram, paper side up, and trace around both wing outlines. Fuse the traced outlines to the *back* of the saved pieces of wing fabric, fusing the front wing outline to the gold side of the fused wing fabric, and the back wing outline to the single layer of organza (use baking parchment to protect the iron and the ironing board). Cut out the wings and remove the paper backing.

2. Using the wing outlines on the diagram below as a guide to placement, position the surface wings (web side down) over the traced abdomen outline on the background fabric, hind wing first, then the slightly overlapping fore wing. With a board under the hoop for support and baking parchment over the wings for protection from the iron, carefully fuse the wings to the background fabric.

3. Using orange rayon thread in a sharps needle, work an outline around the wings in split stitch (next to the edge of the fabric), stitching over the organza for the lower edge of the fore wing.

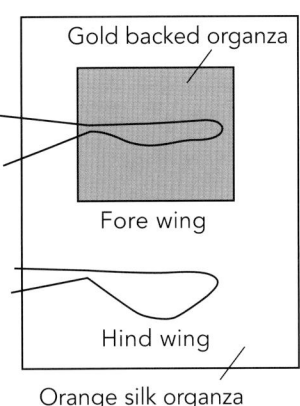

Gold backed organza

Fore wing

Hind wing

Orange silk organza

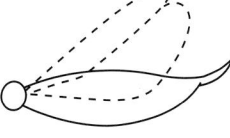

ABDOMEN

The abdomen is worked in raised stem stitch over a layer of padding stitches.

1. Using one strand of lime green thread in a size 10 crewel needle, outline the head, abdomen and ovipositor (narrow pointed 'tail') in split stitch, working the stitches over the fused organza wing (this portion of wing will be covered by the stitched abdomen). The head and ovipositor will be worked later.

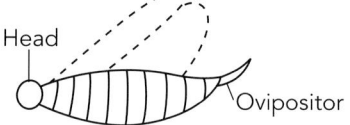

2. With six strands of lime green thread in the smallest yarn darner, pad the abdomen, inside the outline, with long straight stitches, working stitches over each other to increase the padding in the middle of the shape.

3. With one strand of lime green thread, work about eight or nine couching stitches over the padding, enclosing the backstitched outline. Secure the thread.

4. Cover the abdomen with rows of raised stem stitch, worked over the couching stitches with one strand of thread in a tapestry needle. Work some 'short' rows to allow for the width of the abdomen:

   · starting at the lower edge, work four or five rows in lime green

   · work one row in olive green

   · continue working with dark lime green then finish with two or three rows of olive green

5. With one strand of lime green thread, work the ovipositor in slanted satin stitch, enclosing the outline.

HEAD AND WINGS

1. Work the head in padded satin stitch with one strand of lime green thread. Make a 'hole' in the satin stitch for the eye, with a yarn darner, then stitch a purple/green seed bead in the cavity. From the lower edge of the head, work four or five straight stitches, into a point, for the mouth parts.

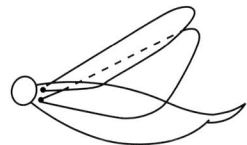

2. Using a yarn darner, insert the wire tails of the detached wings through the abdomen at the points marked on the skeleton outline. Insert the fore wing first, stitching the unbent wire tails behind the head. Then insert the hind wing and carefully bend the wire back under abdomen and stitch to secure (do not trim wires until the grasshopper is finished). Position the detached wings over the corresponding surface wings.

3. A bronze snakeskin collar (pronotum) covers the insertion points of the detached wings. First cut a collar template from paper (or a Post-it note) and check for size (it lies next to the head and needs to reach from the top edge of the abdomen to just over the lower wing insertion point). Then cut a collar shape from bronze snakeskin using the template as a guide. With nylon thread in a sharps needle, apply the snakeskin shape with small stab stitches, first working a stitch at each corner (next to the head), then stitching the top edge of the snakeskin in place.

LEGS

To form a leg, wrap green-covered wire with one strand of olive green thread (following the instructions) then bend into the leg shape with tweezers, using the leg outline diagram as a template. The • end of the leg is stitched to the corresponding • at the edge of the abdomen (use a sharps needle to take a thread through the bend in the wire • and through to the back to secure). The 'foot' end of the leg is inserted through to the back at the stem, using a yarn darner. The wire tail is bent back under the 'foot' and secured with small stitches (always wrap more wire than required to ensure a neat end to the leg). Apply the front leg first, then the back leg and finally the middle leg.

Front Leg

The broader first segment of the front leg is formed by wrapping over two thicknesses of wire.

1. Tie a length of olive green thread to the wire, 1 cm (3/8 in) from one end, leaving a long tail of thread to use for wrapping. Wrap the wire for 2 mm, then bend it in the middle of the wrapped section and squeeze the wires together (the wrapped bend will be the abdomen end • of the leg).

2. Trim the short end of the wire to 4 mm, then, starting at the bend, wrap over both wires (enclosing the short tail of thread) and continue wrapping over the single wire until the wrapped section measures at least 2 cm (3/4 in). Secure the thread (retain the tail).

3. Bend the wrapped wire into three segments to form a front leg shape, using the template as a guide (the wrapped bend • corresponds to • on the diagram). Bend the wire at the end of the 'foot' towards the background (this wrapped tail of wire will be taken through to the back at the stem).

Wrapped tail

4. Apply the leg by stitching the • end over the corresponding point at the edge of the abdomen. At the same time, insert the 'foot' end of the wire through the stem with a yarn darner, adjusting the bends in the legs if required. When the position of the leg has been fine-tuned, secure both ends of the leg and trim the wire.

Back Leg

The broader first segment of the back leg is formed by wrapping over three thicknesses of wire.

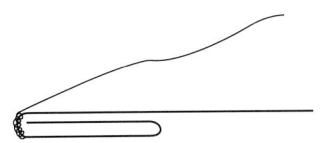

1. Tie a length of olive green thread to the wire, 4 cm (1 ¹/₂ in) from one end, leaving a long tail of thread to use for wrapping. Wrap the wire for 2 mm, then bend it in the middle of the wrapped section and squeeze the wires together (the wrapped bend will be the abdomen end • of the leg).

2. Bend the short end of the wire again, 13 mm (¹/₂ in) away from the wrapped bend—the tail will be enclosed in the resulting space (trim tail to fit). Then, starting at • , wrap over the three thicknesses of wire (enclosing the short tail of thread) and continue wrapping over the single wire until the wrapped section measures 4 cm (1 ¹/₂ in). Secure the thread (retain the tail).

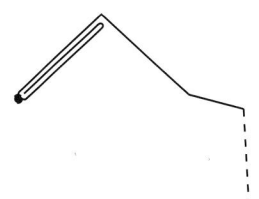

3. Bend the wrapped wire into three segments to form a back leg shape, using the template as a guide (the wrapped bend • corresponds to • on the diagram). Bend the wire at the end of the 'foot' towards the background (this wrapped tail of wire will be taken through to the back at the stem).

4. Apply the leg by stitching the • end over the corresponding point at the edge of the abdomen. At the same time, insert the 'foot' end of the wire at the bottom end of the stem with a yarn darner, adjusting the bends in the legs if required. When the position of the leg has been fine-tuned, secure both ends of the leg and trim the wire.

Middle Leg

Work the middle leg as for the front leg.

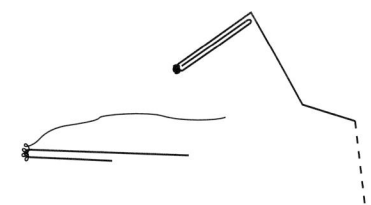

Antennae

Fold the piece of brass wire in half and insert through the head with a small yarn darner. Secure at the back. Shape the wire by pulling through the fingers, then trim to the desired length. Finally, trim the wire tails of the detached wings.

Ladybird

The ladybird, which features in each of the botanical specimens, may be applied wherever you wish—the abdomen outline is not included in the design. The ladybird may also be reduced in size if desired.

The instructions for embroidering the ladybird are on page 43.

Botanical Name

The lower edge of the stitched rectangle, around the specimen, is used to position the guidelines for stitching the botanical name ORNITHOGALUM UMBELLATUM. (Note that if you wish to use upper and lower case letters, only the first word of a botanical name is capitalised.) The letters are stitched by eye as traced lines would be difficult to cover.

The instructions for working the botanical name are on page 45.

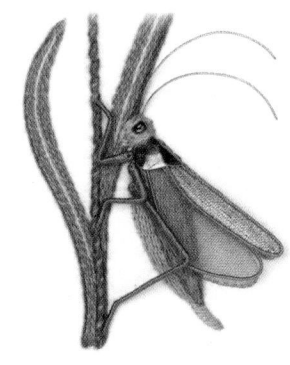

ORNITHOGALUM
UMBELLATUM

Tansy illumination from Les Grandes Heures d'Anne de Bretagne, *Ms Latin 9474, Folio 128, Bibliothèque nationale de France.*

Tansy and Damselfly

The Tansy, Tanacetum vulgare, is a summer-flowering medicinal and culinary herb, with small bright yellow, button-like flowers, and fragrant, green feathery leaves. Valued as an insect-repellent strewing herb, the Tansy was also used in medieval herbal medicine as a purgative, to cure fevers, and to both 'encourage pregnancies and to terminate them'! A popular herbal dye, it produced a rich, mustard-yellow colour.

Tansy, bitter and sharp to our palates, was much used in food preparation in the Middle Ages. As an Easter herb, it was made into puddings with eggs, flour and milk and eaten on Palm Sunday and Easter Sunday.

It was apparently an essential potherb used for sweet and savoury dishes, including a sort of sweet stir-fry consisting of young tansy leaves, green corn and violets, moistened with orange and sugar. Its juice was also used to flavour omelettes.

MIRANDA INNES AND CLAY PERRY, MEDIEVAL FLOWERS, PAGE 92

In Greek mythology, Tansy was regarded as a herb with eternal properties (the Greek word for Tansy is Athanasia, meaning 'immortality'). The long-lasting, golden button-flowers gave rise to the herb's reputation for being deathless, as did the preserving powers of tansy's aromatic, feathery leaves. The leaves were used, with other herbs and spices, to embalm the dead.

This small stumpwork panel features the Tansy, *Tanacetum vulgare*, a summer-flowering medicinal and culinary herb, with small, bright yellow, button-like flowers (worked in French knots) and rich green feathery leaves. One of a series of embroidered medieval botanical specimens and insects, this design also includes a Striped Bug, *Graphosoma lineatum*, its striped detached scutum stretching to the tip of its padded abdomen, an Azure Damselfly, *Coenagrion puella*, with detached gauzy wings and a raised beaded abdomen, and a tiny ladybird with raised detached elytra. The Tansy's botanical name may be worked at the base of this plant.

TANACETUM
VULGARE

Bug abdomen and
leg diagram

Bug detached
scutellum outline

Bug detached
thorax outline

Skeleton outline

Fore wing

Hind wing

**Damselfly detached
wing outlines**

Damselfly
thorax

Damselfly thorax padding
and leg outlines

Ladybird
detached
wing outline

Ladybird
abdomen

*Diagrams are
actual size*

TANACETUM
VULGARE

Botanical name template

Overall Requirements

This is the *complete* list of requirements for this embroidery. For ease of use, the requirements of each individual element are repeated under its heading—for example, Tansy requirements, Striped Bug requirements.

- ivory satin background fabric: 30 cm (12 in) square
- quilter's muslin (or calico) backing fabric: 30 cm (12 in) square (*if working all panels on one piece of fabric, refer to the instructions on page 18*)

- quilter's muslin: 20 cm (8 in) square
- red cotton fabric (homespun): 15 cm (6 in) square
- teal shot crystal organza: 15 cm (6 in) square
- pearl metal organdie: 15 cm (6 in) square
- yellow felt: 10 x 8 cm (4 x 3 in)
- black felt: 5 cm x 8 cm (2 x 3 in)
- paper-backed fusible web: 15 cm (6 in) square *and* 15 x 8 cm (6 x 3 in)
- blue-bronze snakeskin: 2.5 cm (1 in) square

- 25 cm (10 in) embroidery hoop or stretcher bars (if working as a single panel)
- 10 cm (4 in) embroidery hoops
- needles:
  crewel/embroidery sizes 9 and 10
  milliners/straw sizes 8 and 9
  sharps size 12
  tapestry size 28
  sharp yarn darners sizes 14–18
- embroidery equipment (see page 266)

- dark green stranded thread (stems): Soie d'Alger 516 *or* DMC 937

- medium green stranded thread (stems, leaves, buds): Soie d'Alger 2125 *or* DMC 469

- light green stranded thread (buds): Soie d'Alger 2124 *or* DMC 470

- tan stranded thread (flowers): Soie d'Alger 2615 *or* DMC 921

- dark yellow stranded thread (flowers): Soie d'Alger 546 *or* DMC 741

- medium yellow stranded thread (flowers): Soie d'Alger 545 *or* DMC 972

- light yellow stranded thread (flowers): Soie d'Alger 544 *or* DMC 725

- dark orange stranded thread (bug): Soie d'Alger 636 *or* DMC 900

- grey/brown stranded thread (bug): Soie d'Alger 3416 *or* DMC 3371

- black stranded thread (ladybird): DMC 310

- red stranded thread (ladybird): DMC 349

- ivory stranded thread (damselfly): DMC Ecru

- gold/black metallic thread (damselfly): Kreinik Cord 205c

- slate/black metallic thread (damselfly): Kreinik Cord 225c

- steel grey metallic thread (bug): Kreinik Cord 011c

- black metallic thread (ladybird): Kreinik Cord 005c

- black soft metallic thread (damselfly): Madeira Metallic No. 40 col. 70

- blue rayon machine thread (damselfly): Madeira Rayon 40 col. 1028

- grey/green rayon machine thread (botanical name): Madeira Rayon 40 col. 1062

- nylon clear thread: Madeira Monofil 60 col. 1001

This sixteenth century painting of the Tansy from a medieval herbal inspired this piece

- 4 mm blue/green bugle beads
- 3 mm blue/purple bead
- Mill Hill seed beads 374 (blue/purple)
- Mill Hill petite beads 40374 (blue/purple)
- Mill Hill petite beads 42014 (black)

- 33 gauge white covered wire (bug, ladybird): three 10 cm (4 in) lengths (colour red if desired, Copic R17 Lipstick Orange)
- 28 gauge silver uncovered wire (damselfly wings): four 12 cm (4³/₄ in) lengths
- 33 gauge silver uncovered wire (damselfly abdomen): 23 cm (9 in) length

---

- thin card for rectangle template
- heavyweight (110 gsm) tracing paper
- translucent removable tape (e.g. Scotch Removable Magic Tape)

Preparation

1. Mount the satin background fabric and the muslin backing into the 25 cm (10 in) embroidery hoop or frame. If working all panels on one piece of fabric, follow the instructions on page 258.

2. Cut a rectangle from thin card, 7 x 16 cm (2³/₄ x 6¹/₄ in). Place the rectangle template on the satin (checking that it is aligned with the straight grain of the fabric) and insert a fine needle at each corner point. Remove the template. Using rayon machine thread in a sharps needle, make long stitches from each corner point to form a stitched rectangle on the front fabric. This will be used as a reference grid when transferring the skeleton design outline and the lines for the botanical name.

3. Using a fine lead pencil, trace the skeleton outline and rectangle outline of the botanical specimen onto tracing paper. Turn the tracing paper over and draw over the skeleton outline only, not the rectangle. With the tracing paper right side up, transfer the skeleton outline to the background fabric with a stylus, lining up the traced rectangle with the stitched rectangle (it helps to have a board underneath the frame of fabric to provide a firm surface).

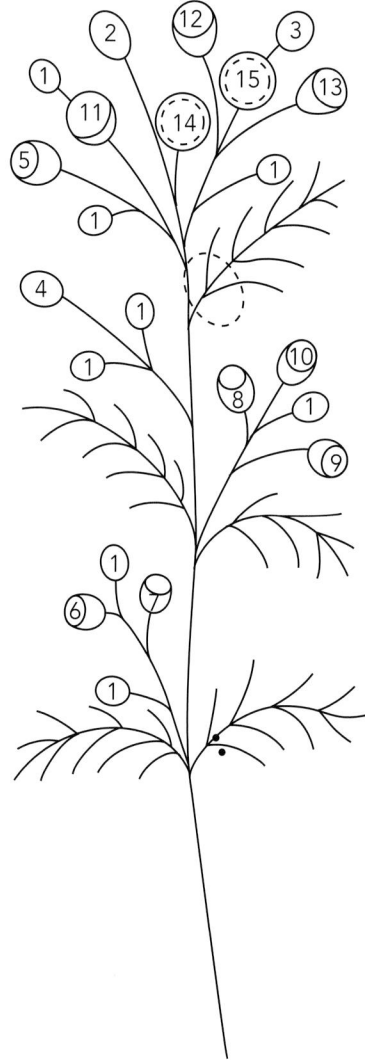

Flower direction diagram

TANSY

Requirements

- yellow felt: 10 x 8 cm (4 x 3 in)
- paper-backed fusible web: 10 x 8 cm (4 x 3 in)
- dark green stranded thread: Soie d'Alger 516 *or* DMC 937
- medium green stranded thread: Soie d'Alger 2125 *or* DMC 469
- light green stranded thread: Soie d'Alger 2124 *or* DMC 470
- tan stranded thread: Soie d'Alger 2615 *or* DMC 921
- dark yellow stranded thread: Soie d'Alger 546 *or* DMC 741
- medium yellow stranded thread: Soie d'Alger 545 *or* DMC 972
- light yellow stranded thread: Soie d'Alger 544 *or* DMC 725

STEMS

Work all the stems in stem stitch with two strands of thread (one each of dark and medium green) in a size 9 crewel needle.

1. Starting at the base, work a row of stem stitch along the main stem line to the fork in the stem near the top (V), then work the side stem to upper flower 15.

2. Work a second row of stem stitch (on the left side of the first row) along the main stem line to the fork in the stem (V), then work the side stem to flower bud 2.

3. Work all remaining side stems in stem stitch, taking the needle underneath flowers when required.

LEAVES

The leaves are embroidered with one strand of medium green thread in a size 10 crewel needle.

1. Work the skeleton outline of the stems and veins of the leaves in split stitch.

2. Starting at the tip of the leaf, work slanted straight stitches on either side of the split stitch veins to form feathery leaves (working the stitches towards the stem, like spaced fishbone stitch, but not crossing in the centre). Work shorter slanted stitches along the main stems of the leaves, if required.

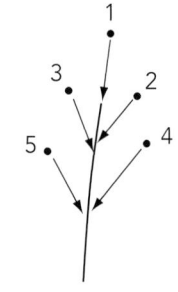

3. Work a few little leaves on the flower stems with split stitch, referring to the photograph for placement.

TANSY BUD AND FLOWER PADDING

The tansy buds and flowers are padded with yellow felt (one or two layers).

Using the skeleton outline as a guide, trace the following padding shapes on to paper-backed fusible web, then fuse to yellow felt (it helps to number the shapes):

- one shape for buds 1 (there are eight of these)
- one shape for buds and flowers 3, 4, 5, 6, 7, 8, 9, 10, 11, 12 and 13
- two shapes for flowers 14 and 15 (one the actual size and one slightly smaller)

Carefully cut out the shapes and put aside until required.

Apply the felt with the fusible web side up—this helps to prevent felt fibres 'fluffing' between the French knots.

TANSY BUDS 1

1. Using light green thread in a size 10 crewel needle, apply the felt bud padding (web side up) with a few stab stitches, then outline the shape in buttonhole stitch (stitches about 1.5 mm apart).

2. Embroider the padded bud in satin stitch, enclosing the outline.

3. Using medium green thread, work three detached chain stitches over the satin stitched bud to form sepals, starting each stitch at the stem end of the bud and ending at the tip.

TANSY BUDS 2, 3 AND 4

1. Using light green thread, apply the bud padding with a few stab stitches, then outline the shape in buttonhole stitch (stitches about 1.5 mm apart).

2. Embroider the padded bud in satin stitch, enclosing the outline.

3. Using two strands of light yellow thread in a size 8 milliners needle, work 3 or 4 French knots (one wrap around the needle) into the top of the bud, working the knots from the background fabric into the edge of the satin stitch.

4. Using medium green thread, work 3 or 4 detached chain stitches over the satin-stitched bud to form sepals, starting each stitch at the stem end of the bud and ending at the French knots.

Tansy Flowers 14 and 15

The tansy flowers are embroidered with concentric circles of French knots, using two strands of thread in a size 8 or 9 milliners needle (with one wrap around the needle). The rows are worked from the outside (the lightest colour) towards the centre (darkest colour). Work flowers 14 and 15 before flowers 5 to 13.

1. Tansy flowers 14 and 15 are padded with two layers of felt, one the actual size and one slightly smaller. Using light yellow thread, apply the felt shapes (web side up) to the background fabric with small stab stitches, applying the smallest shape first, and working the stab stitches 1–1.5 mm apart around the outside edge.

Smaller layer of felt underneath

2. Work the first row of French knots with light yellow thread, bringing the needle up in the felt and down over the edge of the felt into the background fabric. Work a circle of knots around the outside edge, side by side, with no felt edge showing.

Direction of stitch for French knot

3. Continue working concentric rows of French knots, changing from the lightest to the darkest colour, until a very small space is left in the middle. Adjust the colours according to the number of rows required to fill the space (do not be tempted to work the knots with two different colours of thread in the needle!).

   For example:

   · work the second row in light yellow
   · work the third row in medium yellow
   · work the fourth row in medium yellow
   · work the fifth row in dark yellow, and so on.

4. Using tan thread, embroider the centre of the flower with 2 or 3 French knots worked in the small space left in the middle.

TANSY FLOWERS 5 TO 13

The shape of the tansy flowers in this design is influenced by the direction in which the flower is leaning. The flowers may be viewed full-face (flower 15), from the side (flower 5) or from any direction in between. The circles of French knots are worked with directional shading in mind. It is easier to work these flowers if you have worked flowers 14 and 15 first.

1. Apply the felt padding (web side up) with a few stab stitches, using light yellow thread for the top edge (flower edge) and light green for the lower edge (flower base edge). Outline the lower edge of the shape in buttonhole stitch in light green—the length of this line depends on the amount of flower base showing—using the flower direction diagram as a guide.

2. Using the flower direction diagram (see page 108) as a guide, lightly draw in the internal outline of the flower head on the padding (this is optional—the line can be worked by eye). Using light green thread, embroider the base of the flower in satin stitch, working from the edge of the drawn line towards the stem, enclosing the stitched outline.

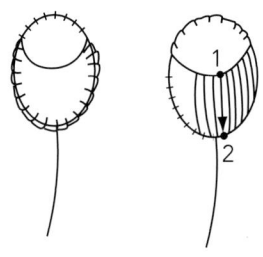

3. The flower is worked in concentric rows of French knots, working from lightest at the edge to darkest in the centre. Work the first row of French knots with light yellow thread, working the circle (or oval) of knots, side by side, over the upper edge of felt and at the edge of the satin stitched base.

4. Continue working concentric rows of French knots, changing from the lightest to the darkest colour, until a very small space is left for one of two French knots in tan thread, for the centre. If the flower is at quite an angle, the number of light and medium colour rows at the top of the flower may be reduced, or eliminated, to give a greater sense of perspective, placing the tan centre of the flower closer to the top edge.

For example, for flowers 5, 6, 7, 8 and 9, the rows may be worked as follows:

- work the first row, in light yellow, along the base edge only
- work the second row around the whole shape in medium yellow
- work successive rows along the lower edge only (inside the outline) leaving a small space for the tan centre knots near the top edge.

5. Using medium green thread, work five or six straight stitches over the satin-stitched base to form sepals, starting each stitch at the stem end of the bud and ending just under the row of French knots.

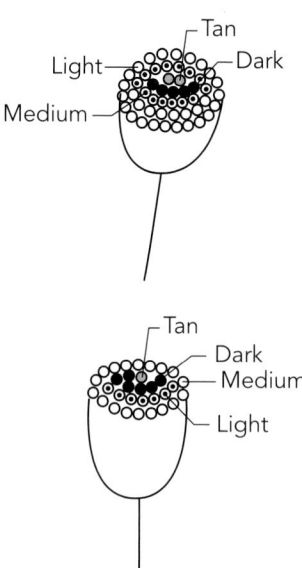

The brightly coloured Striped Bug, Graphosoma lineatum, is a common sight in summer, inhabiting flowering plants in meadows and grass verges.

The distinctive feature of this bug is the large shield-shaped scutellum which stretches from the base of the thorax to the tip of its abdomen, almost covering its crossed wings beneath. Graphosoma lineatum, with its bold stripes of burnt orange and dark greyish brown, can be found embellishing the borders of many illuminated manuscripts.

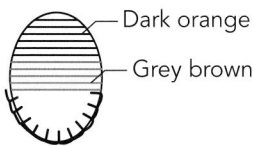

— Dark orange
— Grey brown

Striped Bug

The Striped Bug is made up of a padded abdomen, a detached scutellum (covering the wings), a detached thorax and embroidered head, eyes and legs.

Requirements

- quilter's muslin: 20 cm (8 in) square
- black felt: 5 x 8 cm (2 x 3 in)
- paper-backed fusible web: 5 x 8 cm (2 x 3 in)
- dark orange stranded thread: Soie d'Alger 636 *or* DMC 900
- grey/brown stranded thread: Soie d'Alger 3416 *or* DMC 3371
- steel grey metallic thread: Kreinik Cord 011c
- nylon clear thread: Madeira Monofil 60 col. 1001
- Mill Hill petite beads 40374 (blue/purple)
- 33 gauge white covered wire: two 10 cm (4 in) lengths (colour red if desired, Copic R17 Lipstick Orange)

Abdomen

1. Trace the abdomen outline on to paper-backed fusible web and fuse to black felt. Cut out the shape. Using one strand of dark orange thread in a size 10 crewel needle, apply the felt padding (web side up) to the background fabric with a few stab stitches, then work an outline of buttonhole stitch around the edge of the felt (stitches 1.5 mm apart).

2. The top half of the abdomen is embroidered in satin stitch, worked horizontally, enclosing the outline. Embroider the top third of the abdomen with dark orange thread, then change to grey/brown to work the satin stitches to the half-way line.

3. The Striped Bug has an orange and grey striped flange around the lower half of the abdomen. To embroider the flange, work a band of satin stitch around the lower edge of the abdomen, taking the stitches 2.5–3 mm in to the felt (enclosing the outline), and using dark orange and grey/brown thread to form the stripes. Start by working two satin stitches in grey/brown thread at the tail, then work two satin stitches in dark orange followed by two stitches in grey/brown. Repeat these stitches along the side of the abdomen to form stripes—four stripes each of dark orange and grey/brown—filling any remaining space at the side with grey/brown. Repeat the stripes on the other side of the tail.

4. Using dark orange thread, fill the remaining space, inside the striped flange, with satin stitch.

SCUTELLUM

The scutellum is actually the third division of the thorax as seen from above. It is the very large triangle seen in some bugs (genus *Hemiptera*), often almost covering their 'crossed-over' wings.

1. Mount muslin into a small hoop and trace the outlines for the detached scutellum (including the side markings) and the detached thorax.

2. With one strand of dark orange thread, couch the wire around the scutellum outline with five stitches (work a stitch at each side marking and at the tail), leaving two tails of wire. Buttonhole stitch the wire to the fabric with dark orange or grey/brown thread as follows:

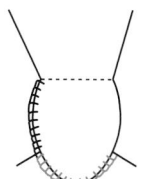

- starting at the top edge, work the side of the scutellum in dark orange thread until the side marking is reached
- change to grey/brown thread to work buttonhole stitches around the lower edge to the other side marking, returning to dark orange to work the remaining side edge.

The buttonholed edge represents the folded wings underneath the scutellum.

3. Using dark orange thread, work a row of split back stitch around the inside edge of the wire and a row of back stitch across the top edge of the scutellum.

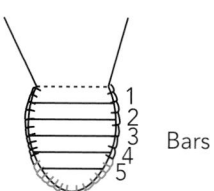

Bars

4. The scutellum is covered with stripes worked in raised stem stitch. With dark orange thread, work five evenly spaced straight stitches across the scutellum, inserting the needle close to the inside edge of the wire. These stitches form the bars over which the raised stem stitch is worked.

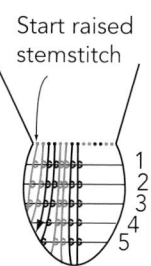

Start raised stemstitch

5. Using one strand of thread in a tapestry needle, fill the shape with raised stem stitch, working each row from the top edge of the scutellum (enclosing the back stitch) towards the tail, inserting the needle inside the edge of the wire. Starting at the top edge corner, work consecutive rows of raised stem stitch, from one side of the scutellum to the other, as follows:

- work 2 rows of grey/brown over 3 bars
- work 2 rows of dark orange over 4 bars
- work 2 rows of grey/brown over 5 bars
- work 2 rows of dark orange over 5 bars (Note: as this is the centre row, insert the needle at the point of the tail)
- work 2 rows of grey/brown over 5 bars
- work 2 rows of dark orange over 4 bars
- finally, work 2 rows of grey over 3 bars.

The spacing of the rows needs to be considered before work commences—make sure the centre row is actually in the centre of the shape. I often find it easier to use a size 10 crewel needle, using the eye of the needle to work the raised stem stitch and the point of the needle to insert the thread close to the wire.

THORAX

1. With one strand of dark orange thread, couch the wire around the thorax outline, leaving two tails of wire at the top edge of the thorax that touch but do not cross.

   Stitch the wire to the fabric with buttonhole stitch, working stripes of dark orange and grey/brown as shown.

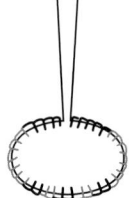

2. Using dark orange thread, work a row of split back stitch around the inside edge of the wire, then work a few padding stitches.

3. Embroider the thorax in satin stitch, working stripes with dark orange and grey/brown thread (two satin stitches in each colour). Starting with a dark orange stripe in the middle of the thorax, work two stripes of each colour on either side of the centre stripe.

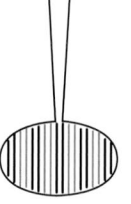

To Complete the Bug

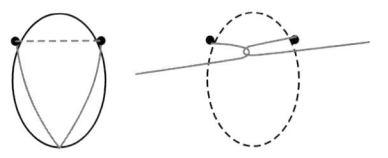

1. Carefully cut out the scutellum and the thorax and shape slightly. Using two yarn darners, insert the wires of the scutellum through to the back at • , on either side of the top edge of the abdomen (check that the tip of the scutellum is the same length as the abdomen). Bend the wires towards each other at the back and twist once, holding the tails of wire at the sides with tape. Do not trim the wire tails until the bug is finished.

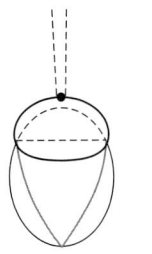

2. Using a yarn darner, insert the wires of the thorax at the top of the abdomen, positioning the thorax so that it overlaps the scutellum by about 1 mm. Bend the wire tails up under the 'head' and hold with tape.

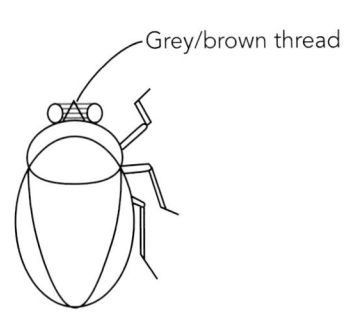

Grey/brown thread

3. Using dark orange thread, work the head in satin stitch, catching in the wire tails at the back and covering the wire insertion point. Change to grey/brown thread and a sharps needle, and stitch a blue/purple petite bead on each side of the head for eyes. Work two straight stitches over the head to form an inverted V in grey/brown thread.

4. With a double strand of steel grey metallic thread in a size 9 milliners needle, work each leg with straight stitches— working two straight stitches (on top of each other) for each of the inner two leg segments, and one stitch for the thinner outer leg segment (refer to the abdomen and leg diagram for a guide to length and placement of stitches). Work two loose straight stitches on either side of the head for the antennae. Gently shape the scutellum and thorax with tweezers then trim the wires.

DAMSELFLY

This damselfly has detached gauzy wings and a detached beaded abdomen.

Requirements

- teal shot crystal organza: 15 cm (6 in) square
- pearl metal organdie: 15 cm (6 in) square
- paper-backed fusible web: 15 cm (6 in) square
- blue-bronze snakeskin: 2.5 cm (1 in) square
- black felt scrap
- blue rayon machine thread: Madeira Rayon 40 col. 1028
- black soft metallic thread: Madeira Metallic 40 col. 70
- gold/black metallic thread: Kreinik Cord 205c
- slate/black metallic thread: Kreinik Cord 225c
- ivory stranded thread: DMC Ecru
- nylon clear thread: Madeira Monofil 60 col. 1001
- 4 mm blue/green bugle beads
- 3 mm blue/purple bead
- Mill Hill seed beads 374 (blue/purple)
- 28 gauge silver uncovered wire (wings): four 12 cm (4³/₄ in) lengths
- 33 gauge silver uncovered wire (abdomen): 23 cm (9 in) length

Smaller and more delicately built than dragonflies, damselflies have a much weaker, more fluttering, dancing flight. The common Azure Damselfly, Coenagrion puella, is mainly seen in summer, flitting over pools, fishponds and slow-moving water, and settling on aquatic plants. The males of the Azure Damselfly are blue, while the females are green to yellowish green. The sexes are also distinguished from each other by the different markings on their slender abdomen.

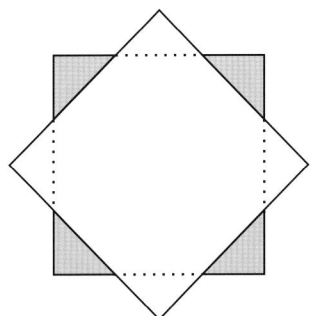

Detached Wings

1. Using paper-backed fusible web, fuse the teal crystal organza to the pearl organdie, rotating one of the layers 45 degrees to be on the bias grain (iron between sheets of baking parchment to protect the iron and the wing fabrics). Mount into a small hoop, teal organza side uppermost.

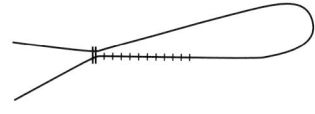

2. Using tweezers, bend the 28 gauge uncovered wire around the wing outline templates—two fore wings and two hind wings—leaving two tails of wire at the base of each wing that touch but do not cross. Place the wire shapes on the hoop of wing fabric, holding the wire tails in place with masking tape. Make sure that you have a right and a left fore wing and a right and a left hind wing.

3. Using one strand of blue rayon machine thread in a sharps needle, stitch the wire to the wing fabric, with small, close, overcast stitches, working several stitches over both wires, at the base of the wing, to begin and end the stitching.

4. To embroider the wing marking (pterostigma) in the upper corner of each wing, work three satin stitches, on top of each other, with black soft metallic thread, knotting the tails of thread together at the back.

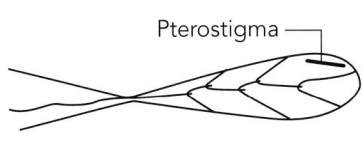

Pterostigma

5. Using gold/black metallic thread in a size 9 milliners needle, work the veins in each wing with a row of feather stitch, using the diagram as a guide. It is safer to keep the tails of thread at the front until the wings have been cut out, then insert them through to the back. The tails of thread are secured after the wing has been applied to the main fabric. Carefully cut out the wings, retaining the tails of thread.

6. Using a large yarn darner, insert the wire (and thread) tails of the two fore wings through the upper dot • marked on the background. Insert the two hind wings through the lower dot • as marked. Bend the wire tails under the wings, holding the tails with masking tape. Do not trim the wires until the damselfly is finished. Stitch the wires to the backing (under the wings) with ecru thread, taking the stitches no further than the span of the wing.

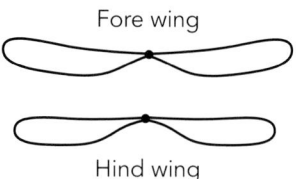

Fore wing

Hind wing

Detached Abdomen

1. Bend the length of 33 gauge uncovered wire in half. Thread the tails of the wire through two blue/purple petite beads and slide them towards the bend in the wire. Using a small yarn darner, shape a tiny loop in the wire at the bend, to prevent the beads sliding off the end of the abdomen. Thread the tails of wire through six blue/green bugle beads to make the abdomen.

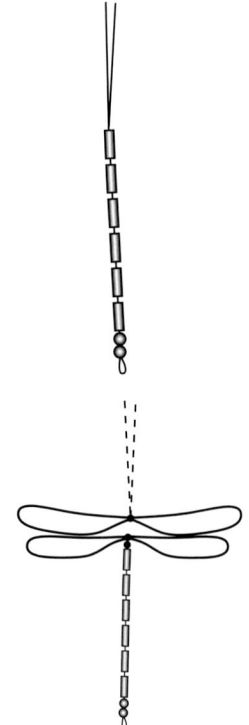

2. Using a yarn darner, insert the wire tails of the abdomen through to the back, close to the insertion point of the hind wings. Hold the tails of wire under the 'head' end of the damselfly with masking tape. Secure the wire with a few stitches. Do not trim the wire or remove the tape until the damselfly is finished.

THORAX

The felt padding and the snakeskin thorax are stitched in place with nylon thread in a sharps needle.

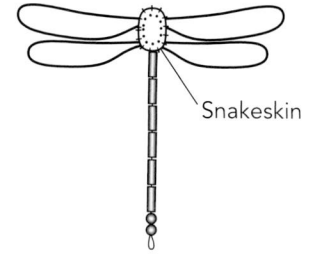

1. To pad the thorax, cut a small piece of black felt (using the diagram as a guide) and apply over the wire insertion points with a few stab stitches around the outside edge.

2. Cut a thorax shape out of snakeskin and check for size (it needs to be just large enough to reach the background fabric over the padding, wings and the top of the abdomen). Apply the snakeskin with small stab stitches, working the stitches from the background fabric into the edge of the snakeskin. Use tweezers to shape the snakeskin into a mound over the felt padding, wings and the top of the abdomen.

Snakeskin

HEAD AND EYES

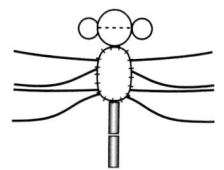

Using nylon thread, stitch a 3 mm bead close to the top of the thorax, for the head, keeping the hole in the bead parallel to the top of the thorax. Bring the needle through to the front and stitch a blue/purple seed bead on either side of the head bead for the eyes, taking the needle through the hole of the head bead several times so that the eyes are suspended on either side. Secure the thread.

LEGS AND ANTENNAE

1. Using a double strand of slate/black metallic thread in a size 9 milliners needle, work each leg with three straight stitches, using the diagram as a guide to length and position. As the legs are stitched towards the thorax, the wings will need to be gently lifted up when working the stitches.

2. Using a single strand of slate/black metallic thread, work a fly stitch above the head for the antennae.

Shape the abdomen and the wings, then trim the wire tails.

LADYBIRD

The ladybird, which features in each of the botanical specimens, may be applied wherever you wish—the abdomen outline is not included in the design. The ladybird may also be reduced in size if desired.

The instructions for embroidering the ladybird are on page 43.

BOTANICAL NAME

The lower edge of the stitched rectangle, around the specimen, is used to position the guidelines for stitching the botanical name TANACETUM VULGARE. (Note that if you wish to use upper and lower case letters, only the first word of a botanical name is capitalised.) The letters are stitched by eye as traced lines would be difficult to cover.

The instructions for working the botanical name are on page 45.

TANACETUM
VULGARE

Venus' Looking Glass and Bumblebee

Venus' Looking Glass, Specularia hybrida, is a summer-flowering member of the campanula family, with purple bell-shaped flowers and oval leaves with wavy edges. A distinctive feature of this plant is its long seed capsules, almost cylindrical in shape, which are present throughout the flowering period.

Also known as a Bellflower, the scientific name, Specularia, comes from the Latin specularius, referring to mirrors and the plant's shiny seeds. In Roman mythology, it is said that Venus, the goddess of love and beauty, had lost her magic mirror (anyone who looked in it would see nothing but beauty). A poor shepherd boy found the mirror, but would not return it because he had become entranced with his own image. Venus sent Cupid to retrieve it, and in his haste, Cupid struck the shepherd's hand. The mirror shattered, and everywhere a piece of it landed, a Venus' Looking Glass flower began to grow.

SPECULARIA
HYBRIDA

This small stumpwork panel is one of a series of embroidered botanical specimens and insects inspired by the illuminated pages of medieval manuscripts. Embroidered on a background of ivory satin, this design features Venus' Looking Glass, *Specularia hybrida*, a summer-flowering member of the campanula family, with purple bell-shaped flowers worked with detached petals, and long seed capsules. Nestled amongst the foliage are a Large Copper Butterfly, *Lycaena dispar*, with raised detached wings, a Buff-tailed Bumblebee, *Bombus terrestris*, with detached gauzy wings and fluffy abdomen, and a tiny ladybird with detached elytra. The botanical name of the flower may be stitched at the base of this specimen.

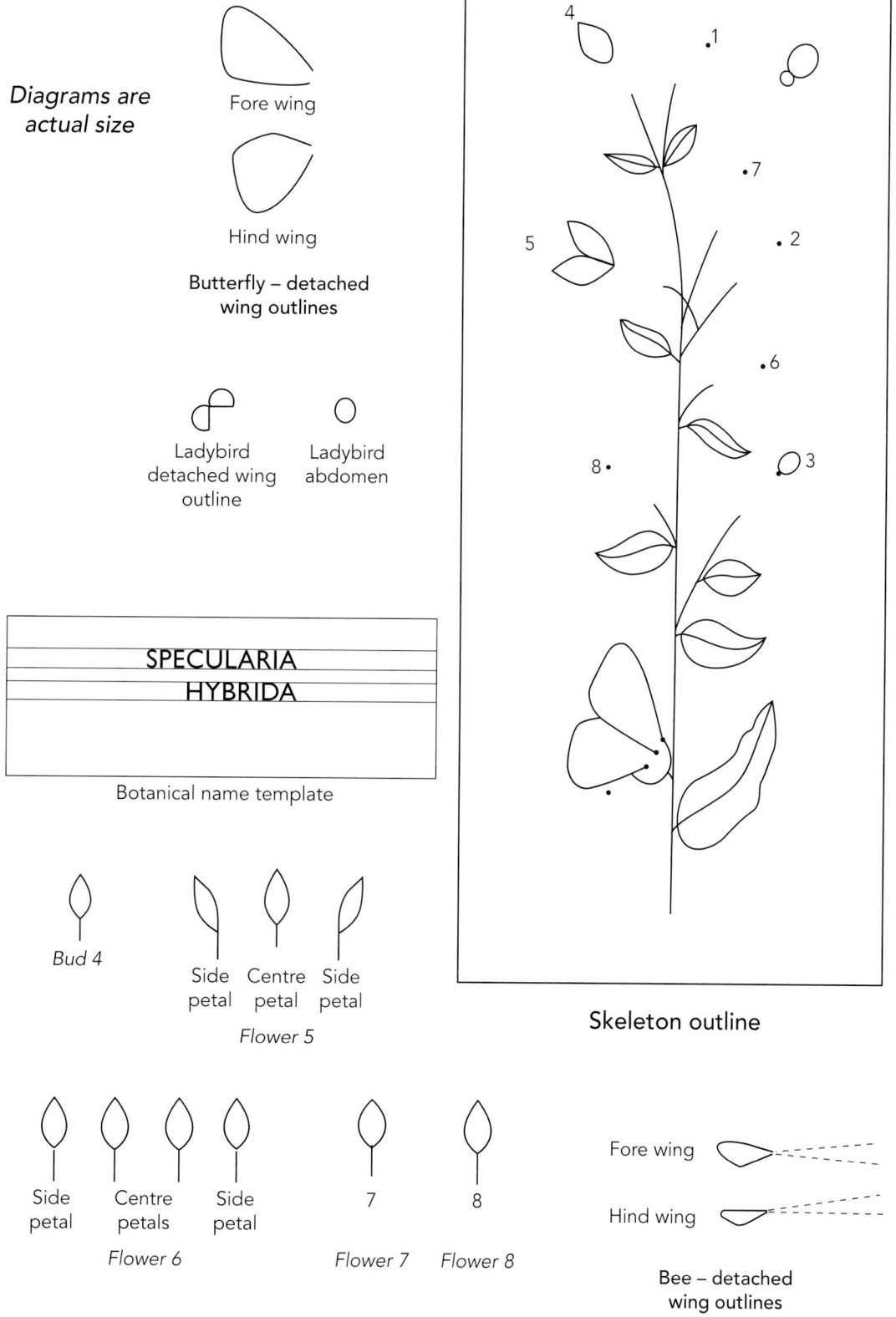

Diagrams are actual size

Fore wing

Hind wing

Butterfly – detached wing outlines

Ladybird detached wing outline

Ladybird abdomen

SPECULARIA

HYBRIDA

Botanical name template

Bud 4

Side petal   Centre petal   Side petal

Flower 5

Side petal   Centre petals   Side petal

Flower 6

Skeleton outline

Side petal   Centre petals   Side petal

Flower 6

7

8

Flower 7   *Flower 8*

Fore wing

Hind wing

Bee – detached wing outlines

Detached petal outlines

Overall Requirements

This is the *complete* list of requirements for this embroidery.
For ease of use, the requirements of each individual element
are repeated under its heading—for example, Venus' Looking
Glass requirements, Buff-tailed Bumblebee requirements.

- ivory satin background fabric: 30 cm (12 in) square
- quilter's muslin (or calico) backing fabric: 30 cm (12 in)
  square (*if working all panels on one piece of fabric, refer to the
  instructions on page 18*)

- quilter's muslin: three 20 cm (8 in) squares
- red cotton fabric (homespun): 15 cm (6 in) square
- honey mottled organza: 15 cm (6 in) square
- pearl metal organdie: 15 cm (6 in) square

- 25 cm (10 in) embroidery hoop or stretcher bars (if working
  as a single panel)
- 10 cm (4 in) embroidery hoops
- needles:
  crewel/embroidery sizes 9 and 10
  milliners/straw size 9
  sharps size 12
  tapestry size 28
  chenille size 18
  sharp yarn darners sizes 14–18
- embroidery equipment (see page 266)

*This illustration of Venus' Looking
Glass from a sixteenth century
French manuscript inspired my
embroidery.*

- dark green stranded thread (stems): Soie d'Alger 3725 *or* DMC 935
- medium green stranded thread (stems, leaves): Soie d'Alger 2126 *or* DMC 937
- light green stranded thread (leaves, seed capsule): Soie d'Alger 2124 *or* DMC 470
- dark purple stranded thread (flowers): Soie d'Alger 3336 *or* DMC 550
- medium purple stranded thread (flowers): Soie d'Alger 3315 *or* DMC 552
- light purple stranded thread (flowers): Soie d'Alger 3313 *or* DMC 553
- medium violet stranded thread (flowers): Soie d'Alger 3314 *or* DMC 3837
- light yellow stranded thread (flowers): Soie d'Alger 621 *or* DMC 745
- dark grey stranded thread (butterfly): Cifonda Art Silk 215 *or* DMC 317
- medium grey stranded thread (butterfly): Cifonda Art Silk 212 *or* DMC 318
- light grey stranded thread (butterfly): Cifonda Art Silk 211 *or* DMC 762
- light blue stranded thread (butterfly): Cifonda Art Silk 181 *or* DMC 159
- medium copper stranded thread (butterfly): Cifonda Art Silk 103 *or* DMC 3776
- light copper stranded thread (butterfly): Cifonda Art Silk 102 *or* DMC 402
- dark yellow stranded thread (butterfly): Cifonda Art Silk 175 *or* DMC 742
- orange stranded thread (butterfly): Cifonda Art Silk 135A *or* DMC 947

- black stranded thread (butterfly): Cifonda Art Silk Black *or* DMC 310
- steel/grey stranded thread (butterfly): Soie d'Alger 3443 *or* DMC 414
- brown/grey stranded thread (bee): DMC 844
- rust stranded thread (bee): DMC 921
- buff stranded thread (bee): DMC 3033
- black stranded thread (ladybird): DMC 310
- red stranded thread (ladybird): DMC 349

- slate/black metallic thread (butterfly): Kreinik Cord 225c
- silver/black metallic thread (butterfly): Kreinik Cord 105c
- copper/black metallic thread (bee): Kreinik Cord 215c
- gold metallic thread (bee): Kreinik Cord 002c
- black metallic thread (ladybird): Kreinik Cord 005c
- thick silver/black metallic thread (butterfly): Madeira Metallic No. 40 col. 442
- variegated pale grey chenille thread (butterfly): col. Neutral
- soft cotton padding thread (seed capsule): DMC Soft Cotton 2470
- cream rayon machine thread (bee): Madeira Rayon 40 col. 1082
- grey/green rayon machine thread (botanical name): Madeira Rayon 40 col. 1062

- 3 mm bronze/blue bead
- Mill Hill Seed Beads 374 (purple/green)
- Mill Hill Petite Beads 42014 (black)

- 33 gauge white covered wire (petals): eighteen 9 cm ($3^{1}/_{2}$ in) lengths (colour purple if desired, Copic BV08 Blue Violet)

- 33 gauge white covered wire (ladybird): 10 cm (4 in) length (colour red if desired, Copic R17 Lipstick Orange)

- 33 gauge white covered wire (butterfly): two 10 cm (4 in) lengths

- 30 gauge green covered wire (stigma): four 10 cm (4 in) lengths

- 28 gauge silver uncovered wire (bee wings): four 10 cm (4 in) lengths

- thin card for rectangle template

- heavyweight (110 gsm) tracing paper

- translucent removable tape (e.g. Scotch Removable Magic Tape)

PREPARATION

1. Mount the satin background fabric and the muslin backing
    into the 25 cm (10 in) embroidery hoop or frame. If
    working all panels on one piece of fabric, follow the
    instructions on page 258.

2. Cut a rectangle from thin card, 7 x 16 cm (2³/₄ in x
    6¹/₄ in). Place the rectangle template on the satin (checking
    that it is aligned with the straight grain of the fabric)
    and insert a fine needle at each corner point. Remove the
    template. Using rayon machine thread in a sharps needle,
    make long stitches from each corner point to form a stitched
    rectangle on the front fabric. This will be used as a
    reference grid when transferring the skeleton design outline
    and the lines for the botanical name.

3. Using a fine lead pencil, trace the skeleton outline
    (including the dots at the end of the seed capsules) and
    rectangle outline of the botanical specimen onto tracing
    paper. Turn the tracing paper over and draw over the
    skeleton outline only, not the rectangle. With the tracing
    paper right side up, transfer the skeleton outline to the
    satin with a stylus, lining up the traced rectangle with the
    stitched rectangle (it helps to have a board underneath the
    frame of fabric to provide a firm surface).

Venus' Looking Glass

Requirements

- quilter's muslin: two 20 cm (8 in) squares
- dark green stranded thread: Soie d'Alger 3725 *or* DMC 935
- medium green stranded thread: Soie d'Alger 2126 *or* DMC 937
- light green stranded thread: Soie d'Alger 2124 *or* DMC 470
- dark purple stranded thread: Soie d'Alger 3336 *or* DMC 550
- medium purple stranded thread: Soie d'Alger 3315 *or* DMC 552
- light purple stranded thread: Soie d'Alger 1313 *or* DMC 553
- medium violet stranded thread: Soie d'Alger 3314 *or* DMC 3837
- light yellow stranded thread: Soie d'Alger 621 *or* DMC 745
- soft cotton padding thread (seed capsule): DMC Soft Cotton 2470
- 33 gauge white covered wire (petals): eighteen 9 cm (3½ in) lengths (colour purple if desired, Copic BV08 Blue Violet)
- 30 gauge green covered wire (stigma): four 10 cm (4 in) lengths

Stems

The stems are worked in stem stitch with two strands of thread (one each of dark and medium green) in a size 9 crewel needle.

1. Starting at the base, work a row of stem stitch along the main stem line, veering to the right to finish at the end of stem 7.

2. Work a second row of stem stitch (on the left side of the first row) along the main stem line, veering to the left to finish at the end of stem 4.

3. Work remaining side stems in stem stitch, working over the main stems for stem 5.

Leaves

The leaves are worked in padded buttonhole stitch with one strand of thread in a size 10 crewel needle.

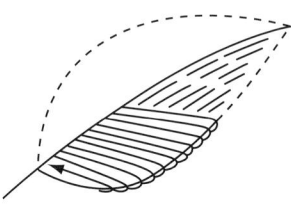

1. Work the central vein in split stitch with light green thread.

2. Using medium green thread, outline the leaf with small back stitches, then work padding stitches inside the outline.

3. Embroider each side of the leaf with long buttonhole stitches (worked at an angle), starting at the base of the leaf and enclosing the backstitch outline. Insert the needle slightly under the central vein (to avoid a gap).

Seed Capsules 1 and 2

The seed capsules are embroidered in raised stem stitch, worked over padding of soft cotton thread. If this thread is not available, substitute 14 strands of light green stranded thread. The sepals at each end of the seed capsules are worked in needle-weaving.

Seed Capsule

1. To pad the seed capsule, make one stitch between the end of the stem and • with a double strand of soft cotton thread in a chenille needle (or fourteen strands of stranded thread, doubled). Cross the tails of padding thread behind the stitch, at the back, and hold at each end with masking tape.

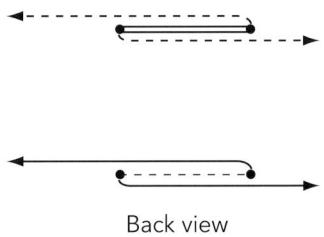

Back view

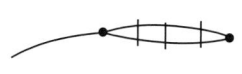

2. With one strand of light green thread in a size 10 crewel needle, work three evenly spaced couching stitches over the padding, catching the tails of padding thread underneath (the tails will be trimmed later). The seed capsule will be embroidered in raised stem stitch over these couching stitches, so they need to be snug but not too tight.

3. Using one strand of thread in a tapestry needle, work eight rows of raised stem stitch to cover the padding, in the following order (to form stripes):

   - two rows with light green thread
   - one row with medium green thread
   - two rows with light green thread
   - one row with medium green thread
   - finish with two rows of light green thread

Trim the tails of padding thread.

Sepals

Using one strand of light green thread, work three sepals at each end of the seed capsule in needle-weaving. Work the side sepals first, then the centre sepal. Use a small crewel needle to stitch the loop and a tapestry needle to work the needle-weaving. To work a sepal:

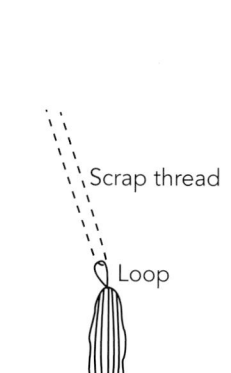

Scrap thread

Loop

1. Bring the needle out at the end of the seed capsule then insert again (through the same hole), making the loop about 3 mm ($^1/_8$ in) long. Pass a length of scrap thread through the loop to enable it to be held under tension while working the needle-weaving.

2. Work a tiny securing stitch at the back before bringing the needle out again at the base of the loop. Change to a tapestry needle. Holding the loop under tension with the scrap thread, slide the needle through the centre of the loop, alternately from the right then the left, to fill the loop with needle-weaving (10–12 weaving stitches), keeping the tension firm and even. Remove the scrap thread, then

insert the needle into the background fabric, allowing the sepal to curve slightly. Secure the thread at the back. Repeat for the remaining sepals.

All the sepals in this piece are worked the same way (there are 39 of them!).

Bud 3

1. Using medium purple thread in a size 10 crewel needle, outline the bud with small back stitches. Embroider the bud in padded satin stitch, enclosing the outline.

2. To pad the seed capsule, make a stitch between the end of the stem and the base of the bud with a double strand of soft cotton thread. Following the instructions for seed capsule 1, complete the seed capsule, working the rows of raised stem stitch towards the base of the embroidered bud.

3. Work three sepals at each end of the seed capsule, curving the ends of the upper sepals around the bud.

Detached Petals

The remaining buds and flowers require eighteen detached petals which, while varying a little in size and colour, are worked the same way. Work all the petals, on two hoops of fabric, and keep aside until required.

1. Mount muslin into a small hoop and trace eight petal outlines—one petal 4 outline, three petal 5 outlines (one centre petal and two side petals) and four petal 6 outlines (two centre petals and two side petals). Number each petal to avoid confusion.

2. Trace five petal 7 and five petal 8 outlines on the remaining hoop of muslin.

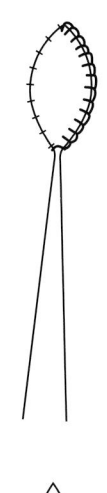

Bud 4 Detached Petal

1. Using one strand of medium purple thread in a size 10 crewel needle, couch wire around the petal outline, leaving two tails of wire at the base that touch but do not cross. Buttonhole stitch the wire to the muslin. Work a row of split stitch around the inside edge of the wire.

2. Embroider the petal in shaded long and short stitch, with dark purple at the base of the petal blending to medium purple at the outer edge.

Flower 5 Detached Petals

1. With medium purple thread, couch wire around the centre petal outline, leaving two tails of wire at the base that touch but do not cross. Buttonhole stitch the wire to the muslin. Work a row of split stitch around the inside edge of the wire.

2. Embroider the petal in shaded long and short stitch, with light purple at the base of the petal blending to medium purple at the outer edge.

3. Using medium purple thread, couch wire around a side petal outline, leaving one tail of wire at the base of the petal (cutting the other tail of wire off at the base of the petal). Buttonhole stitch the wire to the muslin, then embroider as for the centre petal. Work the remaining side petal (removing the opposite tail of wire).

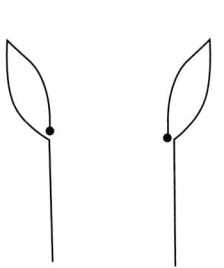

Flower 6 Detached Petals

1. With medium purple thread, couch wire around a centre petal outline, leaving two tails of wire at the base that touch but do not cross. Buttonhole stitch the wire to the muslin. Work a row of split stitch around the inside edge of the wire.

2. Embroider the petal in shaded long and short stitch, with a little dark purple at the base of the petal, blending to medium violet then medium purple at the outer edge. Work the remaining centre petal and both side petals the same way (all petals have two tails of wire).

Flower 7 Detached Petals

1. With medium purple thread, couch wire around the petal outline, leaving two tails of wire at the base that touch but do not cross. Buttonhole stitch the wire to the muslin. Work a row of split stitch around the inside edge of the wire.

2. Embroider the petal in shaded long and short stitch, with a little dark purple at the base of the petal, blending to medium violet then medium purple at the outer edge. Work all five petals.

Flower 8 Detached Petals

1. With medium violet thread, couch wire around the petal outline, leaving two tails of wire at the base that touch but do not cross. Buttonhole stitch the wire to the muslin. Work a row of split stitch around the inside edge of the wire.

2. Embroider the petal in shaded long and short stitch, with a little dark purple at the base of the petal, blending to medium purple then medium violet at the outer edge. Work all five petals.

BUD 4

1. Using medium purple thread, work the top edge of the background petal with a row of close, long and short buttonhole stitch (covering about a third of the petal). Embroider the remainder of the petal in long and short stitch (quite densely worked).

2. Cut out detached petal 4 and shape slightly. Using a yarn darner, insert the wire tails through to the back at the base of the background petal. Bend the wire tails behind the embroidered petal and secure with a few stitches. Do not trim the wire tails until the bud is finished.

3. To pad the seed capsule, make a stitch between the end of the stem and the base of the detached petal with a double strand of soft cotton thread. Following the instructions for seed capsule 1, complete the seed capsule, working the rows of raised stem stitch towards the base of the detached petal.

4. Work three sepals at each end of the seed capsule. Trim wire tails.

FLOWER 5

1. Using medium purple thread, work the top edge of the two background petals with a row of close, long and short buttonhole stitch (covering about a third of the petal). Embroider the petals in shaded long and short stitch, with medium purple at the outer edge blending to light purple at the base.

2. Cut out the three detached petals for flower 5 and shape slightly. Using a yarn darner, insert the side petal wire tails through one hole, at the base of the background petals. Bend the wire tails behind the embroidered petals and hold with masking tape. Apply the centre petal through same hole (below the side petal wires), and bend the wire tails behind the embroidered petals. Secure all wires with a few stitches. Do not trim the wire tails until the flower is finished.

3. To pad the seed capsule, make a stitch between the end of
    the stem and the base of the detached petals with a double
    strand of soft cotton thread. Following the instructions
    for seed capsule 1, complete the seed capsule, working the
    rows of raised stem stitch towards the base of the detached
    petals.

To Work a Stigma

Green-covered wire is wrapped with one strand of medium
green thread to make a stigma.

1. Tie the thread to the wire, 1 cm (3/8 in) from one end,
    leaving one short tail of thread and a longer tail with
    which to wrap.

2. Wrap the wire (back over the short tail of thread) for at
    least 1 cm (3/8 in) and secure the wrapping thread (retain
    the tail of thread).

3. Cut off the unwrapped tip of the wire close to the start of
    the wrapping (as this tip is quite fragile it can be dipped in
    PVA glue if desired). Work four stigmas (for flowers 5, 6, 7
    and 8).

4. Carefully lift up the detached petals and, using a small
    yarn darner, insert the wire tail of the stigma (and the
    tail of thread), through to the back near the base of the
    background petals (the length of the wrapped stigma at
    the front is about 3–4 mm). Secure to the back of the seed
    capsule with a few stitches.

5. Work three sepals at each end of the seed capsule, working
    the end of a sepal into a detached petal if desired. Trim
    wire tails.

FLOWER 6

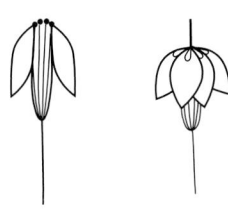

1. To pad the seed capsule, make a stitch between the end of the stem and • (6) with a double strand of soft cotton thread. Following the instructions for seed capsule 1, complete the seed capsule, working the rows of raised stem stitch towards the stem.

2. Work three sepals at the stem end of the seed capsule.

3. Cut out the four detached petals for flower 6 and shape slightly. The wire tails of the detached petals are inserted through four separate holes (as close to each other as possible), at the end of the seed capsule. As the petals will eventually be bent back over the seed capsule, take this into account when inserting the petals. Using a yarn darner, apply the side petals first, then the two centre petals, holding the wire tails behind the seed capsule with masking tape. Bend the petals back over the seed capsule and, when adjusted into position, secure the wire tails with a few stitches. Do not trim the wire tails until the flower is finished.

4. With one strand of light yellow thread in a sharps needle, work a small detached chain stitch into the base of each petal (bring the needle out at the wire insertion point and through the petal to the back).

5. Using a small yarn darner, insert the wire tail of the stigma (and the tail of thread), through to the back at the base of the detached petals (the length of the wrapped stigma at the front is about 3–4 mm). Secure to the back of the seed capsule with a few stitches. Trim all wires.

FLOWER 7

1. To pad the seed capsule, make a stitch between the end of the stem and • (7) with a double strand of soft cotton thread. Following the instructions for seed capsule 1, complete the seed capsule, working the rows of raised stem stitch towards the stem.

2. Work three sepals at the stem end of the seed capsule.

3. Cut out the five detached petals for flower 7 and shape slightly. Draw a circle of five dots (the wire insertion points), very close together, at the end of the seed capsule. Insert the wire tails of the detached petals through five individual holes (as close to each other as possible), using a large yarn darner. Bend the wire tails under each petal and secure to the back with small stitches. Do not trim the wire tails until the flower is finished.

4. Using light yellow thread, work a detached chain stitch into the base of each petal, bringing the needle out from the wire insertion point for each petal.

5. Using a small yarn darner, insert the wire tail of the stigma (and the tail of thread), through to the back through the centre of the flower (the length of the wrapped stigma at the front is about 3–4 mm). Secure to the back of the seed capsule with a few stitches. Using tweezers, gently push each petal towards the centre to make the space as small as possible. Trim all wires.

FLOWER 8

Cut out the five detached petals for flower 8 and work as for flower 7.

Buff-tailed Bumblebees, Bombus terrestris, are very common in woods and gardens where they pollinate a great many plants, in particular cranberries, raspberries, sage, thistles and fruit trees. The queens emerge from hibernation at the beginning of spring to look for a suitable site for a nest; their search is accompanied by a deep buzzing. This species lives mostly in holes in the ground (often an abandoned mouse nest), which the female bee lines with pieces of dry grass and leaves.

Buff-tailed Bumblebee

Requirements

- honey mottled organza: 15 cm (6 in) square
- pearl metal organdie: 15 cm (6 in) square
- brown/grey stranded thread: DMC 844
- rust stranded thread: DMC 921
- buff stranded thread: DMC 3033
- cream rayon machine thread: Madeira Rayon 40 col. 1082
- copper/black metallic thread: Kreinik Cord 215c
- gold metallic thread: Kreinik Cord 002c
- Mill Hill seed beads 374 (purple/green)
- 28 gauge silver uncovered wire: four 10 cm (4 in) lengths

Thorax and Abdomen

1. Outline the abdomen and the small circle next to it (the thorax) with small back stitches using one strand of buff thread.

2. The abdomen is filled with consecutive rows of Turkey knots, worked with two strands of either brown/grey, rust or buff thread in a size 9 crewel needle. Starting at the 'thorax end' of the abdomen, work two rows of Turkey knots in brown/grey, then three rows in rust thread. Work two more rows in brown/grey then three rows in buff for the tail (adjust the number of rows for each stripe, if necessary, to end up with a buff tail). The Turkey knots should pierce the back stitches but not protrude outside them.

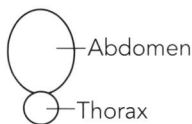

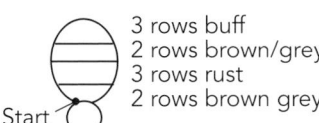

3. Cut the loops between the Turkey knots and comb the threads upwards. Carefully cut and comb the threads to form a velvety mound for the abdomen.

Wings

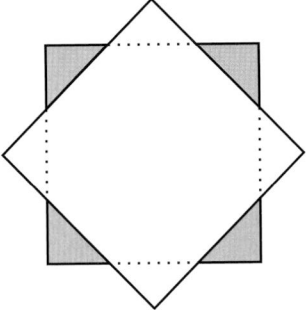

1. Mount the honey mottled organza and the pearl metal organdie (as a backing) into a small hoop, one layer of fabric rotated 45 degrees to be on the bias grain (the wing fabrics are not fused together).

2. Bend uncovered wire around the wing outline templates— two fore wings and two hind wings, leaving two tails of wire at the base of the wing that touch but do not cross. Place the wire shapes on the hoop of wing fabric, holding the wire tails in place with masking tape. Make sure that you have a right and a left fore wing and a right and a left hind wing.

3. Using one strand of cream rayon machine thread in a sharps needle, stitch the wire to the wing fabric with small, close overcast stitches, working several stitches over both wires, at the base of the wing, to begin and end the stitching.

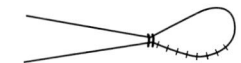

4. With one strand of gold metallic thread in a milliners needle, work a fly stitch in each wing for veins, retaining the tails of thread at the corners of the wings. Carefully cut out the wings, taking care not to cut the tails of metallic thread.

To Complete the Bee

1. Using a yarn darner, insert the wings through two separate holes, inside the stitched thorax outline—the right fore and hind wings together through one hole, and the left fore and hind wings through the other (they will be very close together). Bend the wires to the sides (under the wings) and stitch to the backing with tiny stitches. Do not trim the wire tails until the bee is finished.

2. Using two strands of brown/grey thread, work Turkey knots between the wings to fill the thorax (approximately eight knots), then work three knots in rust thread inside the 'head' end of the thorax. Cut the Turkey knots to form a velvety mound.

3. To form the head/eyes, stitch two purple/green seed beads (side by side with one stitch), very close to the thorax, using brown/grey thread. Work another stitch through both beads then a stitch between the beads (across the previous stitches towards the thorax). Push the beads together with tweezers.

4. With two strands of bronze/black metallic thread in a milliners needle, stitch six legs, working three back stitches for each leg. Work a fly stitch for the antennae with one strand of metallic thread.

BUTTERFLY

This Copper Butterfly has two wings embroidered on the background fabric and two detached wings which are applied over them.

Requirements

- quilter's muslin: 20 cm (8 in) square
- dark grey stranded thread: Cifonda Art Silk 215 *or* DMC 317
- medium grey stranded thread: Cifonda Art Silk 212 *or* DMC 318
- light grey stranded thread: Cifonda Art Silk 211 *or* DMC 762
- light blue stranded thread: Cifonda Art Silk 181 *or* DMC 159
- medium copper stranded thread: Cifonda Art Silk 103 *or* DMC 3776
- light copper stranded thread: Cifonda Art Silk 102 *or* DMC 402
- dark yellow stranded thread: Cifonda Art Silk 175 *or* DMC 742
- orange stranded thread: Cifonda Art Silk 135A *or* DMC 947
- black stranded thread: Cifonda Art Silk Black *or* DMC 310
- steel/grey stranded thread: Soie d'Alger 3443 *or* DMC 414
- slate/black metallic thread: Kreinik Cord 225c
- silver/black metallic thread: Kreinik Cord 105c
- thick silver/black metallic thread: Madeira Metallic 40 col. 442
- variegated pale grey chenille thread: col. Neutral
- 3 mm bronze/blue bead
- 33 gauge white covered wire (butterfly): two 10 cm (4 in) lengths

The Large Copper, Lycaena dispar, is a European butterfly with shiny metallic-looking wings. It inhabits moist areas such as undeveloped riverbanks and wetlands, where it feed on various weedy plants. Sadly, this species of the Lycaenidae family became extinct in Britain in 1864 after its fenland home was reclaimed for agriculture. The upper wings are bright coppery-orange with dark grey borders. The underside of the front wings is bright yellowy-orange with black spots and grey edges; the hind wings are silvery bluish-grey with small black spots and fiery orange borders.

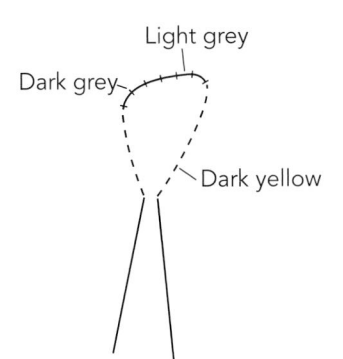

Light grey

Dark grey

Dark yellow

Buttonhole row: dark grey

Row 1: light grey
Row 2: light copper
Row 3: dark yellow
Row 4: medium copper
Row 5: dark yellow
Row 6: medium copper
Row 7: dark yellow

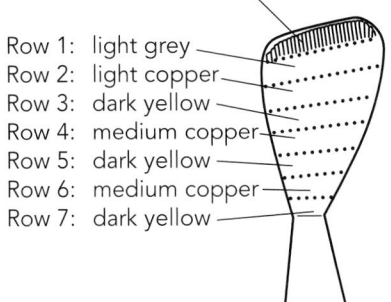

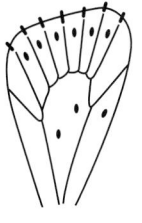

DETACHED FORE WING

1. Using one strand of dark yellow thread in a sharps needle, couch wire around the wing outline leaving two tails of wire at the base of the wing. Buttonhole stitch the wire to the muslin, working the sides of the wing in dark yellow and the corners and outer edge in light grey.

2. To form the markings on the outer edge of the wing, work seven straight stitches over the wire (inside the buttonhole ridge) with dark grey thread

3. The wings are embroidered, inside the wire outline, with rows of buttonhole stitch and encroaching satin stitch. To provide guidelines for these rows, lightly pencil in seven lines as shown. With dark grey thread, work the row at the wing edge first with close, long buttonhole stitches (the ridge of the buttonhole is next to the wire).

4. Work the remainder of the wing with seven rows of straight stitches blending into each other (encroaching satin stitch), blending the first row into the long buttonhole stitches (leaving a narrow strip of dark grey inside the wire). Refer to the diagram for row colours:

5. With the fine silver/black metallic thread in a milliners needle, work the veins with fly and buttonhole stitches, using the diagram and the wing edge markings as a guide to placement.

6. With one strand of black thread, embroider six spots on the edge of the wings (inside the spaces between the veins), and three or four spots at random on the wing surface. Work each spot with three satin stitches.

DETACHED HIND WING

1. Using one strand of light grey thread, couch wire around the wing outline, leaving two tails of wire at the base of the wing, then buttonhole stitch the wire to the muslin.

2. To form the markings on the outer edge of the wing, work seven straight stitches over the wire (inside the buttonhole ridge) with dark grey thread.

3. The wings are embroidered, inside the wire outline, with rows of buttonhole stitch and encroaching satin stitch. To provide guidelines for these rows, lightly pencil in eight lines as shown. With dark grey thread, work the row at the wing edge first with close, long buttonhole stitches (the ridge of the buttonhole is next to the wire).

4. Work the remainder of the wing with eight rows of straight stitches blending into each other (encroaching satin stitch), blending the first row into the long buttonhole stitches (leaving a narrow strip of dark grey inside the wire). Refer to the diagram for row colours:

5. With the fine silver/black metallic thread in a milliners needle, work the veins with fly and buttonhole stitches, using the diagram and the wing edge markings as a guide to placement.

6. With black thread, embroider six spots on the edge of the wings (inside the spaces between the veins), then a row of four spots at the edge of the orange band. Work several more spots at random over the wing surface. Work each spot with three satin stitches.

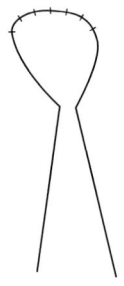

Buttonhole row: dark grey

Row 1: light grey
Row 2: orange
Row 3: light copper
Row 4: light blue
Row 5: medium grey
Row 6: light copper
Row 7: light blue
Row 8: medium grey

BACKGROUND WINGS

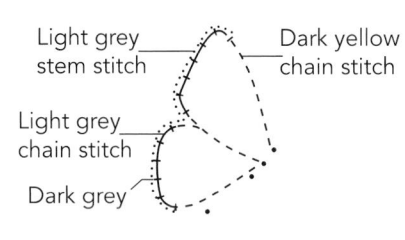

Light grey stem stitch

Dark yellow chain stitch

Light grey chain stitch

Dark grey

1. The background wings, being the 'upper surface' of the butterfly, are the same colour as each other. Work the fore wing first, as it slightly overlaps the hind wing, then adjust the instructions as required to work the hind wing. Work the wing outline in chain stitch with one strand of thread, working the sides of the wing in dark yellow and the corners and outer edge in light grey.

2. To form the markings on the outer edge of the wing, work seven straight stitches over the chain stitch outline, with dark grey thread (six stitches for the hind wing). To replicate the edge of the detached wings, work a row of small stem stitches on the outer edge of the grey chain stitches with light grey thread (*not* next to the yellow chain stitches).

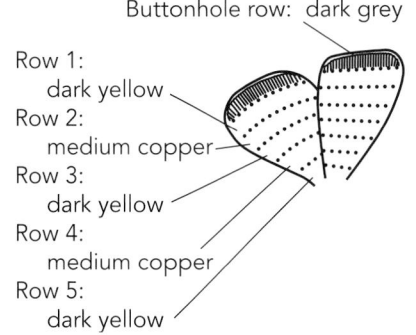

Buttonhole row: dark grey

Row 1:
    dark yellow
Row 2:
    medium copper
Row 3:
    dark yellow
Row 4:
    medium copper
Row 5:
    dark yellow

3. The wings are embroidered, inside the outline, with rows of buttonhole stitch and encroaching satin stitch as for the detached wings. To provide guidelines for these rows, lightly pencil in five lines, as shown. With dark grey thread, work the row at the wing edge first with close, long buttonhole stitches (the ridge of the buttonhole is next to the row of chain stitch).

4. Work the remainder of the wing with five rows of straight stitches blending into each other (encroaching satin stitch), blending the first row into the long buttonhole stitches (leaving a narrow strip of dark grey inside the outline). Refer to the diagram for row colours.

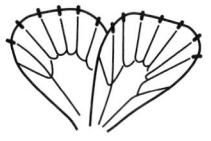

5. With the fine silver/black metallic thread in the milliners needle, work the veins with fly and buttonhole stitches, using the diagram and the wing edge markings as a guide to placement.

To Complete the Butterfly

1. Both the abdomen and the thorax are padded with fourteen strands of steel/grey thread (insert seven strands of steel/grey thread into a chenille needle, make the tails the same length and use the thread double). To pad the abdomen, make one stitch from 3 to 4, holding the tails of thread behind the abdomen with masking tape and retaining the thread in the needle at the back until required to pad the thorax.

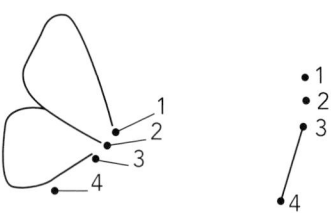

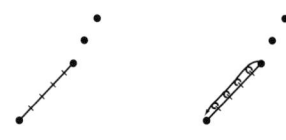

2. With one strand of steel/grey thread in a size 10 crewel needle, work four couching stitches over the padding (catching in the tails of thread behind the abdomen), then, changing to a tapestry needle, cover the abdomen with six rows of raised stem stitch, working over these couching stitches towards the tail.

3. Carefully cut out the detached wings and, using large yarn darners, insert the wire tails through the remaining dots, thus covering the background wings. Apply the fore wing first, inserting the wire tails through dots 1 and 2, then the hind wing through dots 2 and 3 (the wings share hole 2 and the back wing slightly overlaps the front wing). Bend the wire tails under the wings and secure to the back with tiny stitches. Trim the wire tails when the butterfly is finished.

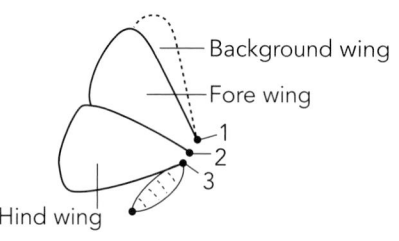

4. Using the retained steel/grey thread, make a padding stitch from 1 to 3; this will be wrapped with chenille thread to form the thorax. With chenille thread in the largest yarn darner, come out near 1, make three wraps around the padding stitch then insert the needle near 3. Make sure the chenille does not twist, and adjust the tension of the wraps (thus the fluffiness of the thorax) as desired. To facilitate the wrapping, do not tighten or secure the padding thread until the stitch has been wrapped with chenille. Use stranded thread to secure all threads at the back.

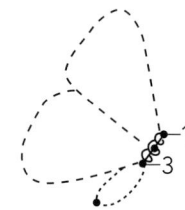

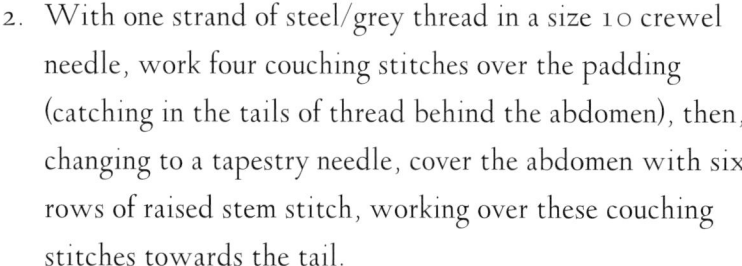

5. With one strand of steel/grey thread, apply a 3 mm bead for the head, working the stitches towards the thorax.

6. Using the thicker silver/black metallic thread, work the antennae with two straight stitches, inserting the base of the stitches through the hole of the head bead. Work a French knot at the end of each straight stitch.

7. With two strands of slate/black metallic thread in the milliners needle, work three legs into the thorax of the butterfly—each leg is worked with three straight stitches.

Ladybird

The ladybird, which features in each of the botanical specimens, may be applied wherever you wish—the abdomen outline is not included in the design. The ladybird may also be reduced in size if desired.

The instructions for embroidering the ladybird are on page 43.

SPECULARIA
HYBRIDA

Botanical Name

The lower edge of the stitched rectangle, around the specimen, is used to position the guidelines for stitching the botanical name SPECULARIA HYBRIDA. (Note that if you wish to use upper and lower case letters, only the first word of a botanical name is capitalised.) The letters are stitched by eye as traced lines would be difficult to cover.

The instructions for working the botanical name are on page 45.

Page of illuminated manuscripts borders, The Grammar of Ornament by Owen Jones,
Plate LXXI, courtesy University of Wisconsin Digital Collections.

Part 2:
Illuminated Panels

*Square ornamental motif from
an illuminated medieval book*

This collection of borders from illuminated manuscripts dating from the 9th to the 14th century provided inspiration for the borders of the panels in this section.

Bittersweet and Butterfly

Bittersweet, *Solanum dulcamara*, one of the most familiar plants in hedgerows and copses, has long trailing stems which depend on stouter hedge plants for support. Also known as Woody Nightshade, the flowers have five purple petals, each with two small green tubercles at its base. Five bright yellow anthers are joined to form a distinctive pyramidal cone in the centre of the flower. The leaves, which vary from heart-shaped to spear-shaped, are very dark green in colour and all have stalks. Its egg-shaped berries go through a series of colour changes—from green through orange then red when ripe.

Bittersweet, so called because of its bitter-tasting branches with their sweetish aftertaste, belongs to the same family as the potato, the tomato and the aubergine, but is not quite so innocuous. Although it is less toxic than its relative Deadly Nightshade, it has long been used in herbal medicine for its soothing, narcotic properties (its botanical name solanum coming from the Latin solamen, 'comfort, solace'), and also to promote healing. One of its ancient names was felonwort, meaning 'abscess'. The berries were cut open and bandaged over sores, a practice still in use in areas where folk medicine is popular. The berries could be particularly harmful to children, so the following remedy is curious!

Teething troubles: make a necklace of dried nightshade berries, let baby wear it, and it will prevent convulsions.

(FROM NOTES COMPILED IN THE 1920S BY DR MARK TAYLOR ON EAST ANGLIAN HERBAL REMEDIES AND FOLKLORE)

... the berries of bittersweet ... were used [to cure chilblains], well rubbed in; they were preserved in bottles for winter use.

FOLK LORE, J.H. BLOOM, 1930

This small stumpwork panel was inspired by the illuminated pages of medieval manuscripts. Embroidered on a background of ivory satin, this design features the hedgerow plant Bittersweet, *Solanum dulcamara*, with detached flower petals, anthers and leaves, and beaded berries. Nestled amongst the foliage are a Copper Butterfly, *Heodes virgaureae*, with raised detached wings, a padded caterpillar, and a beaded hoverfly. The panel is enclosed by an ornate border, worked in silk ribbon, gold thread and beads.

This page from an illuminated sixteenth century manuscript provided inspiration for the
Bittersweet and Butterfly panel.

Upper left
leaf

Upper right
leaf

Lower right
leaf

Lower left
leaf

Detached leaf outlines

Fore wing

Hind wing

**Butterfly detached
wing outlines**

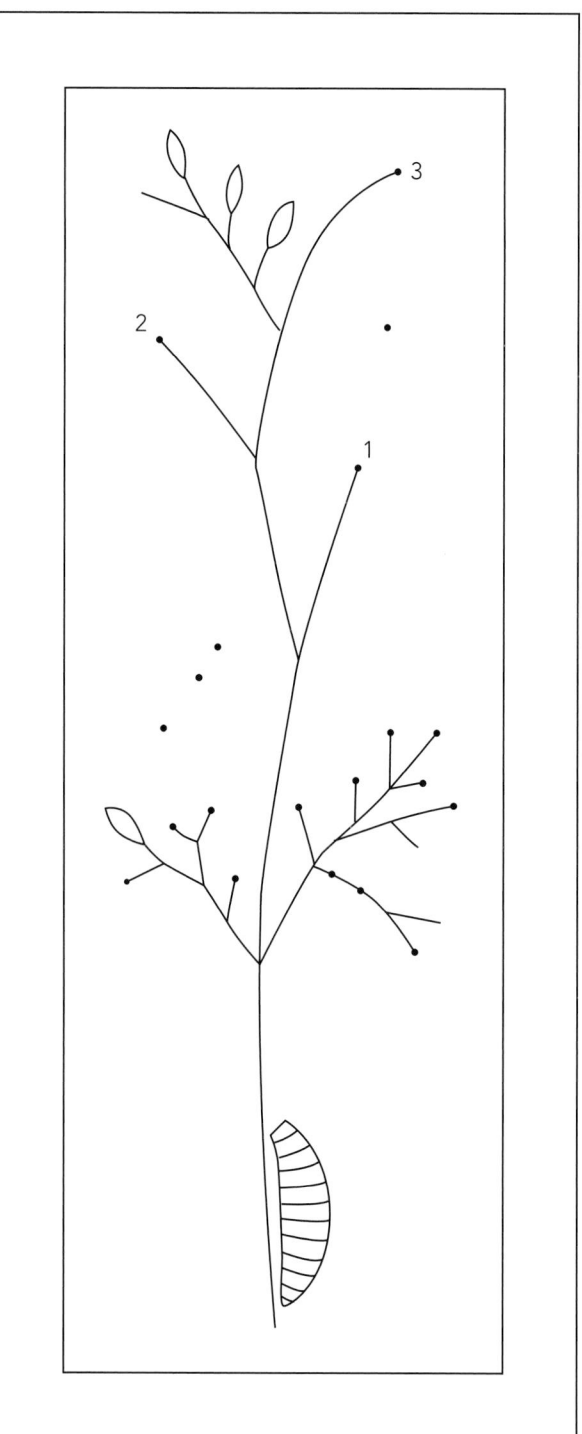

Skeleton outline

Bittersweet
detached
petal outline

Hoverfly wing
outline

Anther
outline

*Diagrams are
actual size*

Overall Requirements

This is the *complete* list of requirements for this panel. For ease of use, the requirements of each individual element are repeated under its heading—for example, Bittersweet requirements, Hover-fly requirements.

- ivory satin background fabric: 30 cm (12 in) square
- quilter's muslin or calico backing fabric: 30 cm (12 in) square
- quilter's muslin: four 20 cm (8 in) squares
- green metal organdie: 4 cm (1 ½ in) square
- paper-backed fusible web: 4 cm (1 ½ in) square
- 25 cm (10 in) embroidery hoop or stretcher bars
- 10 cm (4 in) embroidery hoops
- needles:

  crewel/embroidery sizes 8–10

  milliners/straw sizes 7 and 9

  sharps size 12

  tapestry size 28

  chenille size 18

  sharp yarn darners sizes 14–18
- embroidery equipment (see page 266)

- dark green stranded thread (stems): Soie d'Alger 2115 or DMC 3345
- medium green stranded thread (leaves, berries): Soie d'Alger 2134 or DMC 3346
- dark violet stranded thread (flowers): Soie d'Alger 4916 or DMC 791
- medium violet stranded thread (flowers): Soie d'Alger 4915 or DMC 158
- medium yellow stranded thread (flowers): DMC 972

- red stranded thread (berries): Soie d'Alger 915 or DMC 349
- dark orange stranded thread (berries, caterpillar): Soie d'Alger 635 or DMC 946
- medium orange stranded thread (berries): Soie d'Alger 614 or DMC 970
- light orange stranded thread (butterfly): Soie d'Alger 612 or DMC 3853
- dark yellow stranded thread (butterfly): Soie d'Alger 623 or DMC 742
- mauve stranded thread (butterfly): Soie d'Alger 4635 or DMC 315
- brown stranded thread (butterfly): Soie d'Alger 3416 or DMC 838
- dark lime stranded thread (caterpillar): DMC 581
- medium lime stranded thread (caterpillar): DMC 166
- dark violet stranded thread (border): DMC 791

- gold/black metallic thread (hoverfly): Kreinik Cord 205c
- peacock green metallic thread (hoverfly): Kreinik Blending Filament 085
- gold metallic thread (butterfly, border): Madeira Metallic Art 9803 col. 3007
- gold/bronze metallic thread (butterfly): Madeira Metallic Art 9842 col. 482
- gold couching thread (border): Couching Thread 371 (Dark/Jacobean gold)
- gilt 3-ply twist (border)
- fine gold silk thread (border): YLI Silk stitch 50 col. 79
- dark violet thick pearl cotton (border): DMC Coton Perlé No. 3 col. 791

- variegated copper/brown chenille thread (butterfly): col. Cinnamon
- orange rayon machine thread (hoverfly): Madeira Rayon 40 col. 1078
- nylon clear thread: Madeira Monofil 60 col. 1001

- Hannah bias-cut silk ribbon (border): 1 cm (7/16 in) wide col. Hot Flash

- 4 mm green glass beads (Hot Spotz Glass Beads SBX6-47)
- 4 mm red glass beads (Hot Spotz Glass Beads SBX6-45)
- 3 mm blue/purple glass beads (Hot Spotz Glass Beads SBXL-449)
- Mill Hill seed beads 374 (blue/purple)
- hexagonal-cut 'seed' beads (blue/purple)
- Mill Hill petite beads 40374 (blue/purple)
- Mill Hill petite beads 42037 or 40332 (green)
- Mill Hill petite beads 42028 (ginger)
- gold seed beads: Metallic Delica DBR 31 or Mill Hill Magnifica 10076

- 33 gauge white covered wire (petals): fourteen 9 cm (3 1/2 in) lengths (colour violet if desired, Copic BV08 Blue Violet)
- 33 gauge white covered wire (anthers): three 13 cm (5 in) lengths (colour yellow if desired, Copic Y15 Cadmium Yellow)
- 33 gauge white covered wire (butterfly): four 10 cm (4 in) lengths (colour light orange if desired, Copic YR14 Caramel)

- 33 gauge white covered wire (leaves): two 24 cm (9^1/$_2$ in) lengths and two 12 cm (4^3/$_4$ in) lengths (colour green if desired, Copic G99 Olive)

PREPARATION

1. Mount the satin background fabric and the muslin/calico backing into the 25 cm (10 in) embroidery hoop or frame.

2. Using a fine lead pencil, trace the skeleton outlines of the design and the border onto tracing paper. Turn the tracing paper over and draw over the outlines on the back.

3. With the tracing paper right side up, transfer the design and the border outlines to the satin with a stylus.

4. Using fine gold silk thread in a sharps needle, work a row of tacking/running stitches along both border lines (the lead pencil lines tend to fade). As the border threads will be applied over these stitches, they need to be quite small and accurate.

BITTERSWEET

Requirements

- quilter's muslin: three 20 cm (8 in) squares
- dark green stranded thread: Soie d'Alger 2115 or DMC 3345
- medium green stranded thread: Soie d'Alger 2134 or DMC 3346
- dark violet stranded thread: Soie d'Alger 4916 or DMC 791
- medium violet stranded thread: Soie d'Alger 4915 or DMC 158
- medium yellow stranded thread: DMC 972
- red stranded thread: Soie d'Alger 915 or DMC 349
- dark orange stranded thread: Soie d'Alger 635 or DMC 946
- medium orange stranded thread: Soie d'Alger 614 or DMC 970
- nylon clear thread: Madeira Monofil 60 col.1001
- 4 mm green glass beads (Hot Spotz Glass Beads SBX6-47)
- 4 mm red glass beads (Hot Spotz Glass Beads SBX6-45)
- Mill Hill petite beads 42037 *or* 40332 (green)
- 33 gauge white covered wire (petals): fourteen 9 cm (3$^1/_2$ in) lengths (colour violet if desired, Copic BV08 Blue Violet)
- 33 gauge white covered wire (anthers): three 13 cm (5 in) lengths (colour yellow if desired, Copic Y15 Cadmium Yellow)
- 33 gauge white covered wire (leaves): two 24 cm (9$^1/_2$ in) lengths and two 12 cm (4$^3/_4$ in) lengths (colour green if desired, Copic G99 Olive)

STEMS

The stems, branches and stalks are worked in chain stitch with dark green thread.

1. Starting at the base, with three strands of thread in a size 8 crewel needle, work a row of chain stitch along the main stem line to the middle fork in the stem. Continuing with two strands of thread, work the branch to flower 1.

2. Work the branches to flowers 2 and 3, and the berry branches (main lines) in chain stitch with two strands of thread.

3. Using one strand of thread in a size 10 crewel needle, work the short stalks to the buds and the berries in chain stitch.

DETACHED LEAVES

The detached leaves are worked in dark green and medium green thread. The 24 cm (9¹/₂ in) lengths of wire will be used for the large leaves; the 12 cm (4³/₄ in) lengths for the small leaves.

1. Mount muslin into a small hoop and trace the four leaf outlines (check that they are the right way up).

2. Using one strand of medium green thread in a size 10 crewel needle, couch wire along the central vein, one end of the wire at the tip of the leaf. Overcast stitch the wire to the muslin along the central vein.

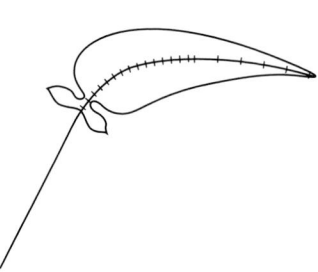

3. Using dark green thread, couch the remaining wire around the leaf outline, bending into a point at the tip (and around the tiny leaflets if working the large leaf), ending with a tail of wire at the base of the leaf (do not trim the wire tail; it will be wrapped later to form a stalk). Buttonhole stitch the wire to the muslin around the outside edge of the leaf.

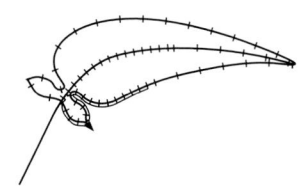

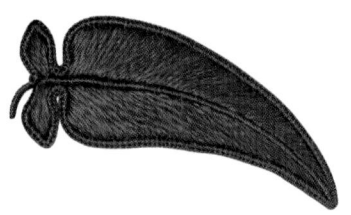

4. Work a row of split stitch around all inside edges of wire, then padding stitches. Embroider the leaf in satin stitch (enclosing the split stitch), working the stitches towards the central vein.

5. With medium green thread, work the side veins of the leaf with straight stitches.

6. Cut out the leaf. Wrap the tail of wire at the base of the leaf with one strand of dark green thread. Attach the thread to the back of the leaf, then closely wrap at least 1 cm (3/8 in) of the wire tail. Secure the thread, retaining the tail. Keep the detached leaves aside until all other work on the panel is finished.

7. Shape the leaf slightly before applying to the finished work. Using a large yarn darner, insert the wrapped wire and thread tails through to the back, at the point on the stem as shown, leaving a short stalk between the leaf and the stem. Secure the tail of wire with a few small stitches at the back of the stem. Shape the leaves with tweezers and trim the wire tails.

FLOWER BUDS

The buds are worked in dark violet and medium green thread.

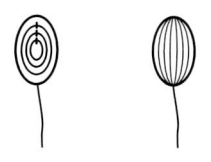

1. With one strand of dark violet thread, outline the bud in split stitch. Using two strands of thread, work several chain stitches, inside the outline, to pad the bud.

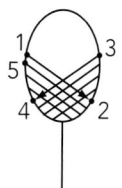

2. Embroider the bud in satin stitch, enclosing the outline.

3. Using one strand of medium green thread, cover the base of the bud with slanted straight stitches, worked alternately from the right, then the left (a variation of fishbone stitch), starting half way up the side of the bud and taking the stitches over the lower edge.

FLOWERS 1, 2 AND 3

The flowers are worked with dark violet, medium violet and medium yellow thread. The detached petals and anthers are worked at the same time, on two hoops of fabric.

Detached Petals

The bittersweet flowers require fourteen detached petals, all the same size and worked the same way.

1. Mount muslin into a small hoop and trace fourteen petal outlines (the petals may be worked on two hoops of fabric, with the detached anthers).

2. Using one strand of medium violet thread in a size 10 crewel needle, couch wire around the petal outline, leaving two wire tails at the base that touch but do not cross. Overcast stitch the wire to the muslin.

3. Using dark violet thread, work a row of split back stitch around the inside the edge of the wire, then embroider the petal in long and short stitch, starting at the base of the petal and working towards the point.

4. With one strand of medium violet thread, work a row of split stitch to form the centre line of the petal. Cut out the petals.

Detached Anthers

The bittersweet flowers require three detached anthers, all the same size and worked the same way. Cut each of the 13 cm (5 in) anther wires into a 9 cm (3¹/₂ in) length and a 4 cm (1¹/₂ in) length.

1. Mount muslin into a small hoop and lightly trace three anther outlines (the anthers may be worked with the detached petals on two hoops of fabric).

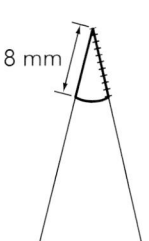

8 mm

2. Bend a 9 cm length of wire in half in an inverted V. Using medium yellow thread, couch the wire around the anther outline, working one stitch at the point and a stitch 8–8.5 mm ($^5/_{16}$ in) down from the point on each side. Stitch the wire to the muslin with overcast stitch.

3. Couch the 4 cm length of wire along the centre of the anther. Starting at the base, overcast stitch the wire to the muslin, working the stitches as close to the point as possible (change to a sharps needle near the tip). Embroider each side of the anther, between the wires, with long and short stitch.

4. Cut out the shape (close to the stitching at the lower edge), avoiding the tails of wire. Carefully bend the centre wire behind the anther and trim to 3 mm ($^1/_8$ in). Using tweezers, squeeze the sides of the anther towards each other (enclosing the trimmed centre tail) to form a cone shape.

To Complete Flowers 1 and 2

Flowers 1 and 2 have five detached petals, while flower 3 has four. If the petals vary in size, select the smaller petals for flower 3.

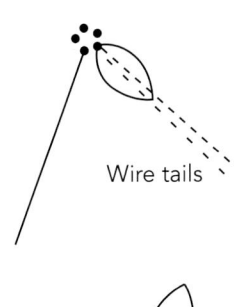

Wire tails

1. Draw a circle of five dots (the wire insertion points), very close together, at the end of stems 1 and 2. Insert the wire tails of the detached petals through five individual holes (as close to each other as possible), using a large yarn darner. Bend the wire tails under each petal and secure with small stitches. Do not cut the wire tails until the flower is finished.

2. Using a yarn darner, insert the two anther wires through one hole in the centre of the flower and secure the tails of wire behind the stem (check that the gap in the anther is at the back).

3. Using tweezers, adjust the shape and position of the petals and anther before applying the green petite beads to form the tubercles at the base of the petals. Using nylon thread in a sharps needle, bring the needle out behind the anther (between two petals), and thread on six green petite beads. Form a circle of beads around the base of the anther and take the needle through to the back between the same two petals. Repeat this step. Work a couching stitch between each bead (to keep the circle of beads close to the base of the petals), then thread the needle through all the beads once more. Secure the thread. Trim the wires.

To Complete Flower 3

1. Draw a semi-circle of four dots (the wire insertion points), very close together, at the end of stem 3. The wire tails of the detached petals are inserted through these four individual holes (as close to each other as possible), using a large yarn darner. Apply the side petals first, then the two centre petals. Bend the wire tails under each petal and secure with small stitches. Do not cut the wire tails until the flower is finished.

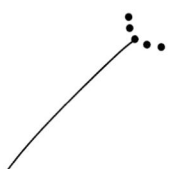

2. Using a yarn darner, insert the two anther wires through one hole at the base of the detached petals and secure the tails of wire behind the stem (check that the gap in the anther is at the back).

3. Using tweezers, adjust the shape and position of the petals and anther before applying the green petite beads to form the tubercles at the base of the petals. Using nylon thread in a sharps needle, bring the needle out behind the anther, and thread on five green petite beads. Form a circle of beads around the base of the anther and take the needle through to the back. Repeat this step. Work a couching stitch between each bead (to keep the circle of beads close to the base of the petals), then thread the needle through all the beads once more. Secure the thread. Trim the wires.

BERRIES

A red or green glass bead is wrapped with one strand of
thread to form a bittersweet berry. The berries are worked in
four different colours—red, dark orange, medium orange and
medium green (use the green beads with the green thread, and
red beads with the other three colours). Select a well-shaped
bead with a large hole.

1. Using a long strand of thread (about 60 cm/24 in) in a size
   28 tapestry needle, bring the needle through the bead,
   leaving a 10 cm (4 in) tail of thread. Continue stitching
   through the hole in the bead (holding onto the thread tail),
   until the bead is covered. Change to a sharps needle if the
   hole gets too small.

2. Work a French knot for the top of the berry, taking the
   needle through the bead to create two tails of thread
   on the other side. Use these tails of thread to apply the
   berries to the background, either singly, at the end of the
   embroidered stalks, or in bunches of three at the dots on
   the lower right stem.

   Work 21 berries, selecting the colours as desired (I worked
   nine in red, three in dark orange, three in medium orange
   and six in medium green). Use the photograph as a guide to
   placement.

Hover-fly

It is easier to work the hover-fly before the detached flower petals are applied.

There are numerous varieties of hoverfly, many of which are beautifully coloured. They are commonly seen from the spring until autumn, clustered around flowers in woods, fields, parks and gardens, near water and in dry regions; in fact, hoverflies of some kind are to be found everywhere.

Requirements

- green metal organdie: 4 cm (1 $^1/_2$ in) square
- paper-backed fusible web: 4 cm (1 $^1/_2$ in) square
- gold/black metallic thread: Kreinik Cord 205c
- peacock green metallic thread: Kreinik Blending Filament 085
- orange rayon machine thread (hoverfly): Madeira Rayon 40 col. 1078
- nylon clear thread: Madeira Monofil 60 col. 1001
- 3 mm blue/purple glass beads (Hot Spotz Glass Beads SBXL-449)
- Mill Hill seed beads 374 (blue/purple)
- hexagonal-cut 'seed' beads (blue/purple)
- Mill Hill petite beads 40374 (blue/purple)
- Mill Hill petite beads 42028 (ginger)

Wings

1. Trace the hover-fly wing outline onto paper-backed fusible web, then fuse to the green metal organdie (use sheets of baking parchment to protect the iron and the wings). Carefully cut out the wing shape and fuse to the background fabric, the centre of the wings (thorax) over the • (use a board underneath the hoop of fabric for support). Check that the wings are going in the right direction—the hover-fly is facing the flower.

2. Couch a line of blending filament around the outside edge of each wing, using nylon thread in a sharps needle to work the couching stitches (work the couching stitches towards the wing so that the edge of the fused fabric does not lift). Using a size 9 milliners needle, insert the tails of blending filament through the centre of the wing (thorax) to the back.

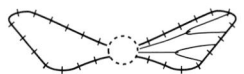

3. With blending filament, work two fly stitches in each wing for the veins.

Body

Select the following beads to work the thorax and the abdomen of the hover-fly:

- one 3 mm blue/purple bead for the thorax
- two blue/purple seed beads (374) for the abdomen
- four blue/purple hexagonal beads for the abdomen
- three blue/purple petite beads (40374) for the abdomen

1. Using nylon thread in a sharps needle, stitch the 3 mm bead over the centre of the wings for the thorax (keeping the hole in the bead at right angles to the wings), working several stitches through the bead to make it secure.

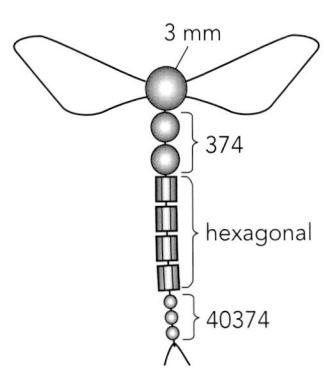

2. Take the needle through the thorax bead, then thread on the remaining blue/purple beads in the order listed above. Insert the needle into the background fabric (applying the abdomen beads with one long stitch), then couch between each bead, shaping the body into a curve as you go (make sure the original long stitch is longer than the beads to allow for the couching stitches). Take the needle back through all beads one more time then secure the thread at the back.

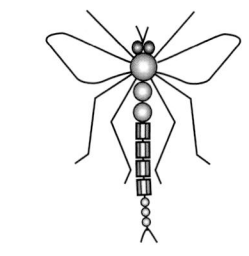

3. Using orange rayon machine thread in a sharps needle, work a fly stitch for the tail at the end of the abdomen beads, taking the 'tie-down' stitch through all the beads towards the thorax. Stitch two ginger petite beads, side by side, next to the thorax, for the eyes, making several stitches through both beads then working one firm stitch, between the beads, towards the thorax.

4. With one strand of gold/black metallic thread in a size 9 milliners needle, work the legs with straight stitches, and the antennae with a small fly stitch.

CATERPILLAR

This caterpillar is the larva of a Copper Butterfly.

Requirements

- dark lime stranded thread: DMC 581
- medium lime stranded thread: DMC 166
- dark orange stranded thread: Soie d'Alger 635 or DMC 946
- 3 mm blue/purple glass beads (Hot Spotz Glass Beads SBXL-449)

1. A caterpillar has twelve discernible body segments behind the head. These segments are indicated by the eleven internal lines on the caterpillar outline. Using one strand of medium lime thread in a size 10 crewel needle, outline the caterpillar in back stitch, working one back stitch per segment and one stitch across the head end.

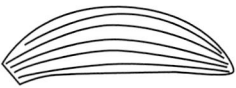

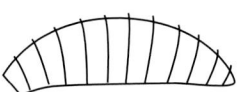

2. Using six strands of medium lime thread in a chenille needle, pad the caterpillar body (inside the outline), with laid satin stitches worked the length of the body. First work a few shorter stitches to pad the middle section, then cover with the longer stitches. With one strand of thread, work eleven couching stitches over the padding, using the back stitches as a guide to placement. The caterpillar will be embroidered in raised stem stitch over these couching stitches, so they need to be snug but not too tight.

3. Using one strand of thread, stitch a 3 mm bead at the end of the caterpillar for the head (keeping the hole in the bead at right angles to the end of the caterpillar).

4. With one strand of medium lime thread in a tapestry needle, work a row of raised stem stitch along the lower edge of the caterpillar, starting at the head end and inserting the needle at the tail. Continue working rows of raised stem stitch to cover the body of the caterpillar, adding a stripe in dark orange near the base and the top (start some rows through the head bead and work some short rows, to allow for the shape of the body).

5. Using three strands of dark lime thread in a size 7 milliners needle, work eight French knots (below the appropriate segments) to represent the eight pairs of legs:

   - work a French knot below the first three segments behind the head

   - miss two segments, then work French knots below the next four segments

   - miss two segments, then work a knot below the tails segment.

   Using tweezers, gently squeeze the legs to define their shape.

6. With one strand of dark lime thread in a size 9 milliners needle, work French knots for the spiracles, just above the lower orange line. Work a knot in every segment except the first three and the last (eight knots in all). Work the French knots across a row of raised stem stitch (so they don't fall into the padding). Don't pull the stitches too tight.

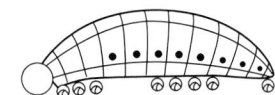

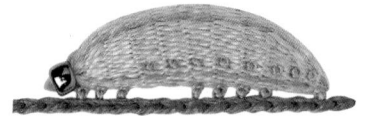

Butterfly

Requirements

- quilter's muslin: 20 cm (8 in) square
- light orange stranded thread: Soie d'Alger 612 or DMC 3853
- dark yellow stranded thread: Soie d'Alger 623 or DMC 742
- mauve stranded thread: Soie d'Alger 4635 or DMC 315
- brown stranded thread: Soie d'Alger 3416 or DMC 838
- gold metallic thread: Madeira Metallic Art 9803 col. 3007
- gold/bronze metallic thread: Madeira Metallic Art 9842 col. 482
- variegated copper/brown chenille thread: col. Cinnamon
- nylon clear thread: Madeira Monofil 60 col. 1001
- 3 mm blue/purple glass beads (Hot Spotz Glass Beads SBXL-449)
- Mill Hill petite beads 40374 (blue/purple)
- 33 gauge white covered wire (butterfly): four 10 cm (4 in) lengths (colour light orange if desired, Copic YR14 Caramel)

The Scarce Copper, Heodes virgaureae, is one of the brilliant orange-red lycaenid butterflies. These small, swift flyers only occur in the mountainous areas of central Europe, where they feed on flower-rich meadows on the banks of streams or at the edges of woods. The male, with its iridescent copper-gold wings, is very different from the duller brown female.

Preparation

Mount muslin into a small hoop and trace the outlines for the detached wings—a right and a left fore wing and a right and a left hind wing.

Fore and Hind Wings

1. Using one strand of light orange thread in a size 10 crewel needle, couch wire around the wing outline, leaving two tails of wire at the base of the wing. Buttonhole stitch the wire to the muslin.

2. Work a row of long and short buttonhole stitch at the outer edge of the wings, inside the wire outline, with light orange thread. Changing to dark yellow thread, embroider the remainder of the wing in long and short stitch, blending the stitches into the outer band of light orange.

3. With one strand of gold metallic thread in a size 9 milliners needle, work the veins with fly stitch and buttonhole stitch, using the diagram as a guide. Embroider the spots with French knots with one strand of mauve thread.

To Complete the Butterfly

1. Both the abdomen and the thorax are padded with fourteen strands of brown thread (insert seven strands of brown thread into a chenille needle, make the tails the same length and use the thread double). To pad the abdomen, make one stitch from 3 to 4, holding the tails of thread behind the abdomen with masking tape and retaining the thread in the needle at the back until required to pad the thorax.

2. With one strand of brown thread in a size 10 crewel needle, work four couching stitches over the padding (catching in the tails of thread behind the abdomen), then, changing to a tapestry needle, cover the abdomen with six rows of raised stem stitch, working over these couching stitches towards the tail.

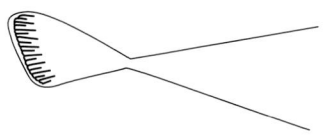

Fore wing   Hind wing

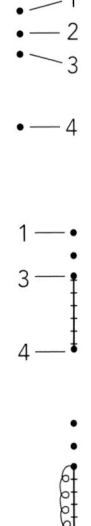

3. Carefully cut out the wings and apply by inserting the wire tails through the upper three dots as shown, using large yarn darners. Apply the hind wings first, inserting the wire tails through 2 and 3, then the fore wings through dots 1 and 2 (the wings share hole 2). Bend the wire tails under the wings and secure to the backing fabric with tiny stitches, making sure that the stitches do not protrude outside the wing span. Trim the wire tails when the butterfly is finished.

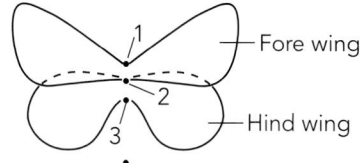

4. Using the retained brown thread, make a padding stitch from 1 to 3—this will be wrapped with chenille thread to form the thorax. With chenille thread in the largest yarn darner, come out near 1, make three wraps around the padding stitch then insert the needle near 3. Make sure the chenille does not twist, and adjust the tension of the wraps (thus the fluffiness of the thorax) as desired. To facilitate the wrapping, do not tighten or secure the padding thread until the stitch has been wrapped with chenille. Use stranded thread to secure all threads at the back.

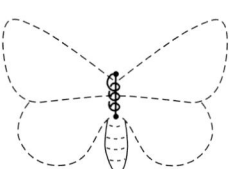

5. With one strand of brown thread, apply a 3 mm bead for the head, working the stitches towards the thorax. To form the eyes, apply two blue/purple petite beads, one stitch through both beads, above the head bead. Work a couching stitch between the beads.

6. With gold/bronze metallic thread in a size 9 milliners needle, make a fly stitch for the antennae then work a French knot at each end.

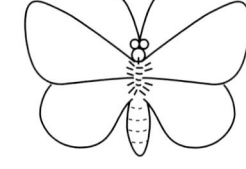

BORDER

This border, inspired by the richly decorated margins in a sixteenth century Book of Hours, is great fun to work; however, it requires precision in the placement of the silk ribbon, the border threads and the beads. Because of the accuracy required, no conversions for the metric measurements are supplied. Before commencing the border, check that the two lines of tacking/running stitch (the border lines) are still straight; adjust if necessary. There is no need to remove these stitches.

Requirements

- Hannah bias-cut silk ribbon: 1 cm (7/16 in) wide col. Hot Flash
- gilt 3-ply twist
- dark violet thick pearl cotton: DMC Coton Perlé No. 3 col. 791
- dark violet stranded thread: DMC 791
- gold couching thread: Couching Thread 371 (Dark/ Jacobean gold)
- gold metallic thread: Madeira Metallic Art 9803 col. 3007
- fine gold silk thread: YLI Silk stitch 50 col. 79
- nylon clear thread: Madeira Monofil 60 col. 1001
- gold seed beads: Metallic Delica DBR 31 *or* Mill Hill Magnifica 10076

RIBBON BACKGROUND

The background of the border is a rich orange-red bias-cut silk ribbon. The ribbon is optional (I have seen this border worked very successfully without it).

Cut 75 cm of bias-cut silk ribbon. Using fine silk sewing thread in a sharps needle, stitch the ribbon to the border with large herringbone stitches (keeping the ends of the stitches 1–2 mm inside the edges of the ribbon). The ribbon should *just* cover the stitched border lines, so it may need to be eased as you stitch (bias ribbon makes this easier). Starting in the lower left corner (turning under 0.5 cm of ribbon), herringbone stitch the ribbon over the left side of the border until the top edge is reached. Work a row of running stitch *across* the ribbon at the top edge, then fold the ribbon down and to the right, making a form of mitre at the corner (secure with a long stitch inside

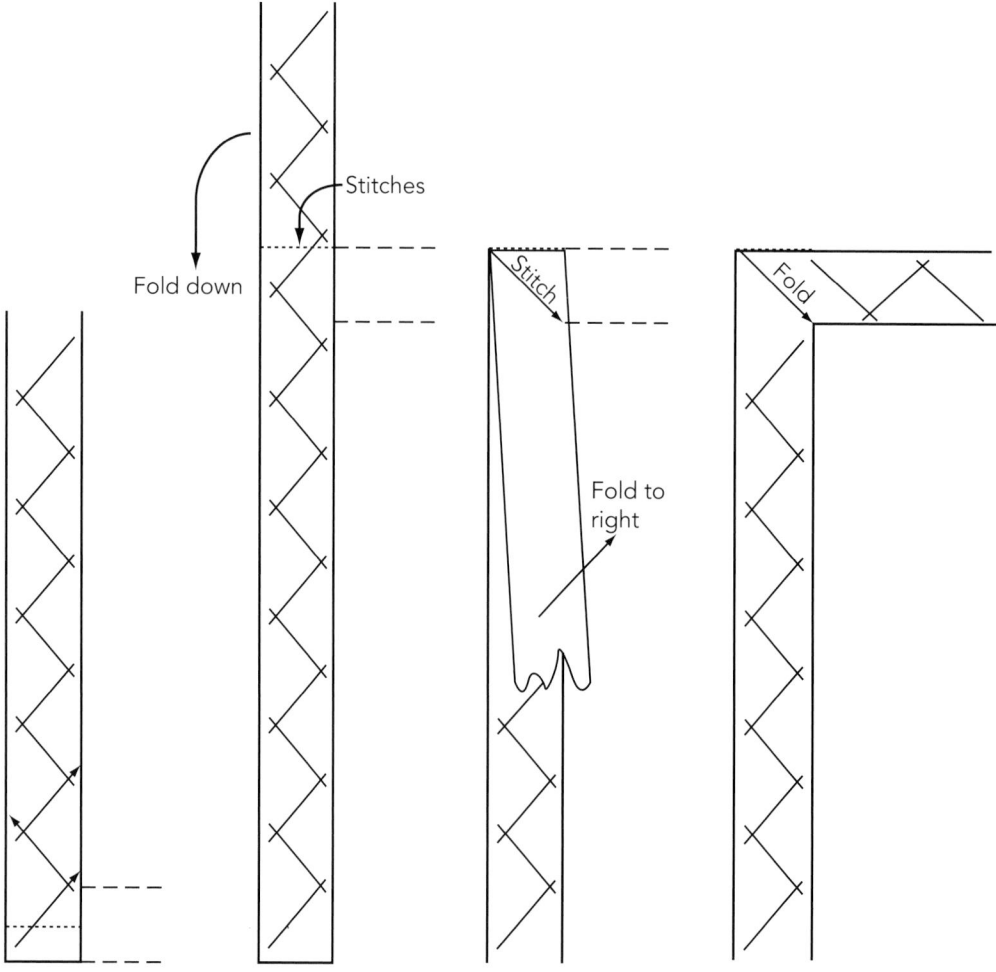

the fold). Continue stitching and folding the ribbon until the lower left-hand corner is reached again, folding in a triangular corner of ribbon to complete. The herringbone stitches remain until the border is finished (they are then carefully unpicked).

EDGES

The border edges consist of couched rows of gilt 3-ply twist and dark violet Coton Perlé No. 3. The lines of couched thread need to be kept very straight (a clear plastic ruler, held next to the rows of thread, is a great help). Holding the gold or purple threads under tension, while working the couching stitches, also helps to keep the rows straight.

1. Using *either* nylon thread in a sharps needle *or* one strand of gold metallic thread in a size 9 milliners needle, couch a line of gilt twist over the edge of the ribbon, along the inner border line (the running stitches of the border lines should be just under the edges of the ribbon), working the stitches 3–4 mm apart, *towards* the centre of the ribbon (this catches in the edge of the ribbon, which may be uneven). Using a chenille needle, sink the tails of gilt thread through to the back at the corner and secure.

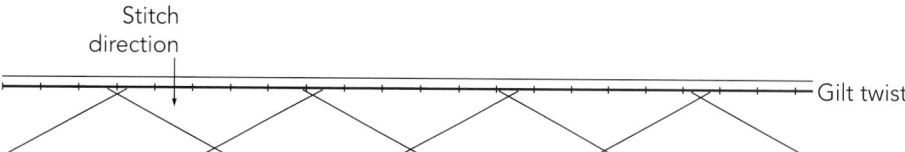

2. Using one strand of matching DMC stranded thread in a sharps needle (the Soie d'Alger equivalent is a slightly different colour), couch a line of dark violet Coton Perlé next to the gilt twist (covering any protruding edges of the ribbon), starting the purple Perlé at a different corner than that of the gilt twist. Work the couching stitches 3–4 mm apart (in a brick pattern, between the stitches in the previous row), angling the needle towards and slightly under the gilt twist to avoid a gap between the threads. Using a chenille needle, sink the tails of purple Perlé through to the back at the corner and secure.

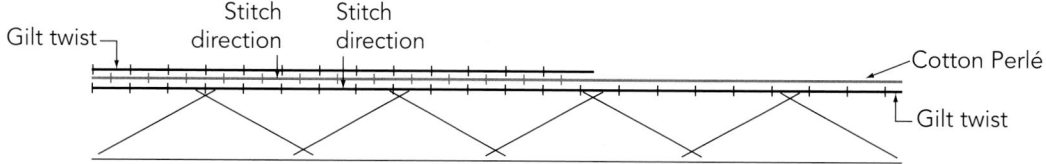

3. Starting at a different corner again, for the neatest result, couch another line of gilt twist next to the Coton Perlé (in a brick pattern), angling the needle slightly under the purple Perlé to avoid a gap between the threads.

4. Couch a line of gilt twist over the remaining edge of the ribbon (along the outer border line), working the stitches *towards* the centre of the ribbon. Continue as for the inner border, sinking the tails of thread at different corners for the neatest result.

Beading

The inside of the border is embellished with gold couching thread, inserted through gold beads in a zig-zag pattern. Check that the gold thread fits through the gold beads.

1. Using a fine lead pencil, mark dots on both sides of the ribbon, 1 cm apart, close to the lines of gilt twist (if necessary, adjust the placement of the dots so that they are evenly spaced *and* opposite each other—see diagram). Use a board underneath the hoop for support.

2. Using nylon thread, stitch a gold bead over every dot, working two back stitches per bead (the hole in the bead is parallel to the edge). To make the first back stitch, come out next to the hole, take the needle through the bead, then go straight down. For the second back stitch, bring the needle out at the edge of the gilt twist, through the bead, then down again near the gilt twist (this second stitch pulls the bead towards the border, so that when the couching thread is laced through the beads, it will not pull them away from the gilt twist to leave a gap). Apply the beads to one entire border edge before working the other (not in a zig-zag movement).

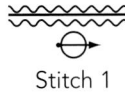

Stitch 1

Stitch 2

3. Cut two 1 metre lengths of gold Couching Thread 371. Starting at the upper left corner, insert one of the lengths of couching thread through the corner bead, producing two tails of equal length (50 cm). Thread the tails through the beads in a zig-zag fashion (one tail to the right and the other to the left of the corner), following the lacing pattern as shown, until the tails of thread meet in the diagonally opposite corner (lower right). Sink the tails through to the back and secure. Starting in this lower right corner, insert the remaining length of couching thread through the corner bead, as above, repeating the lacing pattern with these tails of thread until the upper left corner is reached. Sink the tails and secure. Carefully remove the herringbone stitches.

   Hint: Use tweezers to guide the ends of the couching thread through the beads. The ends of the couching thread may be dipped in a little PVA glue, if desired, to help prevent fraying and to facilitate the threading.

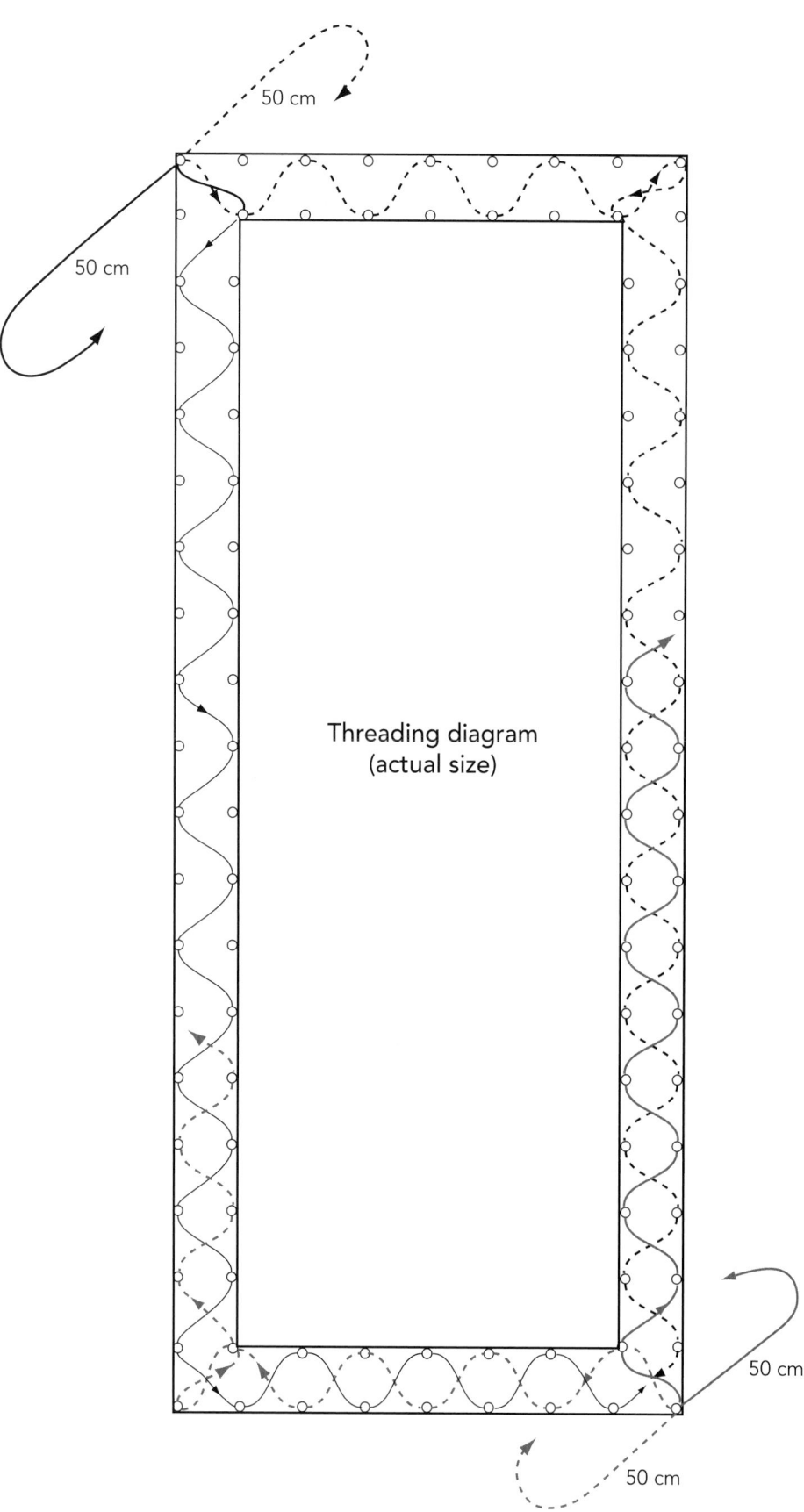

50 cm

50 cm

Threading diagram
(actual size)

50 cm

50 cm

Snowdrop and Cranefly

The snowdrop, Galanthus nivalus, has been grown since early medieval times, when it was probably known as a 'bulbous white violet'. This elegant, winter-flowering bulb is made up of 'an outer whorl of three propeller-like white sepals protecting the inner "trumpet" of true petals, each stained with a delicate inverted green heart'. The graceful white flower, attached to the long, smooth stems by an arched green pedicel, is protected by the spathe (a pair of narrow green bracts). The green leaves are long and narrow.

The name Galanthus is derived from the Greek gala, 'milk', and anthos, 'flower', while 'snowdrop' originated from the sixteenth century German Schneetropfen, 'pendant'. Known throughout Europe for centuries, the snowdrop arrived in Britain during the 1850s, in the baggage of soldiers returning from the Crimean War. It became linked to Candlemas Day, the Church's candle blessing ritual on February 2, where altars were decorated with these simple white flowers. This ceremony also gave rise to the popular name for the snowdrop, Candlemas Bells. Since Victorian times, plant hunters have coveted and collected snowdrops to produce over 500 named cultivars.

This small stumpwork embroidery features the Snowdrop, *Galanthus nivalis*, a winter-flowering bulb, with detached flower petals and wrapped-wire stems. Inspired by the decorated pages of medieval manuscripts this design includes a Black-and-yellow Cranefly, *Nephrotoma maculosa*, with gauzy detached wings and extraordinarily long legs, and a Scarlet Tiger Moth, *Callimorpha dominula*, with silk-embroidered raised wings. An ornate border, worked in silk ribbon, gold thread and beads, surrounds the panel.

The sixteenth century illustration of the Snowdrop that provided the inspiration for my panel.

Bud petal
outline

Inner petal
outline

Petal outline 2

Petal outline 4

**Snowdrop detached
petal outlines**

Fore wing

Hind wing

**Tiger moth detached
wing outlines**

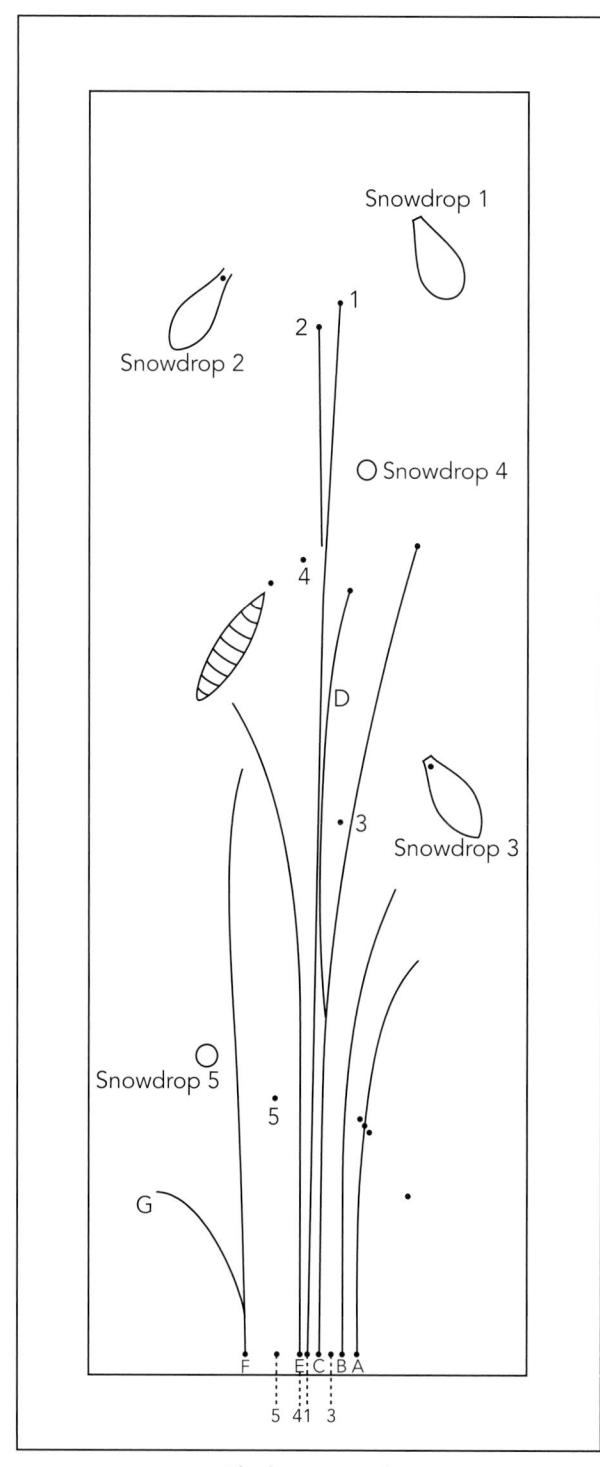

Skeleton outline

*Diagrams are
actual size*

Cranefly detached
wing outline

Thorax outline

Overall Requirements

This is the *complete* list of requirements for this panel. For ease of use, the requirements of each individual element are repeated under its heading—for example, Snowdrop requirements, Cranefly requirements.

- ivory satin background fabric: 30 cm (12 in) square
- quilter's muslin or calico backing fabric: 30 cm (12 in) square
- quilter's muslin: four 20 cm (8 in) squares
- purple/gold shot crystal organza: 15 cm (6 in) square
- pearl metal organdie: 15 cm (6 in) square
- paper-backed fusible web: 15 cm (6 in) square
- black snakeskin: 2.5 cm (1 in) square
- 25 cm (10 in) embroidery hoop or stretcher bars
- 15 cm (6 in) embroidery hoop
- 10 cm (4 in) embroidery hoops
- needles:

  crewel/embroidery sizes 8–10

  milliners/straw sizes 8 and 9

  sharps size 12

  tapestry size 28

  chenille size 18

  sharp yarn darners sizes 14–18
- embroidery equipment (see page 266)

- dark green stranded thread (stems, leaves): Soie d'Alger 2115 *or* DMC 3345
- medium green stranded thread (pedicel): Soie d'Alger 2114 *or* DMC 3346 *or* 3347
- white stranded thread (flowers): Soie d'Alger Blanc *or* DMC Blanc

- yellow stranded thread (flowers): Soie d'Alger 536 *or* DMC 726
- dark gold stranded thread (cranefly, moth): Soie d'Alger 2526 *or* DMC 783
- medium gold stranded thread (cranefly): Soie d'Alger 2525 *or* DMC 728
- dark purple stranded thread (cranefly): Soie d'Alger 3326 *or* DMC 939
- dark navy stranded thread (moth): Soie d'Alger 165 *or* Noir *or* DMC 310
- scarlet stranded thread (moth): Soie d'Alger 636 *or* DMC 349
- cream stranded thread (moth): Soie d'Alger 2522 *or* DMC 3823
- rust stranded thread (moth): Soie d'Alger 2636 *or* DMC 919
- dark gold stranded thread (border): DMC 783

- brown/black metallic thread (cranefly): Kreinik Cord 201c
- black metallic thread (moth): Kreinik Cord 005c
- red metallic thread (moth): Kreinik Cord 003c
- gold/bronze metallic thread (moth): Madeira Metallic Art 9842 col. 482
- grey metallic thread (cranefly): Madeira Metallic 40 col. 360
- black soft metallic thread (cranefly): Madeira Metallic 40 col. 70
- gold metallic thread (border): Madeira Metallic Art 9803 col. 3007
- gold couching thread (border): Couching Thread 371 (Dark/Jacobean gold)
- gilt 3-ply twist (border)

- fine gold silk thread (border): YLI Silk stitch 50 col. 79
- dark gold thick pearl cotton (border): DMC Coton Perlé No. 3 col. 783
- variegated gold/black chenille thread (moth): col. Fire
- slate rayon machine thread (cranefly): Madeira Rayon 40 col. 1164
- polyester machine thread for couching wire: any colour
- nylon clear thread: Madeira Monofil 60 col. 1001
- Hannah bias-cut silk ribbon: 1 cm ($7/16$ in) wide col. African Violet (border)

- 4 mm green pearl beads
- 3 mm bronze/purple bead
- Mill Hill seed beads 374 (blue/purple)
- Mill Hill petite beads 40374 (blue/purple)
- Mill Hill petite beads 42014 (black)
- gold seed beads: Metallic Delica DBR 31 *or* Mill Hill Magnifica 10076

- 33 gauge white covered wire (bud, outer petals): twelve 15 cm (6 in) lengths
- 33 gauge white covered wire (inner petals): eight 9 cm ($3^1/_2$ in) lengths
- 33 gauge white covered wire (pedicel 4 and 5): two 12 cm ($4^3/_4$ in) lengths
- 33 gauge white covered wire (moth): four 12 cm ($4^1/_2$ in) lengths (colour wire red and purple if desired, Copic R17 Lipstick Orange, Copic BV08 Blue Violet)
- 30 gauge green covered wire (spathe): two 36 cm (14 in) lengths
- 30 gauge green covered wire (stem): one 18 cm (7 in) lengths

- 30 gauge green covered wire (spathe, stem): four 15 cm (6 in) lengths

- 30 gauge green covered wire (stem): one 6 cm ($2^1/_4$ in) lengths

- 28 gauge uncovered wire (cranefly wings): two 11 cm ($4^1/_4$ in) lengths

- clear self-adhesive plastic (used for covering books): five 6 cm ($2^1/_2$ in) squares

- brown Pigma Micron 01 marking pen (optional)

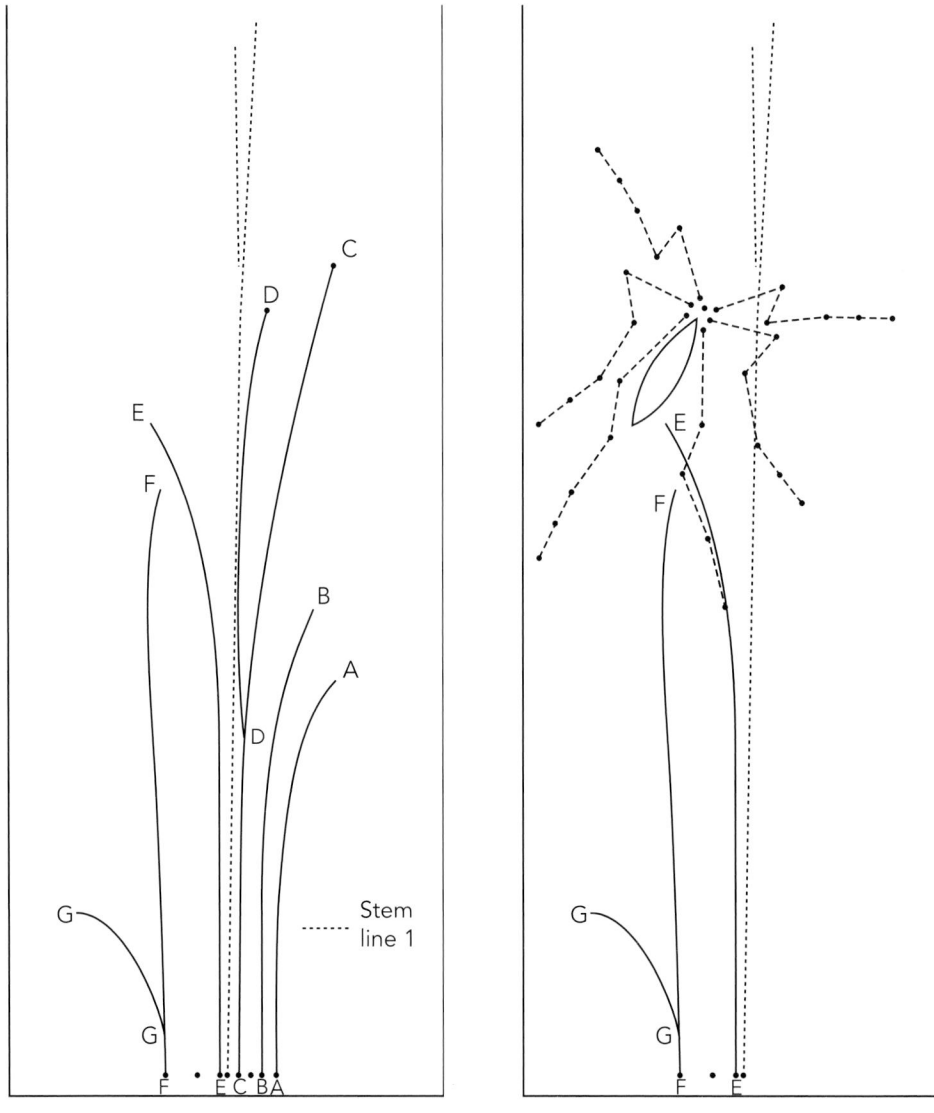

Leaf lines diagram
(diagram actual size)

Cranefly leg template
(diagram actual size)

PREPARATION

1. Mount the satin background fabric and the muslin/calico backing into the 25 cm (10 in) embroidery hoop or frame.

2. Using a fine lead pencil, trace the skeleton outlines of the design and the border onto tracing paper (including the dots at the end of each stem). Turn the tracing paper over and draw over the outlines on the back.

3. With the tracing paper right side up, transfer the design and the border outlines to the satin with a stylus.

4. Using fine gold silk thread in a sharps needle, work a row of tacking/running stitches along both border lines (the lead pencil lines tend to fade). As the border threads will be applied over these stitches, they need to be quite small and accurate.

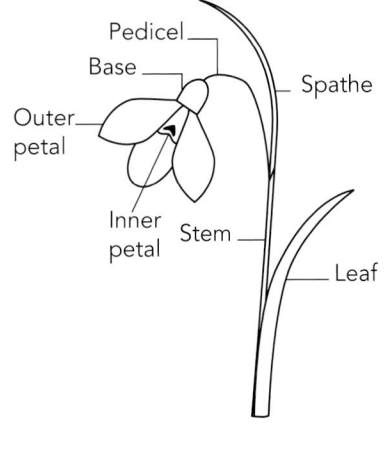

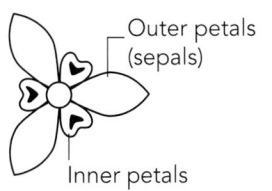

THE SNOWDROP

It will help to know a little about this winter-flowering bulb before you start the embroidery. The flowers are borne at the end of smooth green stems which rise above the long flat leaves. A snowdrop flower is made up of an outer circle of three propeller-shaped white petals (actually sepals) surrounding an inner circle of three smaller 'true' petals (these petals are white, with a green inverted heart shape near the edge). Bright yellow stamens are found in the centre of the flower. The green bead-like base of the snowdrop is attached to the stem by an arched green pedicel. Enclosing the base of the pedicel (where it joins the stem) is the spathe, a pair of narrow green bracts (leaves) which protect the flowers.

Requirements

- quilter's muslin: three 20 cm (8 in) squares
- dark green stranded thread: Soie d'Alger 2115 *or* DMC 3345
- medium green stranded thread: Soie d'Alger 2114 *or* DMC 3346 *or* 3347
- white stranded thread: Soie d'Alger Blanc *or* DMC Blanc
- yellow stranded thread: Soie d'Alger 536 *or* DMC 726
- polyester machine thread for couching wire: any colour
- nylon clear thread: Madeira Monofil 60 col. 1001
- 4 mm green pearl beads
- 33 gauge white covered wire (bud, outer petals): twelve 15 cm (6 in) lengths
- 33 gauge white covered wire (inner petals): eight 9 cm ($3^1/_2$ in) lengths
- 33 gauge white covered wire (pedicel 4 and 5): two 12 cm ($4^3/_4$ in) lengths
- 30 gauge green covered wire (spathe): two 36 cm (14 in) lengths
- 30 gauge green covered wire (stem): one 18 cm (7 in) lengths
- 30 gauge green covered wire (spathe, stem): four 15 cm (6 in) lengths
- 30 gauge green covered wire (stem): one 6 cm ($2^1/_4$ in) lengths
- clear self-adhesive plastic (used for covering books): five 6 cm ($2^1/_2$ in) squares
- brown Pigma Micron 01 marking pen (optional)

LEAVES

The leaves, which form the background behind the raised stems, are worked with consecutive rows of stem stitch, using one strand of dark green thread in a size 10 Crewel needle. Start each row at the base and work towards the tip of the leaf, staggering the ends of the rows to shape the leaves and form the point. Refer to the Leaf Lines Diagram and follow the recommended order of work when embroidering the leaves.

Order of work

1. Work a row of stem stitch along leaf line A. Work four more rows of stem stitch on the *right* side of this line.

2. Work a row of stem stitch along leaf line B. Work four more rows of stem stitch on the *right* side of this line.

3. Work a row of stem stitch along leaf line C. Work four more rows of stem stitch on the *right* side of this line.

4. Starting at the edge of leaf C, work a row of stem stitch along leaf line D. Work four more rows of stem stitch on the *right* side of this line, starting at the edge of leaf C.

5. Work a row of stem stitch along leaf line E. Work four more rows of stem stitch on the *left* side of this line.

6. Work a row of stem stitch along leaf line F. Work four more rows of stem stitch on the *right* side of this line.

7. Starting at the base of leaf line F, work a row of stem stitch along leaf line G. Work four more rows of stem stitch on the *left* side of this line.

8. When all the leaves are embroidered, transfer the cranefly leg template diagram to the background fabric.

The Snowdrop, Galanthus nivalus, *flowers the next year from bulbs, but takes five years to flower from seed*

To Transfer Cranefly Leg Template to Background Fabric
As the legs are very long and very fine, they cannot be traced
onto the background fabric. The best time to transfer the
cranefly leg template is after the leaves have been stitched.

Trace the leg template dots onto tracing paper—include
the abdomen, leaf E and F outlines and part of the border
outlines to ensure accurate placement. Hold the tracing over
the background fabric, lining up the abdomen, leaf and border
lines, and insert a fine needle at each dot (leg joint). Mark the
dots lightly on the back with a lead pencil (or a brown Pigma
marking pen), or make tiny tacking stitches with fine silk
thread.

Stems

The stems are worked in dark green thread. The stems for
snowdrops 1 and 2 are embroidered on the background in
whipped stem stitch. Snowdrops 3, 4 and 5 have detached,
wrapped-wire stems, which are applied on top of the
embroidered leaves.

Background Stems 1 and 2

1. With three strands of thread in a size 8 crewel needle,
    work a row of stem stitch along stem line 1 (between leaves
    C and E), starting at the base and working until 2 mm
    (^{1}/8 in) away from the end of the stem • 1 (park the thread
    to use later).

2. Starting at the edge of stem 1, work a row of stem stitch
    along stem line 2 until 2 mm (^{1}/8 in) away from the end of
    the stem • 2 (park the thread to use later).

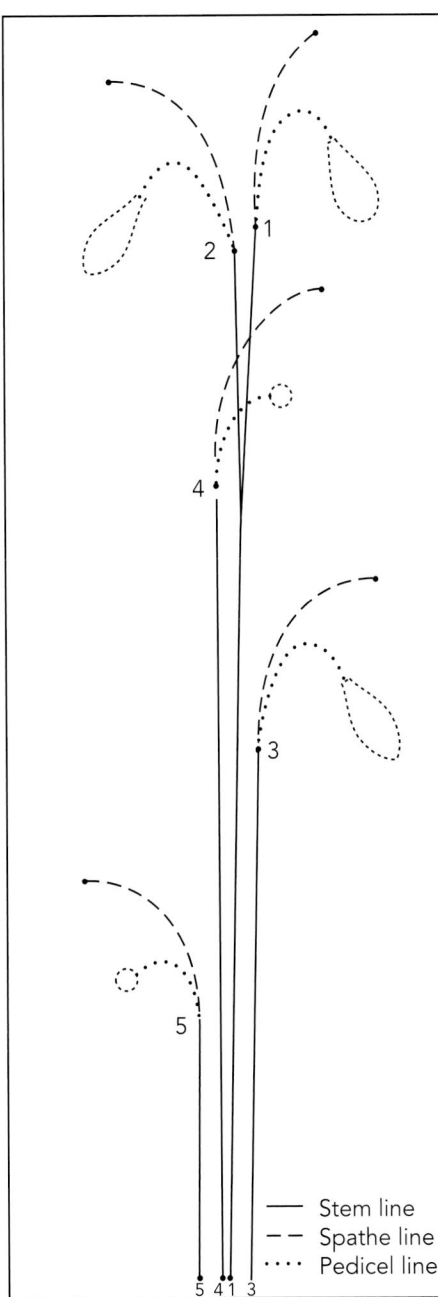

**Stem, pedicel and spathe
outlines diagrams
(stems 3, 4 and 5 are detached)**

— Stem line
– – Spathe line
···· Pedicel line

To Transfer Spathe Placement Dots

Using the stem, pedicel and spathe outlines diagram, trace the dots at the ends of the spathes onto the original tracing of the skeleton outline. Hold the tracing over the completed stems and insert a fine needle through the marked dots. Transfer the dots at the end of the spathes with a tacking stitch (as pencil may show) or mark the dots lightly on the back with a lead pencil (or a brown Pigma marking pen).

DETACHED PETALS

The snowdrops require twenty detached petals which, while varying a little in size and colour, are worked the same way. To avoid soiling the white edges of the petals with a traced lead pencil outline, the wires are bent into a petal shape first, before applying to the muslin. Use tweezers, and the appropriate detached petal outline as a template, to bend the wires into the required petal shapes. Work all the petals, on two hoops of fabric, and keep aside until required.

1. Mount a square of muslin into a 10 cm (4 in) hoop and apply the wires for the detached petals for bud 1, and the detached petals for snowdrops 2 and 3. Number each petal to avoid confusion.

2. Mount a square of muslin into a 15 cm (6 in) hoop and apply the wires for the detached petals for snowdrops 5 and 6.

Bud 1 Detached Petals

Using petal outline 1 as a template, work two detached bud petals as follows:

1. Shape a 15 cm (6 in) length of wire around the petal outline, leaving two tails of wire at the base that touch but do not cross. Make the tails of wire equal in length and do not trim. They will be wrapped later to form the arched pedicel at the top of the flower.

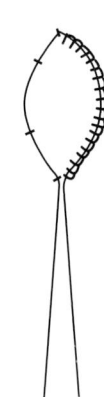

2. With one strand of white thread in a size 10 crewel needle, couch the wire petal outline to the muslin, then buttonhole stitch the wire to the muslin. Work a row of split stitch around the inside edge of the wire.

3. Using a new length of white thread, embroider the petal in long and short stitch (covering the split stitch), working from the base of the petal towards to tip

Snowdrops 2 and 3 Detached Outer Petals
Using petal outline 2 as a template, work four detached outer petals following the instructions for Bud 1 (two detached petals for each snowdrop).

Snowdrops 4 and 5 Detached Outer Petals
Using petal outline 4 as a template, work six detached outer petals following the instructions for bud 1 (three detached petals for each snowdrop).

Snowdrops 2, 3, 4 and 5 Detached Inner Petals
Using the inner petal outline as a template, work eight detached inner petals (one each for snowdrops 2 and 3, and three each for snowdrops 4 and 5) as follows:

1. Shape a 9 cm (3¹/₂ in) length of wire around the inner petal outline, leaving two tails of wire at the base that touch but do not cross.

2. Using white thread, couch the wire petal outline to the muslin, then buttonhole stitch the wire to the muslin.

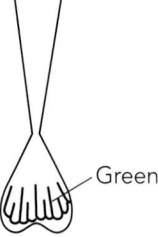
Green

3. Using one strand of dark green thread, embroider the green marking, on the inside edge of the wire, with a row of long and short buttonhole stitch (half way down the petal). Embroider the remainder of the petal in white (blending into the green).

Bud 1

Background petal

Outline the background petal in back stitch with one strand of white thread in a size 10 crewel needle. Work a row of close, long and short buttonhole stitch around the lower edge of the petal, enclosing the back-stitch outline. Embroider the remainder of the petal in long and short stitch.

Detached Petals and Pedicel

The wire tails of the detached bud petals are inserted through a green pearl then wrapped with medium green thread to form the pedicel. This is shaped into a smooth curve then inserted at the top of the stem.

1. Cut out the two detached bud petals. As the petals will overlap each other to form the bud, select the 'better' (or larger) one to be the upper petal. Cut a 40 cm (16 in) length of medium green thread and attach to the back of the lower petal, near the wire tails (this thread will be used for wrapping the wires). Insert the four wire tails, and the tail of thread, through a 4 mm green pearl bead. Arrange the petals so that the upper petal is above the lower, and shape slightly (the upper petal to the right and the lower petal to the left). Identify the 'outside' wire of each petal and trim flush with the top of the pearl. (*Hint:* slide the pearl gently up the wires, carefully cut off the 'outside' wire of each petal leaving a 3 mm tail, then slide the bead back in place.)

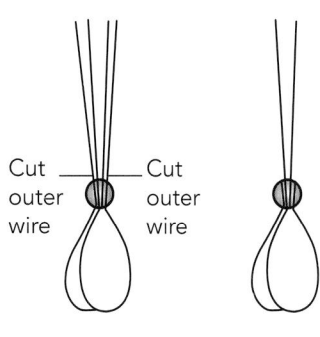

Cut outer wire — Cut outer wire

2. To form the pedicel, wrap the remaining two wire tails with the medium green thread, keeping the wires side by side. Wrap about 3 cm (1¼ in) then secure the thread, retaining the tail (the wrapped wire needs to be longer than the length of the curved pedicel). Carefully shape the wrapped wire with tweezers, using the pedicel line on the diagram sheet as a guide.

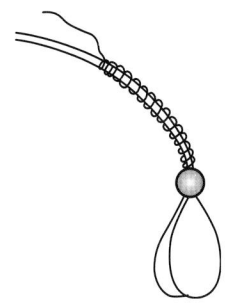

3. To apply the detached petals, insert the wire tails of the wrapped pedicel (and the tail of thread) through • at the top of stem 1, using a yarn darner (keep the wire tails loose at the back until the petals are secured to allow for adjustments). Position the detached petals over the background petal, with the green pearl at the top edge. Attach a length of nylon thread (in a sharps needle) to the top of the background petal, at the back. To secure the detached petals over the background petal, bring the needle out at the top of the background petal, make a stitch over both of the detached petals (below the bead), and insert the needle back into the background petal (almost through the same hole). Repeat, pulling the petals together at the top. To hold the pearl close to the top of the petals, bring the needle out again (from the same point), slide it under the pearl and the wrapped wire, take it over the wire then back under the pearl to the back. Make another stitch if necessary. Finally, make a few tiny stitches into the side edges of the petals to hold them in place.

4. Adjust the position of the pedicel then stitch the wire tails to the back of the stem and trim.

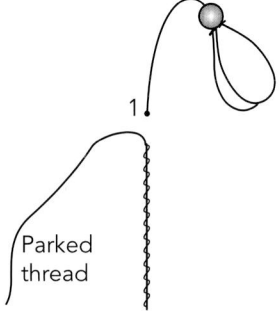

1

Parked
thread

Spathe 1

The spathe (the pair of narrow green bracts which curve behind the pedicel) is made with wire, covered with buttonhole stitch.

1. Mount a piece of muslin into a small hoop (this will be used to support the spathe wire whilst working the buttonhole stitch). Trace spathe 1 outline onto a 5 cm (2 in) square of paper. Attach the square of paper (outline side up) to the hoop of muslin with a larger square of clear, self-adhesive plastic. This will be used as a template to shape the wire for the spathe.

Upper

B

A

Lower

C

Spathe 1 outline
Actual size

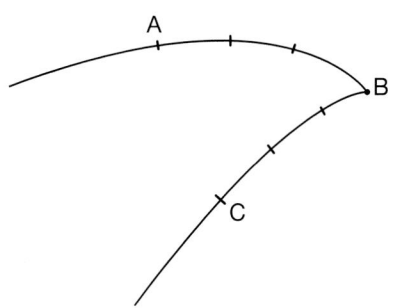

2. Bend a 15 cm (6 in) piece of green-covered wire in half,
   making a distinct point at the bend. Using machine thread,
   couch the wire to the spathe outline with stitches at A,
   B and C (and one or two stitches in between), stitching
   through the plastic, paper and muslin. Secure the thread
   and temporarily hold the tails of wire to the muslin with
   masking tape.

3. Using one strand of thread in a tapestry needle, cover the
   wire spathe with buttonhole stitch (sliding the needle
   between the wire and the plastic), working the ridge of the
   buttonhole on the *inside* of the wire shape. The upper edge
   of the wire, A to B, is worked with dark green thread, the
   lower edge of the wire, B to C, is worked with medium
   green thread. Leave a tail of thread at each end of the
   buttonhole stitches (one tail at both A and C, two tails at
   B). Do not take the green threads through to the back at
   any stage.

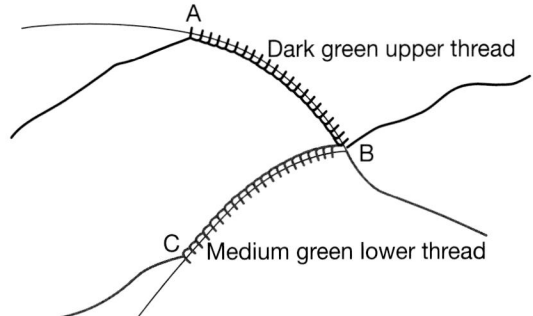

4. Cut and remove the couching stitches (from the back) and
   lift the wire spathe from the plastic (do not trim the thread
   tails). Push the buttonholed edges of the wire together (the
   ridge of the buttonhole just touching), and curve into shape
   using the spathe line on the diagram sheet as a guide.

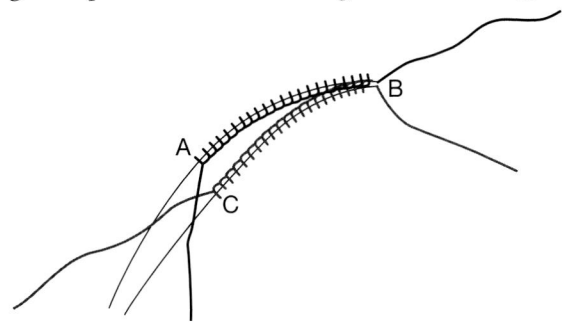

5. Using a small yarn darner, carefully insert the lower edge wire tail (and thread) under the pedicel (about 2 mm above • 1). Insert the upper edge wire tail (and thread) at the top of the stem • 1 (next to the pedicel insertion point). Adjust the shape of the wires, inserting the tails of thread at B through to the back at (or near) the tacked dot. Secure the tails of thread and wire, and trim.

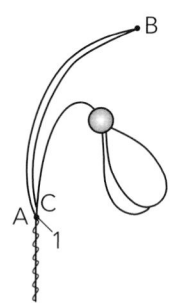

6. Using the 'parked' tails of stem thread, complete the stem with one or two stem stitches to • , neatly covering the insertion points of the pedicel and spathe.

7. Using three strands of dark green thread in a tapestry needle, whip the stem stitch to give a more raised effect, if desired.

8. Shape the detached petals of the snowdrop bud and trim wire tails.

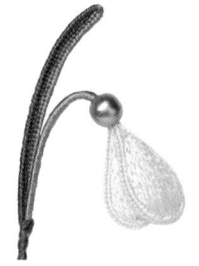

SNOWDROP 2

Background Petal

Outline the background petal in backstitch with one strand of white thread. Work a row of close, long and short buttonhole stitch around the lower edge of the petal, enclosing the backstitch outline. Embroider the remainder of the petal in long and short stitch.

Inner Detached Petal

Cut out the detached inner petal and shape slightly. Using a yarn darner, insert the wire tails through one hole in the background petal at the • as marked (1 mm below top edge). Adjust the position of the inner petal so that the lower edge comes about halfway down the background petal—hold the wire tails at the back, above the top of the petal, with masking tape. Using white thread in a sharps needle, stitch the top of the inner petal to the top of the background petal (near the wire insertion point), making short stitches into the sides and centre of the petal (disguising the wire insertion point). Do not trim the wires until the flower is finished.

Detached Outer Petals and Pedicel

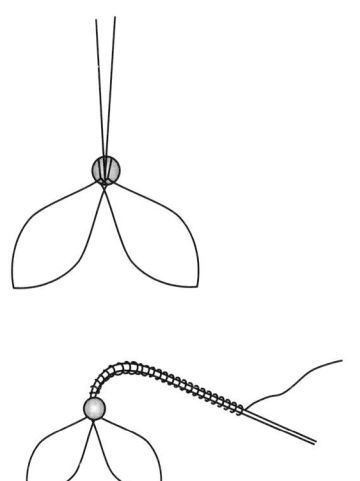

1. Cut out the two detached outer petals. Cut a 40 cm (16 in)
    length of medium green thread and attach to the back of one
    of these petals, near the wire tails (this thread will be used
    for wrapping the wires). Insert the four wire tails, and the
    tail of thread, through a 4 mm green pearl bead. Arrange
    the petals so that they are side by side, and shape slightly.
    Identify the 'outside' wire of each petal and trim flush with
    the top of the pearl.

2. To form the pedicel, wrap the remaining two wire tails
    with the medium green thread, keeping the two wires side
    by side. Wrap about 3 cm (1¼ in), then secure the thread
    retaining the tail. Carefully shape the wrapped wire with
    tweezers, using the pedicel line on the diagram sheet as a
    guide.

3. To apply the detached petals, insert the tails of the
    wrapped pedicel through • at the top of stem 2, using
    a yarn darner. Position the detached petals over the
    background petal and detached inner petal, with the green
    pearl at the top edge. Attach a length of nylon thread to
    the top of the background petal, at the back. Secure the
    detached petals to the background by working a few tiny
    stitches into the top edges of each petal, just below the
    pearl. To hold the pearl close to the top of the petals, bring
    the needle out at the top of the background petal, slide
    it under the pearl and the wrapped wire, take it over the
    wire, then back under the pearl to the back. Make another
    stitch if necessary.

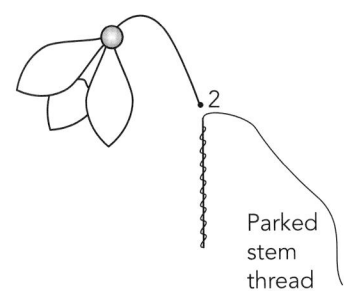

Parked
stem
thread

4. Adjust the position of the pedicel then stitch the wire tails
    to the back of the stem and trim.

Spathe 2

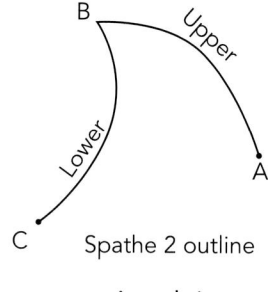

Spathe 2 outline

Actual size

1. Mount a piece of muslin into a small hoop. Trace spathe 2 outline onto a 5 cm (2 in) square of paper and attach to the hoop of muslin with a larger square of clear, self-adhesive plastic. This will be used as a template to shape the wire for the spathe.

2. Bend a 15 cm (6 in) piece of green-covered wire in half, making a distinct point at the bend. Using machine thread, couch the wire to the spathe outline with stitches at A, B and C (and one or two stitches in between), stitching through the plastic, paper and muslin. Secure the thread and temporarily hold the tails of wire to the muslin with masking tape.

3. Using one strand of thread in a tapestry needle, cover the wire spathe with buttonhole stitch (sliding the needle between the wire and the plastic), working the ridge of the buttonhole on the *inside* of the wire shape. The upper edge of the wire, A to B, is worked with dark green thread, the lower edge of the wire, B to C, is worked with medium green thread. Leave a tail of thread at each end of the buttonhole stitches (one tail at both A and C, two tails at B). Do not take the green threads through to the back at any stage.

4. Cut and remove the couching stitches and lift the wire spathe from the plastic (do not trim the thread tails). Push the buttonholed edges of the wire together (the ridge of the buttonhole just touching), and curve into shape using the spathe line on the diagram sheet as a guide.

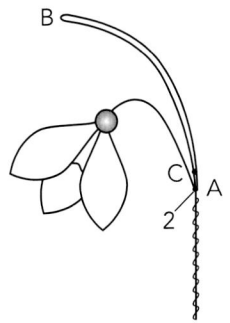

5. Using a small yarn darner, carefully insert the lower edge wire tail (and thread) under the pedicel (about 2 mm above • 2). Insert the upper edge wire tail (and thread) at the top of the stem • 2 (next to the pedicel insertion point). Adjust the shape of the wires, inserting the tails of thread at B through to the back at (or near) the tacked dot. Secure the tails of thread and wire, and trim.

6. Using the 'parked' tails of stem thread, complete the stem with one or two stem stitches to • , neatly covering the insertion points of the pedicel and spathe.

7. Using three strands of dark green thread in a tapestry needle, whip the stem stitch to give a more raised effect, if desired.

8. Shape the detached petals of the snowdrop and trim wire tails.

SNOWDROP 3

Background Petal

Outline the background petal in back stitch with one strand of white thread. Work a row of close, long and short buttonhole stitch around the lower edge of the petal, enclosing the back-stitch outline. Embroider the remainder of the petal in long and short stitch.

Inner Detached Petal

Cut out the detached inner petal and shape slightly. Using a yarn darner, insert the wire tails through one hole in the background petal at the • as marked (1 mm below top edge). Adjust the position of the inner petal so that the lower edge comes about halfway down the background petal—hold the wire tails at the back with masking tape. Using white thread in a sharps needle, stitch the top of the inner petal to the top of the background petal, making short stitches into the sides and centre of the petal. Do not trim the wires until the flower is finished.

Detached Outer Petals and Pedicel

1. Cut out the two detached outer petals. Cut a 40 cm (16 in) length of medium green thread and attach to the back of one of these petals, near the wire tails. Insert the four wire tails, and the tail of thread, through a 4 mm green pearl bead. Arrange the petals so that they are side by side, and shape slightly. Identify the 'outside' wire of each petal and trim flush with the top of the pearl.

2. To form the pedicel, wrap the remaining wire tails with the medium green thread, keeping the two wires side by side. Wrap about 3 cm (1¼ in), retaining the tail of thread. Carefully shape the wrapped wire with tweezers, using the pedicel line on the diagram sheet as a guide.

3. To apply the detached petals, insert the wire tails of the wrapped pedicel (and the tail of thread) through upper • 3 (this will be the position of the top of wrapped stem 3), using a yarn darner (keep the wire tails loose at the back until the petals are secured to allow for adjustments). Position the detached petals over the background petal and detached inner petal, with the green pearl at the top edge. Using nylon thread, secure the detached petals to the background by working a few tiny stitches into the top edges of each petal, just below the pearl. To hold the pearl close to the top of the petals, bring the needle out (at the top of the background petal), slide it under the pearl and the wrapped wire, take it over the wire then back under the pearl to the back. Make another stitch if necessary.

4. Adjust the position of the pedicel then stitch the wire tails to the back (behind leaf C) and trim.

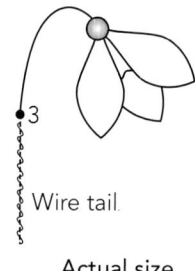

•3

Wire tail.

Actual size

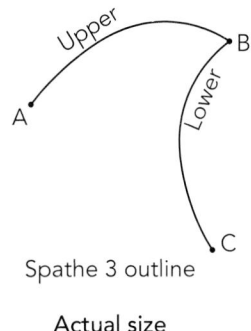

Upper

Lower

A

B

C

Spathe 3 outline

Actual size

Spathe and Stem 3

Cut a 36 cm (14 in) length of green-covered wire for the combined spathe and stem (the long tails of wire are wrapped to form the detached stem for snowdrop 3).

1. Mount a piece of muslin into a 15 cm (6 in) hoop. Trace spathe 3 outline onto a 5 cm (2 in) square of paper and attach to the hoop of muslin with a larger square of clear, self-adhesive plastic. This will be used as a template to shape the wire for the spathe.

2. Bend a 36 cm (14 in) length of green-covered wire in half, making a distinct point at the bend. Using machine thread, couch the wire to the spathe outline with stitches at A, B and C (and one or two stitches in between), stitching through the plastic, paper and muslin. Secure the thread and temporarily hold the long tails of wire to the muslin with masking tape (take care not to bend the tails of wire).

3. Using one strand of thread in a tapestry needle, cover the wire spathe with buttonhole stitch, working the ridge of the buttonhole on the *inside* of the wire shape. The upper edge of the wire, A to B, is worked with dark green thread, the lower edge of the wire, B to C, is worked with medium green thread. Leave a tail of thread at each end of the buttonhole stitches (one tail at both A and C, two tails at B).

4. Cut and remove the couching stitches and lift the wire spathe from the plastic (do not trim the thread tails). Push the buttonholed edges of the wire together (the ridge of the buttonhole just touching), and curve into shape using the spathe line on the diagram sheet as a guide (adjust the number of buttonhole stitches, if necessary, to make points A and C lie side by side). Loosely tie thread tails A and C together at the back with a square knot (it needs to be able to be undone later—the thread tails will be used to secure the spathe to background).

B

A C

5. Add a third piece of green wire (15 cm/6 in long) to the
    long tails of wire, the cut end flush with the base of the
    spathe (A-C). These three wires will be wrapped with
    one strand of dark green thread to form the stem of the
    snowdrop as follows:

    • Slide a length of dark green thread between the two
      long tails of wire, leaving a tail of thread at A-C (next
      to the knotted tails of thread). Holding the three wires
      together (the third wire at the back), wrap closely for
      about 2.5 cm (1 in), taking care not to twist the wires.
      Secure the wrapping thread with a half-hitch knot
      (buttonhole loop) around the wires, retaining the tail of
      thread.

    • Slide a new length of thread between the wires (leaving
      a tail of thread next to the retained tail), and continue
      wrapping the wires closely for another 2.5 cm (1 in),
      as before (the join between the two wrapped sections
      should be invisible). Secure the wrapping thread with
      a half-hitch knot around the wires, retaining the tail of
      thread. The retained tails of thread will be used later to
      attach the stem to the background fabric.

    • Slide another length of thread between the wires
      (leaving a tail of thread next to the retained tail), and
      continue wrapping the wires closely for about 4 cm
      (1 $^1/_2$ in). Secure the thread at the end of the wrapping,
      retaining the tail of thread (the wrapped length of the
      stem needs to be longer than the actual stem to ensure a
      neat insertion point).

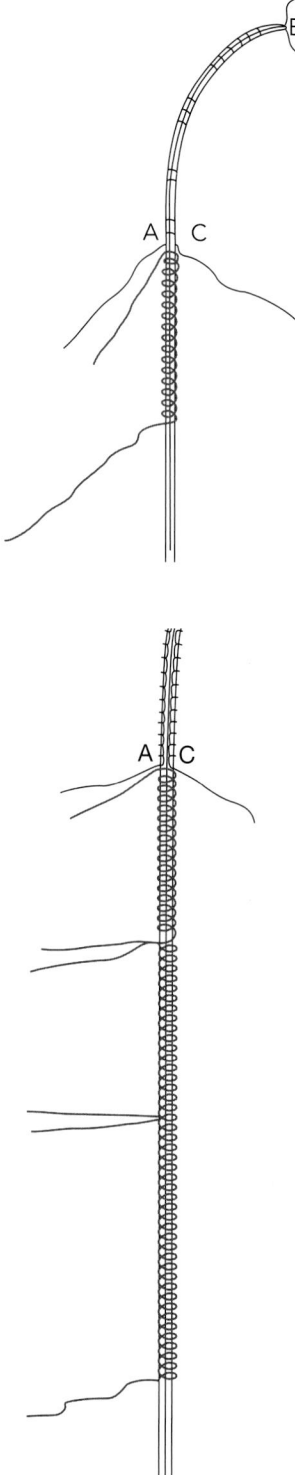

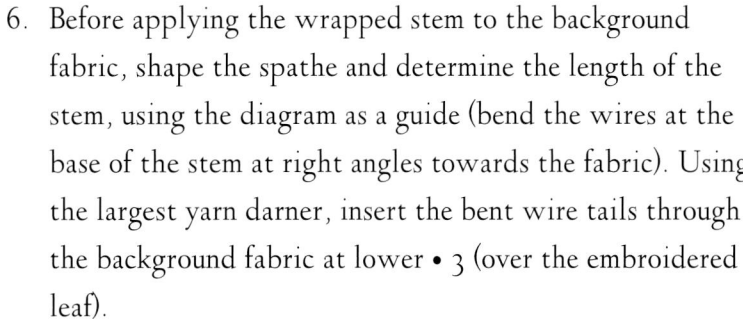

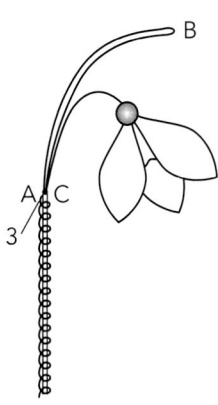

6. Before applying the wrapped stem to the background fabric, shape the spathe and determine the length of the stem, using the diagram as a guide (bend the wires at the base of the stem at right angles towards the fabric). Using the largest yarn darner, insert the bent wire tails through the background fabric at lower • 3 (over the embroidered leaf).

7. Undo the knot at A-C and take the three tails of thread through to the back at the top of the stem at upper • 3. Adjust the curve and position of the spathe and insert the tails of thread at B through to the back at (or near) the tacked dot. Keep all wire and thread tails loose to allow for final adjustments. When satisfied with the shape and position of the spathe and stem, secure all tails of wire and thread (bend the wire tails behind the stem, stitch and trim, grading the lengths of the tails to prevent a lump). Finally, take the retained tails of wrapping thread through to the back to secure the wrapped stem.

8. Shape the detached petals of the snowdrop and trim wire tails.

SNOWDROP 4

Snowdrop 4 has three detached outer petals, three detached inner petals, and a detached spathe and stem.

To Apply Detached Petals

1. Cut out the three detached outer petals for snowdrop 4 and shape slightly. Draw three equally spaced dots on the small circle outline on the background fabric (these are the detached outer petal insertion points). Insert the wire tails of the detached outer petals, through three individual holes, using a yarn darner. Bend the wire tails under each petal and secure with small stitches. Do not cut the wire tails until the flower is finished.

2. Cut out three detached inner petals for snowdrop 4 and shape slightly. Using a yarn darner, insert the wire tails of the detached inner petals, through three individual holes between the outer petals (just in from the circle outline). Bend the wire tails under each petal and secure with small stitches. Do not cut the wire tails until the flower is finished.

3. Using two strands of yellow thread in a size 8 milliners needle, work six or seven French knots in the centre of the snowdrop for the stamens.

Pedicel

1. Bend a 12 cm (4³/₄ in) length of white wire in half. Secure a length of medium green thread to the bend, leaving a 10 cm (4 in) tail of thread. To form the pedicel, wrap the wire tails, from the bend, with the medium green thread, keeping the two wires side by side. Wrap about 3 cm (1¹/₄ in) and secure the thread, retaining the tail. Carefully shape the wrapped wire with tweezers, using the pedicel line on the diagram as a guide.

2. To apply the pedicel, insert the wire and thread tails through upper • 4 (this will be the position of the top of wrapped stem 4), using a yarn darner (keep the wire tails loose at the back until the other end of the pedicel is secured to allow for adjustments).

3. To secure the 'flower end' of the pedicel, take the tail of thread through to the back (under the petals), near the centre of the flower.

4. Adjust the position of the pedicel, secure the thread tail, then stitch the wire tails to the back (behind where the detached stem will lie). Trim wire.

Pedicel
wire tail

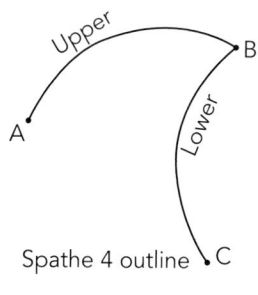

Spathe 4 outline

Actual size

Spathe and Stem 4

Cut a 36 cm (14 in) length of green-covered wire for the combined spathe and stem (the long tails of wire are wrapped to form the detached stem for snowdrop 4).

1. Mount a piece of muslin into a 15 cm (6 in) hoop. Trace spathe 4 outline onto a 5 cm (2 in) square of paper and attach to the hoop of muslin with a larger square of clear, self-adhesive plastic. This will be used as a template to shape the wire for the spathe.

2. Bend a 36 cm (14 in) length of green-covered wire in half, making a distinct point at the bend. Using machine thread, couch the wire to the spathe outline with stitches at A, B and C (and one or two stitches in between), stitching through the plastic, paper and muslin. Secure the thread and temporarily hold the long tails of wire to the muslin with masking tape (take care not to bend the tails of the wire).

3. Cover the wire spathe with buttonhole stitch, working the ridge of the buttonhole on the *inside* of the wire shape. The upper edge of the wire, A to B, is worked with dark green thread, the lower edge of the wire, B to C, is worked with medium green thread. Leave a tail of thread at each end of the buttonhole stitches (one tail at both A and C, two tails at B).

4. Cut and remove the couching stitches and lift the wire spathe from the plastic. Push the buttonholed edges of the wire together, and curve into shape using the spathe line on the diagram sheet as a guide (adjust the number of buttonhole stitches, if necessary, to make points A and C lie side by side). Loosely tie thread tails A and C together at the back with a square knot.

5. Add a third piece of green wire (15 cm/6 in long) to the long tails of wire, the cut end flush with the base of the spathe (A-C). These three wires will be wrapped with one strand of dark green thread to form the stem of the snowdrop as follows:

- Slide a length of dark green thread between the two long tails of wire, leaving a tail of thread at A-C (next to the knotted tails of thread). Holding the three wires together (the third wire at the back), wrap closely for about 2.5 cm (1 in), taking care not to twist the wires. Secure the wrapping thread with a half-hitch knot (buttonhole loop) around the wires, retaining the tail of thread.

- Slide a new length of thread between the wires (leaving a tail of thread next to the retained tail), and continue wrapping the wires closely for another 2.5 cm (1 in), as before (the join between the two wrapped sections should be invisible). Secure the wrapping thread with a half-hitch knot around the wires, retaining the tail of thread. The retained tails of thread will be used later to attach the stem to the background fabric.

- Slide a new length of thread between the wires and work as above.

- Slide a final length of thread between the wires (leaving a tail of thread next to the retained tail), and continue wrapping the wires closely for about 4 cm ($1^1/_2$ in). Secure the thread at the end of the wrapping, retaining a tail of thread (the wrapped length of the stem is longer than the actual stem to ensure a neat insertion point).

6. Before applying the wrapped stem to the background fabric, shape the spathe and determine the length of the stem, using the diagram as a guide (bend the wires at the base of the stem at right angles towards the fabric). Using the largest yarn darner, insert the bent wire tails through the background fabric at lower • 4 (over embroidered leaf E).

7. Undo the knot at A-C and take the three tails of thread through to the back at upper • 4 (the top of the stem). Adjust the curve and position of the spathe and insert the tails of thread at B through to the back at (or near) the tacked dot. Keep all wire and thread tails loose to allow for final adjustments. When satisfied with the shape and position of the spathe and stem, secure all tails of wire and thread (bend the wire tails behind the stem, stitch and trim, grading the lengths of the tails to prevent a lump). Finally, take the retained tails of wrapping thread through to the back to secure the wrapped stem.

8. Using tweezers, shape the snowdrop petals, gently pushing each petal towards the centre to make the space as small as possible. Trim all wires.

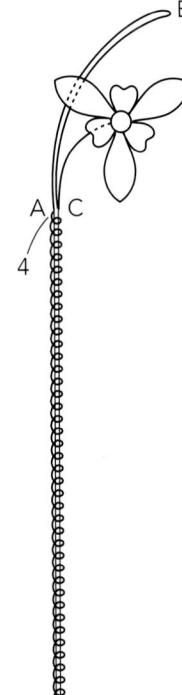

Actual size

SNOWDROP 5

Snowdrop 5 also has three detached outer petals, three detached inner petals, and a detached spathe and stem.

To Apply Detached Petals

Cut out the three detached inner petals and three detached outer petals for snowdrop 5. Apply and complete as for snowdrop 4.

Pedicel

Prepare and apply the pedicel as for snowdrop 4.

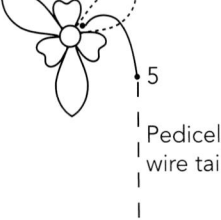

Spathe and Stem 5

Cut an 18 cm (7 in) length of green-covered wire for the combined spathe and stem (the tails are wrapped to form the detached stem for snowdrop 5).

B, Upper, A, Lower, C — Spathe 5 outline

Actual size

1. Mount a piece of muslin into a hoop. Trace spathe 5 outline onto paper and attach to the hoop of muslin with self-adhesive plastic. This will be used as a template to shape the wire for the spathe.

2. Bend an 18 cm (7 in) length of green-covered wire in half, making a distinct point at the bend. Using machine thread, couch the wire to the spathe outline with stitches at A, B and C (and one or two stitches in between), stitching through the plastic, paper and muslin. Secure the thread and temporarily hold the tails of wire to the muslin with masking tape.

3. Cover the wire spathe with buttonhole stitch, as for snowdrop 4.

4. Remove the wire spathe from the plastic, push the buttonholed edges of the wire together, and curve into shape using the spathe line on the diagram sheet as a guide. Loosely tie thread tails A and C together at the back with a square knot.

5. Add a third piece of green wire (6 cm/2¼ in long) to the tails of wire, the cut end flush with the base of the spathe (A-C). These three wires will be wrapped with one strand of dark green thread to form the stem of the snowdrop as follows:

   • Slide a length of dark green thread between the two long tails of wire, leaving a tail of thread at A-C. Wrap the three wires closely for about 2 cm (³/₄ in). Secure the wrapping thread with a half-hitch knot, retaining the tail of thread.

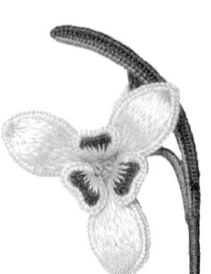

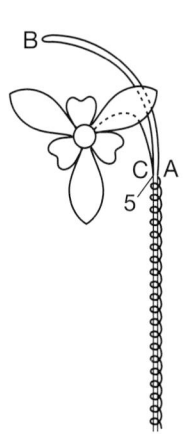

- Slide a new length of thread between the wires (leaving a tail of thread next to the retained tail), and continue wrapping the wires closely for another 2.5 cm (1 in). Secure the thread at the end of the wrapping, retaining a tail of thread.

6. Before applying the wrapped stem to the background fabric, shape the spathe and determine the length of the stem, using the diagram as a guide (bend the wires at the base of the stem at right angles towards the fabric). Using the largest yarn darner, insert the bent wire tails at lower • 5.

7. Undo the knot at A-C and take the three tails of thread through to the back at upper • 5 (the top of the stem). Adjust the curve and position of the spathe and insert the tails of thread at B through to the back at (or near) the tacked dot. Keep all wire and tails of thread loose to allow for final adjustments. When satisfied with the shape and position of the spathe and stem, secure all tails of wire and thread. Finally, take the retained tails of wrapping thread through to the back to secure the wrapped stem.

8. Using tweezers, shape the snowdrop petals, gently pushing each petal towards the centre to make the space as small as possible. Trim all wires.

CRANEFLY

The cranefly's extraordinarily long legs are stitched over the completed stems and leaves.

Requirements

- purple/gold shot crystal organza: 15 cm (6 in) square
- pearl metal organdie: 15 cm (6 in) square
- paper-backed fusible web: 15 cm (6 in) square
- black snakeskin: 2.5 cm (1 in) square
- dark gold stranded thread: Soie d'Alger 2526 *or* DMC 783
- medium gold stranded thread: Soie d'Alger 2525 *or* DMC 728
- dark purple stranded thread: Soie d'Alger 3326 *or* DMC 939
- brown/black metallic thread: Kreinik Cord 201c
- grey metallic thread: Madeira Metallic 40 col. 360
- black soft metallic thread: Madeira Metallic 40 col. 70
- slate rayon machine thread: Madeira Rayon 40 col. 1164
- nylon clear thread: Madeira Monofil 60 col. 1001
- Mill Hill seed beads 374 (blue/purple)
- Mill Hill petite beads 40374 (blue/purple)
- 28 gauge uncovered wire: two 11 cm (4¹/₄ in) lengths

The Black-and-yellow Cranefly, Nephrotoma maculosa, is also known as Daddy-long-legs because of its extraordinarily long legs. The harmless Cranefly, with its strongly striped abdomen, is common in fields and gardens where it likes to rest on vegetation, and is a familiar sight on warm summer evenings, clustered around electric lights.

ABDOMEN

1. Using dark gold thread in a size 10 crewel needle, outline the abdomen in back stitch, using the internal segment lines as a guide to length (nine back stitches on each side).

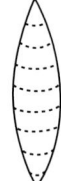

2. Using six strands of medium gold thread in a chenille needle, pad the abdomen, inside the outline, with six long straight stitches. With one strand of thread, work eight couching stitches over the padding, using the back stitches as a guide to placement. The abdomen will be embroidered in raised stem stitch over these couching stitches, so they need to be snug but not too tight.

3. To form a slightly textured centre line, work a row of raised chain stitch down the centre of the abdomen, working over the couched bars towards the tail, with one strand of dark purple thread in a tapestry needle.

4. Work four rows of raised stem stitch, on either side of the centre line, to cover the abdomen, working all rows towards the tail. First, work two rows in medium gold, next to the centre line, making the second row shorter to allow for the tapered tail. Then, using dark gold thread, work two rows on each side, to complete the abdomen.

5. To form the point at the tail of the abdomen, work a stitch (1.5 mm long) with one strand of dark purple thread in a sharps needle.

Detached Wings

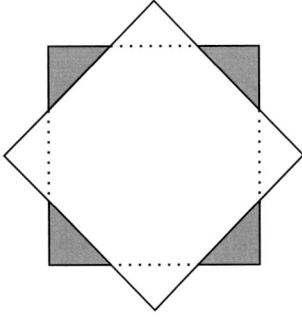

1. Using paper-backed fusible web, fuse the purple crystal organza to the pearl organdie, rotating one of the layers 45 degrees to be on the bias grain (iron between sheets of baking parchment to protect the iron and the wing fabrics). Mount into a small hoop, purple organza side uppermost.

2. Using tweezers, bend the uncovered wire around the wing outline template to shape the two wings, leaving two tails of wire at the base of each wing that touch but do not cross. Place the wire shapes on the hoop of wing fabric, holding the wire tails in place with masking tape. Make sure that you have a right and a left wing.

3. Using one strand of slate rayon machine thread in a sharps needle, stitch the wire to the wing fabric with small, close, overcast stitches, working several stitches over both wires, at the base of the wing, to begin and end the stitching.

4. To embroider the wing marking (pterostigma) in the upper corner of both wings, work three satin stitches, on top of each other, with black soft metallic thread, knotting the tails of thread together at the back.

5. Using grey metallic thread in a size 9 milliners needle, work the veins in each wing with three fly stitches, using the diagram as a guide. It is safer to keep the tails of thread at the front until the wings have been cut out, then insert them through to the back. The tails of thread are secured after the wing has been applied to the main fabric. Carefully cut out the wings, retaining the tails of thread.

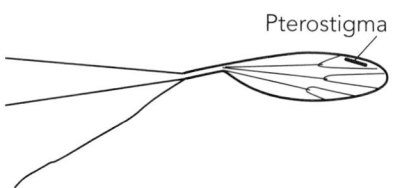

Pterostigma

Thorax

1. Using a large yarn darner, insert the wire (and thread) tails of the wings through the dot • at the top of the abdomen. Bend the wire tails under the abdomen and secure with a few stitches. Do not trim the wires until the cranefly is finished.

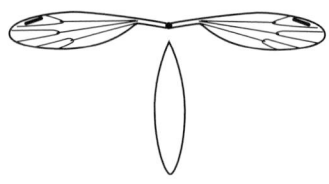

2. Using six strands of dark purple thread, pad the thorax with five stitches over the base of the wings (covering the wire insertion point), stitching towards the abdomen.

3. Cut the thorax shape out of snakeskin and check for size (it needs to be *just* large enough to reach the background fabric over the padding and wings and to cover the first 'segment' of the abdomen). Using nylon thread in a sharps needle, apply the snakeskin with small stab stitches, working from the background into the edge of the snakeskin. Work the first two stitches at the lower corners of the thorax (covering the first segment of the abdomen), then a stitch on either side above the wings and one stitch at the top edge. Use tweezers to shape the snakeskin into a mound over the padding and wings.

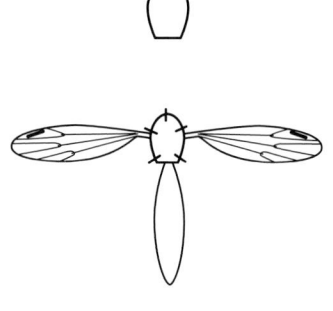

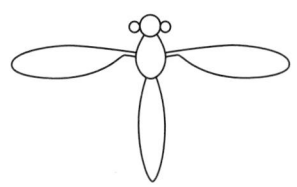

4. Using nylon thread, stitch a blue/purple seed bead close to the top of the thorax, for the head, keeping the hole in the bead parallel to the top of the thorax. Bring the needle through to the front and stitch a blue/purple petite bead on either side of the head bead for the eyes, taking the needle through the hole of the seed bead several times so that the eyes are suspended on either side. Secure the thread.

Legs and Antennae

As the legs are very long and very fine, they cannot be traced onto the background fabric. The best time to transfer the cranefly leg template is after the leaves have been stitched (see page 190 for leg template and page 194 for instructions). As the legs all start at the thorax (under the wings), gently raise the wings out of the way when working the stitches.

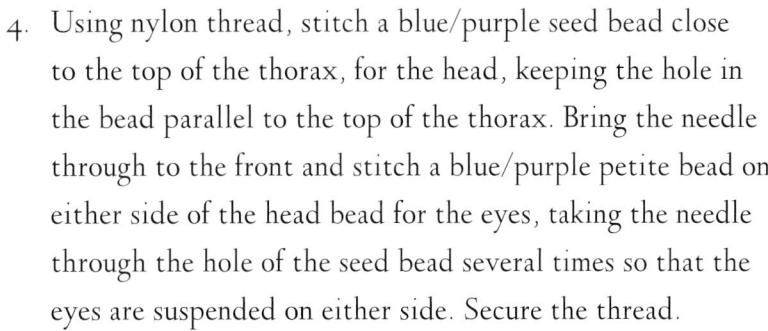

1. Using a double strand of brown/black metallic thread in a size 9 milliners needle, work each leg with long straight stitches, over stems and leaves, using the leg template dots marked on the back as a guide to length and placement (the position of the legs may be varied if desired). Work two stitches (on top of each other) for the long, thicker leg segment closest to the body, then four long back stitches for remaining leg segments.

2. Using a single strand of brown/black metallic thread, make a stitch on either side of the head bead for the antennae (taking the needle through the head bead if desired).

3. Using tweezers, gently squeeze the abdomen (to neaten and raise) and position the wings. Trim the wire tails.

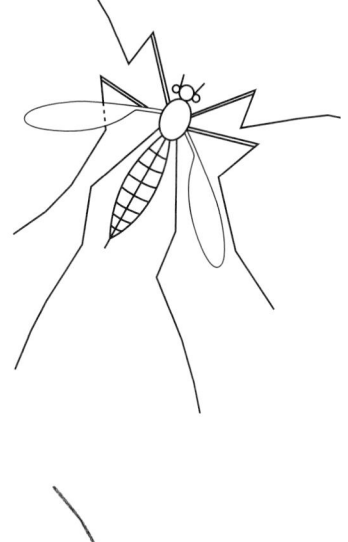

TIGER MOTH

Work a Scarlet Tiger Moth over the leaves and stems at the base of the snowdrops. Use the dots on the skeleton outline of the design for placement of the abdomen and wings.

Requirements

- quilter's muslin: 20 cm (8 in) square
- dark navy stranded thread: Soie d'Alger 165 *or* Noir *or* DMC 310
- scarlet stranded thread: Soie d'Alger 636 *or* DMC 349
- dark gold stranded thread: Soie d'Alger 2526 *or* DMC 783
- cream stranded thread: Soie d'Alger 2522 *or* DMC 3823
- rust stranded thread: Soie d'Alger 2636 *or* DMC 919
- black metallic thread: Kreinik Cord 005c
- red metallic thread: Kreinik Cord 003c
- gold/bronze metallic thread: Madeira Metallic Art 9842 col. 482
- variegated gold/black chenille thread: col. Fire
- nylon clear thread: Madeira Monofil 60 col. 1001
- 3 mm bronze/purple bead
- Mill Hill petite beads 42014 (black)
- 33 gauge white covered wire: four 12 cm (4½ in) lengths (colour wire red and purple if desired, Copic R17 Lipstick Orange, Copic BV08 Blue Violet)

Most tiger moths are brightly coloured, a characteristic that often leads them to be mistaken for butterflies when their wings are spread. They are named after the tiger-like stripes on their fore wings. The Scarlet Tiger Moth, Callimorpha dominula, *a vividly coloured, day-flying member of the family, frequents damp meadows, wooded valleys and the banks of streams. During summer it flies at night as well as during the daytime. Its black fore wings have a metallic green sheen, and cream and orange spots that may vary greatly in shape. The hind wings, often hidden beneath the fore wings, are a vivid scarlet with black blotches. It has comb-like (pectinate) antennae and the scarlet abdomen has a central black stripe.*

PREPARATION

1. Mount the muslin into a small hoop and trace four wing outlines (including the inside wing markings)—a right and a left fore wing and a right and a left hind wing.

2. Using tweezers, shape a length of wire around the wing outline diagram, leaving two tails of wire at the base of the wing. Shape a right and a left fore wing and a right and a left hind wing. If desired, colour the wires red and purple (or black) using the diagram as a guide (leave the dark gold section of the fore wing uncoloured).

FORE WINGS

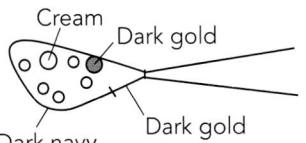

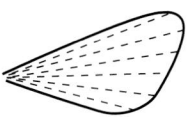

1. Using one strand of dark navy thread in a crewel needle, couch the shaped wire around the traced fore-wing outline, working a couching stitch on either side of the dark gold marking on the lower edge of the wing. Buttonhole stitch the wire to the muslin, working the lower marking with dark gold thread, and the rest of the wing with dark navy.

   The wings are embroidered with one strand of thread in a combination of buttonhole stitch and long and short stitch (for the background of the wings), and satin stitch (for the spots).

   Hint: To help achieve a smooth surface, work *all* stitches in the direction of imaginary lines, radiating from the base of the wings to the outer edge.

2. Embroider the spots in the wings, with either cream or dark gold thread, as follows:

   · Outline the spot in back stitch and work some padding stitches inside the outline (if the spot is large).

   · Embroider the spot in satin stitch, enclosing the outline, taking care with the direction of the stitches.

3. Using dark navy thread, embroider the outer edge of
    the wing (inside the wire) with a row of long and short
    buttonhole stitch, varying the length of the stitches to
    work to the edge of the spots as required. Embroider the
    remainder of the wing surface (between the spots) in long
    and short stitch.

4. With black metallic thread in a milliners needle, work the
    veins with fly and single feather stitches, using the diagram
    as a guide.

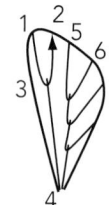

Hind Wings

1. Using one strand of scarlet thread, couch the shaped wire
    around the traced hind-wing outline, working the couching
    stitches to correspond with the colour changes at the edge
    of the wing. Buttonhole stitch the wire to the muslin, in
    either dark navy or scarlet, according to the edge markings.

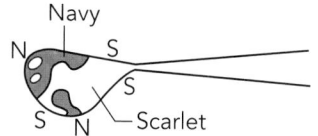

2. Using scarlet thread, outline the two red spots (at the
    outer corners) in back stitch, then embroider in satin stitch,
    enclosing the outline.

3. Outline the remaining internal lines in back stitch with
    dark navy thread, then embroider these areas in satin stitch
    (enclosing the outline), taking care with the direction of the
    stitches.

4. Starting at the edge of the wing, embroider the remainder
    of the wing surface (between the spots) in long and short
    stitch, using scarlet thread.

5. With red metallic thread in a milliners needle, work the
    veins with three fly stitches, using the diagram as a guide.

To Complete the Moth

1. To pad the abdomen, make one stitch from 3 to 4, with fourteen strands of rust thread in a chenille needle (seven strands doubled). Cross the tails of padding thread behind the stitch (at the back), and hold each end with masking tape.

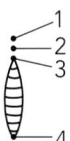

2. With one strand of rust thread in a size 10 crewel needle, work five evenly spaced couching stitches over the padding, catching in the tails of padding thread behind the abdomen (the tails will be trimmed later). The abdomen will be embroidered in raised stem stitch over these couching stitches so they need to be snug but not too tight.

3. With one strand of thread in a tapestry needle, work seven rows of raised stem stitch—three rows in rust, the centre row in dark navy, then three more rows in rust, working each row towards the tail.

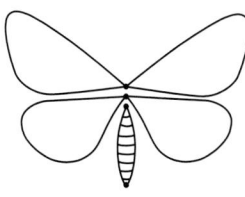

4. Carefully cut out the wings and apply by inserting the wire tails through the two upper two dots as shown, using large yarn darners. Apply the hind wings first, inserting both wire tails through dot 2, then the fore wings through dot 1 (the wings will slightly overlap). Bend the wire tails under the wings and secure to the backing fabric with tiny stitches, making sure that the stitches do not protrude outside the wing span. Trim the wire tails when the moth is finished.

5. The thorax is worked with three straight stitches across the centre of the wings (from 1 to 3), using chenille thread in the largest yarn darner. Using variegated chenille, select a dark yellow section and make two stitches. Work a stitch on top/between with black chenille to form a centre stripe (for maximum control of the chenille, all stitches can be made with separate lengths of thread, all inserted from the front). Make sure the chenille does not twist, and adjust the tension of the stitches (thus the fluffiness of the thorax), as desired. Secure the tails of chenille with nylon thread after the head is applied (to allow for final adjustments).

6. Using nylon thread in a sharps needle, stitch a 3 mm bead close to the top of the thorax, for the head (keeping the hole in the bead parallel to the top of the thorax). Bring the needle through to the front and stitch a black petite bead on either side of the head bead for the eyes, taking the needle through the hole of the bead several times so that the eyes are suspended on either side.

7. With one strand of gold/bronze metallic thread in a sharps needle, make a stitch on either side of the head bead for the antennae (taking the needle through the head bead if desired).

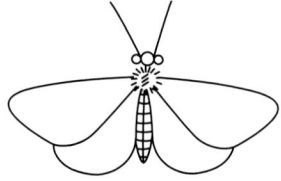

Border

This border, inspired by the richly decorated margins in a sixteenth century Book of Hours, is great fun to work; however, it requires precision in the placement of the silk ribbon, the border threads and the beads. Because of the accuracy required, no conversions for the metric measurements are supplied. Before commencing the border, check that the two lines of running stitch (the border lines) are still straight; adjust if necessary. There is no need to remove these stitches.

Requirements

- Hannah bias-cut silk ribbon: 1 cm (7/16 in) wide col. African Violet

- gilt 3-ply twist

- dark gold thick pearl cotton: DMC Coton Perlé No. 3 col. 783

- dark gold stranded thread: DMC 783

- gold couching thread: Couching Thread 371 (Dark/Jacobean gold)

- gold metallic thread: Madeira Metallic Art 9803 col. 3007

- fine gold silk thread: YLI Silk stitch 50 col. 79

- nylon clear thread: Madeira Monofil 60 col. 1001

- gold seed beads: Metallic Delica DBR 31 *or* Mill Hill Magnifica 10076

Ribbon Background

The background of the border is a rich violet-purple bias-cut silk ribbon. The ribbon is optional (I have seen this border worked very successfully without it).

Cut 75 cm of bias-cut silk ribbon. Using fine silk sewing thread in a sharps needle, stitch the ribbon to the border with large herringbone stitches, following the instructions for the ribbon background for the Bittersweet on page 178.

EDGES

The border edges consist of couched rows of gilt 3-ply twist and dark gold Coton Perlé No. 3.

1. Following the instructions for the border edges for the Bittersweet, couch the gold twist, with *either* nylon thread in a sharps needle *or* one strand of gold metallic thread in a size 9 milliners needle.

2. Couch the dark gold Coton Perlé with one strand of matching stranded thread (DMC 783) in a sharps needle.

BEADING

The inside of the border is embellished with gold couching thread, inserted through gold beads in a zig-zag pattern, following the beading instructions for the Bittersweet on page 180.

Wild Pea and Longhorn Moth

The pea family, including the genus Lathyrus, has been known to mankind
for as long as there has been agriculture, providing crops for the Neolithic
settlements throughout the Nile delta and the Near East as far back as 6000
BC. The name Lathyrus is derived from the Ancient Greek word for a
stimulant, thoures, as the Greeks believed the seed of the pea had stimulating
properties. Numbering over 160 species, annual and perennial, cultivated and
wild, Lathyrus can be found in every colour of the rainbow, from crimson
to violet, white, yellow and even green-flowered. It is easy to understand their
family name, Papilionaceae, 'like butterflies'.

The Wild Pea, Lathyrus sylvestris, is a narrow-leaved everlasting pea
with broadly winged stems and branched tendrils. Native to Britain, this
vigorous climbing perennial may be found scrambling over bushes and shrubs
at woodland edges, roadsides and especially on wet sea cliffs. Each stem
produces clusters of three to twelve greenish-pink to magenta flowers, making
a magnificent display for many weeks in summer. The long, brownish-green
seed pods disperse their seeds with an audible snap when ripe. The Wild Pea
attracts legume-feeding beetles and weevils, caterpillars and bees.

Inspired by the illuminated pages of medieval manuscripts, this small stumpwork panel features the Wild Pea, *Lathyrus sylvestris*, a summer-flowering perennial, with detached flower petals and leaves, and a beaded seed pod. A Longhorn Moth, *Adela reamurella*, with golden raised wings and extraordinarily long antennae, and a tiny Two-spot Ladybird, *Adalia bipunctata*, with detached elytra complete the design. The ornate border is worked in silk ribbon, gold thread and beads.

This Wild Pea from a sixteenth century French manuscript provided the inspiration for my embroidered panel.

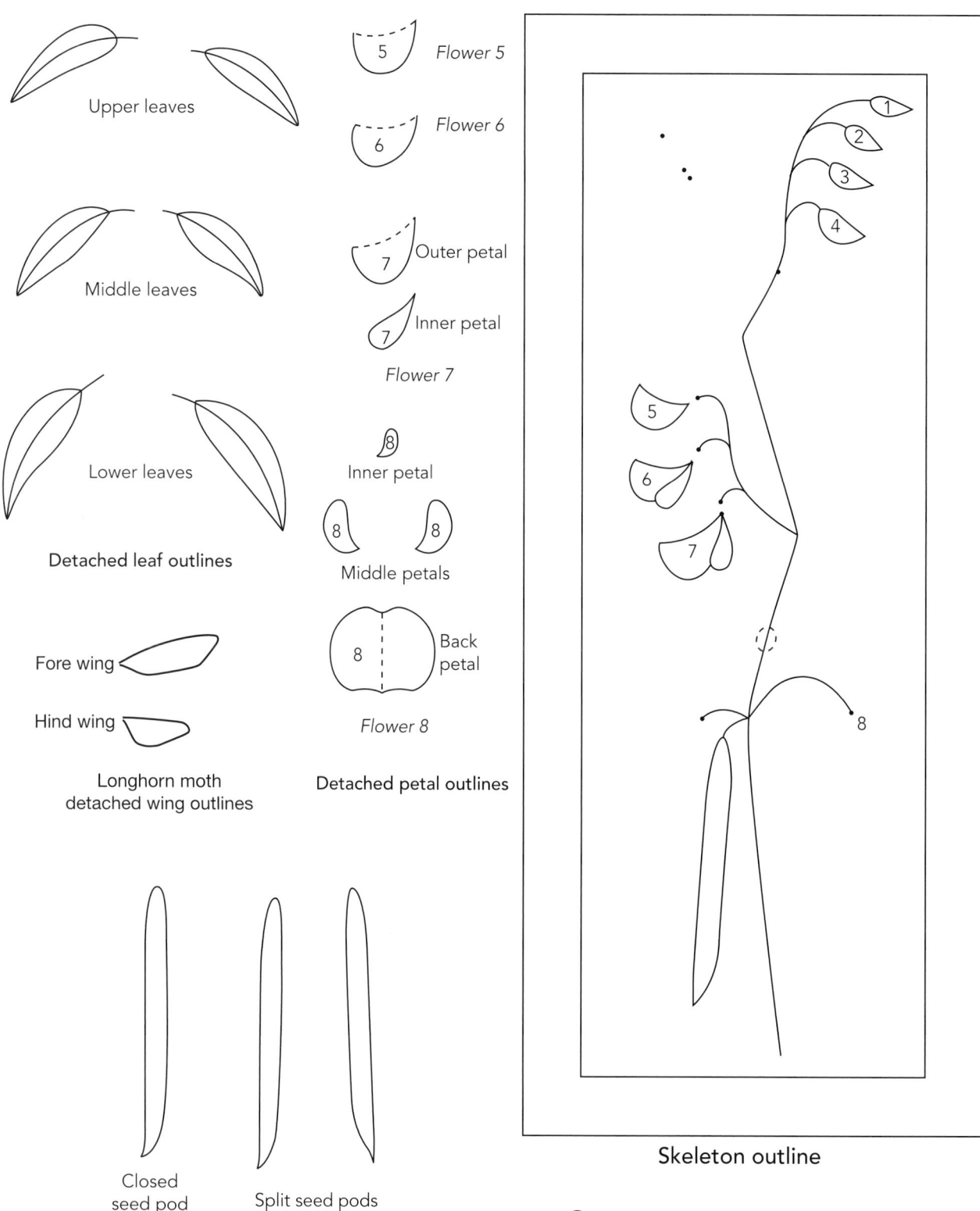

Upper leaves

Middle leaves

Lower leaves

Detached leaf outlines

Fore wing

Hind wing

Longhorn moth
detached wing outlines

Closed
seed pod

Split seed pods

Detached seed pod outlines

5   *Flower 5*

6   *Flower 6*

7   Outer petal

7   Inner petal

Flower 7

8   Inner petal

8   8   Middle petals

8   Back
petal

Flower 8

Detached petal outlines

5

6

7

8

Skeleton outline

Ladybird
wing outline

Ladybird
abdomen outline

*Diagrams are
actual size*

Overall Requirements

This is the *complete* list of requirements for this panel. For ease of use, the requirements of each individual element are repeated under its heading—for example, Wild Pea requirements, Ladybird requirements.

- ivory satin background fabric: 30 cm (12 in) square
- quilter's muslin or calico backing fabric: 30 cm (12 in) square
- quilter's muslin: four 20 cm (8 in) squares
- light gold shot crystal organza: 15 x 7.5 cm (6 x 3 in)
- wine/black shot crystal organza: 15 x 7.5 cm (6 x 3 in)
- gold metal organdie:15 cm (6 in) square
- paper-backed fusible web: 15 cm (6 in) square
- 25 cm (10 in) embroidery hoop or stretcher bars
- 15 cm (6 in) embroidery hoops
- 10 cm (4 in) embroidery hoops
- needles:
  crewel/embroidery sizes 8–10
  milliners/straw sizes 8 and 9
  sharps size 12
  chenille size 18
  sharp yarn darners sizes 14–18
- embroidery equipment (see page 266)

- dark green stranded thread (stems, leaves): Soie d'Alger 1835 *or* DMC 986
- medium green stranded thread (stems, leaves): Soie d'Alger 1833 *or* DMC 988
- olive stranded thread (seed pod): Soie d'Alger 2133 *or* DMC 3364

- magenta stranded thread (flowers): Soie d'Alger 1043 *or* DMC 718

- violet stranded thread (flowers): Soie d'Alger 3314 *or* DMC 3837

- medium mauve stranded thread (flowers): Soie d'Alger 3313 *or* DMC 3835

- light mauve stranded thread (flowers): Soie d'Alger 3311 *or* DMC 3836

- very pale mauve stranded thread (flowers): Soie d'Alger 3331 *or* DMC 819

- pale lime stranded thread (flowers): Soie d'Alger 242 *or* DMC 3348

- dark brown stranded thread (moth): Soie d'Alger 4146 *or* DMC 838

- red stranded thread (ladybird, border): DMC 349

- black stranded thread (ladybird): DMC 310

- black metallic thread (ladybird): Kreinik Cord 005c

- wine/black metallic thread (moth): Kreinik Cord 208c

- pale gold metallic thread (moth): Madeira Metallic 30 col. 6032

- gold metallic thread (border): Madeira Metallic Art 9803 col. 3007

- gold couching thread (border): Couching Thread 371 (Dark/Jacobean gold)

- gilt 3-ply twist (border)

- fine gold silk thread (border): YLI Silk stitch 50 col. 79

- red thick pearl cotton (border): DMC Coton Perlé No. 3 col. 349

- black chenille thread (moth): Au Ver à Soie Chenille à Broder col. Noir

- pale gold rayon machine thread (moth): Madeira Rayon 40 col. 1338
- pale plum rayon machine thread (moth): Madeira Rayon 40 col. 1358
- nylon clear thread: Madeira Monofil 60 col. 1001

Lathyrus sylvestris

- Hannah bias-cut silk ribbon: 1 cm (7/16 in) wide col. Cabernet (border)
- Mill Hill antique glass beads 3036 (wine/bronze)
- Mill Hill petite beads 42014 (black)
- gold seed beads: Metallic Delica Beads DBR 31 *or* Mill Hill Magnifica 10076

- 33 gauge white covered wire (leaves): six 12 cm (4¹/₂ in) lengths (colour wire green if desired, Copic G28 Ocean Green)
- 33 gauge white covered wire (petals): seven 9 cm (3¹/₂ in) lengths (colour three wires magenta if desired, Copic RV09 Fuchsia)
- 33 gauge white covered wire (flower 8 outer petal): one 12 cm length
- 33 gauge white covered wire (seed pods): three 18 cm (7 in) lengths
- 33 gauge white covered wire (ladybird): one 12 cm (4³/₄ in) length (colour wire red if desired, Copic R17 Lipstick Orange)
- 33 gauge white covered wire (moth wings): four 9 cm (3¹/₂ in) lengths (colour wire pale gold if desired, Copic YR24 Pale Sepia)
- 28 gauge brass wire (moth antennae): one 15 cm length
- 28 gauge uncovered wire (tendrils): four 11 cm (4¹/₄ in) lengths

PREPARATION

1. Mount the satin background fabric and the muslin/calico backing into the 25 cm (10 in) embroidery hoop or frame.

2. Using a fine lead pencil, trace the skeleton outlines of the design and the border onto tracing paper. Turn the tracing paper over and draw over the outlines on the back.

3. With the tracing paper right side up, transfer the design and the border outlines to the satin with a stylus.

4. Using fine gold silk thread in a sharps needle, work a row of tacking/running stitches along both border lines (the lead pencil lines tend to fade). As the border threads will be applied over these stitches, they need to be quite small and accurate.

WILD PEA

Requirements

- quilter's muslin: four 20 cm (8 in) squares
- dark green stranded thread: Soie d'Alger 1835 *or* DMC 986
- medium green stranded thread: Soie d'Alger 1833 *or* DMC 988
- olive stranded thread: Soie d'Alger 2133 *or* DMC 3364
- magenta stranded thread: Soie d'Alger 1043 *or* DMC 718
- violet stranded thread: Soie d'Alger 3314 *or* DMC 3837
- medium mauve stranded thread: Soie d'Alger 3313 *or* DMC 3835
- light mauve stranded thread: Soie d'Alger 3311 *or* DMC 3836
- very pale mauve stranded thread: Soie d'Alger 3331 *or* DMC 819

- pale lime stranded thread: Soie d'Alger 242 *or* DMC 3348
- nylon clear thread: Madeira Monofil 60 col. 1001
- 33 gauge white covered wire (leaves): six 12 cm (4¹/₂ in) lengths (colour wire green if desired, Copic G28 Ocean Green)
- 33 gauge white covered wire (petals): seven 9 cm (3¹/₂ in) lengths (colour three wires magenta if desired, Copic RV09 Fuchsia)
- 33 gauge white covered wire (flower 8 outer petal): one 12 cm length
- 33 gauge white covered wire (seed pods): three 18 cm (7 in) lengths
- 28 gauge uncovered wire (tendrils): four 11 cm (4¹/₄ in) lengths

Stems

A distinctive feature of the wild pea is the winged (leaf-like) nature of the branching plant stems; the flower and bud stems are not winged. The stems are worked in stem stitch with dark and medium green threads.

1. Work the central vein of the main stem in stem stitch with two strands of medium green thread in a size 9 crewel needle, starting at the lower end and working to the base of the upper bud stem (•). Continue with the same thread to work the upper bud stem, reducing to one strand to work the finer stems to the individual buds.

2. Work the left flower stem in stem stitch with two strands of medium green thread, reducing to one strand to work the individual flower stems. Work the lower flower and seed pod stems with two strands of thread.

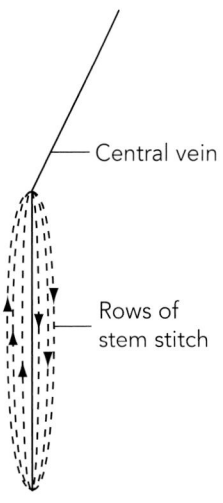

Central vein

Rows of stem stitch

3. To embroider the 'wings' on the main plant stem, work consecutive rows of stem stitch on either side of the central vein, using one strand of dark green thread in a size 10 crewel needle. Starting at the base, work three rows of stem stitch on either side of the lower stem segment, tapering the end of each row to form a slight indentation at each end of the segment (it is easier to complete one stem segment before proceeding to the next). Work three rows of stem stitch on either side of the next segment and two rows of stem stitch on either side of the upper two segments.

DETACHED LEAVES

The detached leaves are worked in dark and medium green thread.

1. Mount muslin into a 15 cm (6 in) hoop and trace the six leaf outlines. Label each pair of leaves to identify them (upper, middle and lower leaves).

2. Using one strand of medium green thread, couch wire along the central vein, one end of the wire at the tip of the leaf. Overcast stitch the wire to the muslin along the central vein.

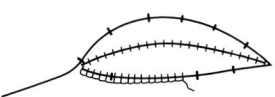

3. Using dark green thread, couch the remaining wire around the leaf outline, bending into a point at the tip and ending with one tail of wire at the base of the leaf. Buttonhole stitch the wire to the muslin around the outside edge of the leaf.

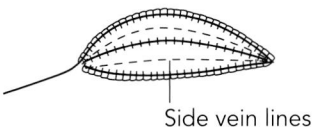

Side vein lines

4. Embroider the surface of the leaf with consecutive rows of stem stitch, starting next to the central vein with dark green thread and working two side veins in medium green thread. Work all rows towards the tip of the leaf, adjusting the length of the rows as required to fill the shape.

5. Carefully cut out the leaves and keep aside until all other work on the panel is finished.

6. Shape the leaf slightly before applying to the finished work. Using a large yarn darner, insert the wire tails through to the back at the stem segment indentations. Secure the tails of wire with a few small stitches at the back of the stem. Shape the leaves with tweezers and trim the wire tails.

Buds 1 and 2

1. Using one strand of pale lime thread, outline the bud shape in back stitch. Embroider the bud with long, close buttonhole stitches worked in a fan shape, the ridge of the buttonhole at the lower edge of the bud, enclosing the outline.

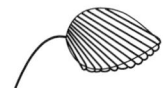

2. To form the sepals, work three detached chain stitches from the end of the stem, over the base of the bud, with one strand of medium green thread.

Bud 3

Work in the same way as bud 1, using very pale mauve thread.

Bud 4

Work in the same way as bud 1, using light mauve thread.

Flower 5

Background Petal

Outline the background petal in back stitch with one strand of light mauve thread. Work a row of close, long and short buttonhole stitch around the curved lower edge of the petal, enclosing the outline. Embroider the remainder of the petal in long and short stitch.

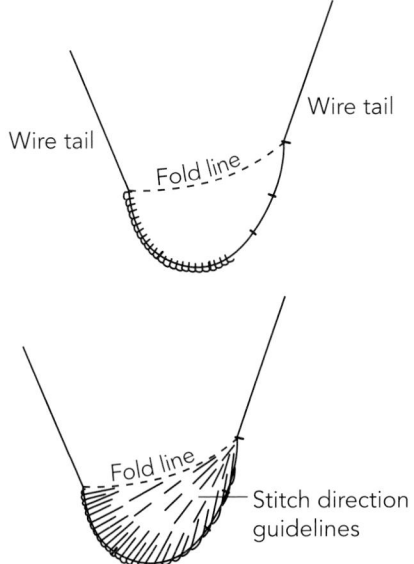

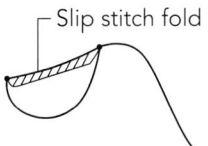

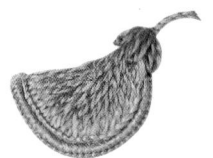

Detached Petal

1. Mount muslin into a small hoop and trace the detached petal outlines for flowers 5, 6 and 7. With one strand of light mauve thread, couch wire around the lower edge of petal outline 5, leaving a wire tail at each end of the upper 'fold' line. Buttonhole stitch the wire to the muslin.

2. Using light mauve thread, work a row of long and short buttonhole stitch around the lower edge of the petal (inside the wire), using the diagram as a guide to stitch direction. Embroider the remainder of the petal in long and short stitch with medium mauve thread, blending into the light mauve and working up to the 'fold' line.

3. Cut out the petal close to the wire edge, leaving a small turning (2 mm/^{1}/$_8$ in) at the 'fold' edge. Finger-press the turning under. Using a fine yarn darner, apply the detached petal over the embroidered background petal, inserting one wire tail at the end of the stem and the other at the outer edge. Bend wires behind the flower and hold with tape—secure and trim when the flower is complete. Tuck the fold under and, using a matching thread, slip stitch the edge to the background fabric, just above the top edge of the embroidered petal (or lift the petal up and carefully back stitch along the fold). Shape the detached petal over the background petal with tweezers.

4. To embroider the sepals, work three detached chain stitches, from the end of the stem into the base of the flower, with one strand of medium green thread.

Flower 6

Background Petals

Outline the background petals in back stitch, the upper petal in medium mauve thread and the lower petal in magenta. Embroider the upper petal first, using medium mauve thread. Work a row of close, long and short buttonhole stitch around the lower edge of the petal, enclosing the outline then embroider the remainder of the petal in long and short stitch.

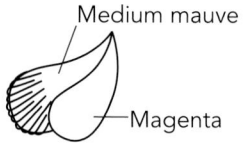

Medium mauve

Magenta

Embroider the lower petal in the same way using magenta thread.

Detached Petal

1. With one strand of medium mauve thread, couch wire around the lower edge of petal outline 6, leaving a wire tail at each end of the upper 'fold' line. Buttonhole stitch the wire to the muslin.

2. Using medium mauve thread, work a row of long and short buttonhole stitch around the lower edge of the petal, then embroider the remainder of the petal in long and short stitch with violet thread (blending in to the medium mauve).

3. Cut out the petal close to the wire edge, leaving a small turning (2 mm/^{1}/$_8$ in) at the 'fold' edge. Using a fine yarn darner, apply the detached petal over the embroidered background petals, inserting the wire tails at the end of the stem and at the outer edge. Bend wires behind the flower and hold with tape—secure and trim when the flower is complete. Tuck the fold under and slip stitch the edge to the background fabric, just above the top edge of the background petals. Shape the detached petal over the background petals with tweezers.

4. To embroider the sepals, work three detached chain stitches, from the end of the stem into the base of the flower, with one strand of medium green thread.

FLOWER 7

Background Petals

Outline the background petals in back stitch, the upper petal in violet thread and the lower petal in very pale mauve. Embroider the upper petal first, using violet thread. Work a row of close, long and short buttonhole stitch around the lower edge of the petal, enclosing the outline then embroider the remainder of the petal in long and short stitch. Embroider the lower petal in the same way using very pale mauve thread.

Detached Petals

1. Flower 7 has an inner and outer detached petal. With one strand of violet thread, couch wire around the lower edge of outer petal outline 7, leaving a wire tail at each end of the upper 'fold' line. Buttonhole stitch the wire to the muslin.

2. Using violet thread, work a row of long and short buttonhole stitch around the lower edge of the petal, then embroider the remainder of the petal in long and short stitch in violet thread blending to magenta at the inner corner of the petal. Cut out the petal close to the wire edge, leaving a small turning (2 mm/⅛ in) at the 'fold' edge. Finger-press the turning under.

3. With one strand of magenta thread, couch wire around the inner petal outline 7, leaving two wire tails that touch but do not cross at the inner corner of the petal. Buttonhole stitch the wire to the muslin. Using magenta thread, work a row of long and short buttonhole stitch around the lower edge of the petal, then embroider the remainder of the petal in long and short stitch. Cut out the petal close to the wire edge.

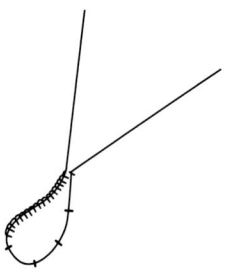

4. Using a fine yarn darner, apply the detached inner petal over the embroidered background petals, inserting the wire tails at the base of the petals, allowing a little of the lower petal to protrude. Secure wire tails behind the background petals. Apply the detached outer petal over the background petals, inserting the wire tails at the end of the stem and at the outer edge. Bend wires behind flower and hold with tape—secure and trim when flower is complete. Tuck the fold under and slip stitch the edge to the background, just above the top edge of the background petals. Shape the detached petal over the background petals with tweezers.

Detached inner petal

5. To embroider the sepals, work four detached chain stitches, from the end of the stem into the base of the flower, with one strand of medium green thread.

Flower 8

Detached Petals

1. Mount muslin into a small hoop and trace the detached petal outlines for flower 8.

2. With one strand of medium mauve thread, couch the 12 cm (4¹/₂ in) length of wire around the back petal outline, leaving two wire tails at the base that touch but do not cross. Buttonhole stitch the wire to the muslin. Work a row of long and short buttonhole stitch around the edge of the petal, inside the wire, using the diagram as a guide to stitch direction. Embroider the remainder of the petal in long and short stitch with violet thread (blending in to the medium mauve). Work a row of split stitch along the 'fold' line in the centre of the petal with magenta thread. Carefully cut out the petal.

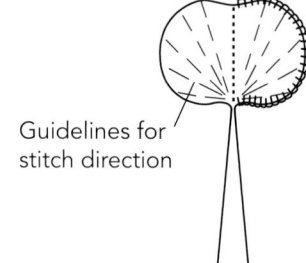

Guidelines for stitch direction

3. With one strand of magenta thread, couch wire around a middle petal outline, leaving two wire tails at the base that touch but do not cross. Buttonhole stitch the wire to the muslin. Work a row of long and short buttonhole stitch around the lower edge, then embroider the remainder of the petal in long and short stitch. Repeat for the remaining middle petal (check that it is a mirror image). Carefully cut out the petals.

4. With one strand of very pale mauve thread, couch wire around the inner petal outline, leaving two wire tails at the base that touch but do not cross. Buttonhole stitch the wire to the muslin. As the inner petal will be viewed on both sides, it needs to be embroidered on both sides. Cut out the petal, then carefully work satin stitch on both sides of the petal as follows:

   - bring the needle out on one side of the petal, inside the wire near the base

   - work a satin stitch across the petal, inserting the needle through the outer edge of the buttonhole (between the wire and the outer ridge of the buttonhole stitch—a size 12 needle helps with this)

   - work a satin stitch across the other side of the petal, inserting the needle near the base.

   Repeat until both sides of the petal are covered with satin stitch

To Complete Flower 8

1. To shape the back petal, fold it in half along the magenta 'fold' line, right sides facing, then open out again and shape slightly, leaving an indentation along the fold line. Using a yarn darner, apply the detached back petal at • at the end of the stem, fold the wires behind the stem and secure. Do not trim wire tails until the flower is complete.

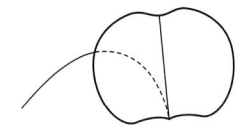

2. Insert the wire tails of the inner petal also at • . Fold the wires behind the stem, checking that the petal is pointing upwards, and secure (do not trim tails yet).

3. Shape the middle petals before applying on either side of the inner petal at • (they need to cup around the inner petal, the inner petal protruding slightly below the lower edges of the petals). Check that the petals are pointing upwards. Secure all wire tails behind the stem. Trim when you are satisfied with the shaping of the petals.

Closed Seed Pod

1. Mount muslin into a small hoop and trace the three detached seed pod outlines—one closed seed pod outline and two split seed pod outlines (check that the lower tips are all pointing the correct way). Embroider all detached seed pod shapes before cutting out.

2. Work a row of stem stitch around the closed seed pod outline on the background fabric with one strand of medium green thread. This outline will be used as a guide when applying the detached seed pod shape.

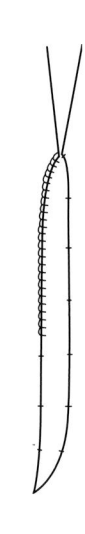

3. Using medium green thread, couch an 18 cm (7 in) length of wire around the detached closed seed pod outline, leaving two wire tails at the top of the pod that touch but do not cross. Buttonhole stitch the wire to the muslin. Embroider the seed pod with consecutive rows of stem stitch, working all rows from the top of the seed pod towards the pointed tip.

4. Carefully cut out the seed pod and shape slightly before applying, gently pushing the long edges towards each other to raise the centre of the pod into a smooth curve. To apply the detached seed pod to the background fabric, insert the wire tails at the end of the stem, using a yarn darner, and position the shape over the back stitched outline (the detached shape should be slightly wider than the outline, thus allowing for the raised centre of the pod when it is stitched into place). Using nylon thread in a size 12 sharps needle, stitch the detached seed pod over the outline with small 'invisible' stitches. Secure the wire tails behind the stem and trim.

5. To embroider the sepals, work three detached chain stitches, from the end of the stem into the top of the pod, with one strand of medium green thread.

Split Seed Pod

As the pea seed pod matures it starts to dry out and change colour. When the seed pod splits open, each side of the pod twists into a spiral (one clockwise, the other anticlockwise), releasing the seeds as they twist.

1. Using one strand of olive thread, couch an 18 cm (7 in) length of wire around a detached split seed pod outline, leaving two wire tails at the top of the pod that touch but do not cross. Buttonhole stitch the wire to the muslin— checking that the wires on either side of the pod are parallel and no more than 4 mm apart.

2. Embroider the seed pod with six rows of stem stitch, working all rows from the top of the seed pod towards the pointed tip. As the back of the detached shape will be visible, split the back of the stitch when working the stem stitches (instead of 'sharing the hole'), and start and finish the thread carefully, so that the back looks neat. Repeat for the remaining pea pod shape, checking that the lower tip is pointing in the opposite direction! Carefully cut out both pea pods, as close to the stitched edge as possible.

3. Using nylon thread in a size 12 sharps needle, stitch a row of wine/bronze antique beads to the *back* of the seed pods leaving a bead-width gap between each bead. Start the row of beads about 5 mm (3/16 in) down from the top of the pod, and leave a space of about 4 mm at the lower tip (12 or 13 beads on each side). To avoid stitches showing on the front surface of the pod, apply the beads with a type of 'back stitch', sliding the needle through the stitching behind the beads. Gently shape the sides of the pod around the beads.

4. Starting at the top, carefully twist the seed pods, twisting the right side pod to the right and the left side pod to the left (refer to the photograph). Using nylon thread, stitch the tops of the pods together then insert the wire tails at the end of the seed pod stem, using a large yarn darner. Secure the wires to the back of the stem.

5. To embroider the sepals, work three detached chain stitches, from the end of the stem into the top of the pod, with one strand of olive thread. If necessary, secure the seed pods to the background with a few invisible stitches worked with nylon thread.

TENDRILS

Apply the detached leaves before inserting the tendrils. The pea tendrils are formed by wrapping 11 cm ($4^1/_4$ in) lengths of uncovered wire with one strand of medium green thread.

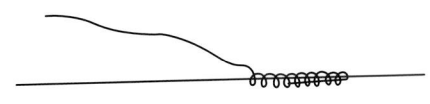

1. Knot a length of thread to the wire, 1 cm ($^3/_8$ in) from one end, leaving a short tail of thread (or attach tail with a minute amount of PVA glue to avoid the knot). Keeping the 1 cm of wire at one end, wrap about 4 or 5 cm (2 in) of wire, enclosing the knot and the short tail of thread. Secure the wrapping thread with a knot, retaining the tails of wire and thread.

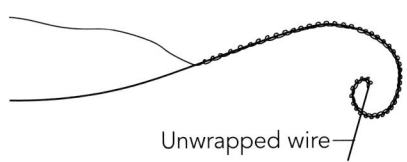

Unwrapped wire

2. Holding on to the 1 cm unwrapped end of wire, twist the wrapped wire into a coil around a knitting needle or yarn darner to form a tendril (the finer the needle the smaller the coil), or use tweezers to shape the wrapped wire as desired. Do not cut the short end of wire until the tendril is in place and secured (this prevents the thread unravelling at the end of the tendril). Make four tendrils.

3. Using a fine yarn darner, insert the retained wire and thread tails through to the back of the work—the upper two tendrils at the end of the upper stem segment, and the lower two tendrils between the middle pair of leaves. Adjust the tendrils and secure to the back of the stems.

4. Carefully cut off the unwrapped 1 cm of wire, close to the tip of the tendril.

LONGHORN MOTH

Work a Longhorn Moth above the wild pea, using the dots on the skeleton outline of the design for placement of the abdomen and wings.

Requirements

- light gold shot crystal organza: 15 x 7.5 cm (6 x 3 in)
- wine/black shot crystal organza: 15 x 7.5 cm (6 x 3 in)
- gold metal organdie: 15 cm (6 in) square
- paper-backed fusible web: 15 cm (6 in) square
- pale gold rayon machine thread: Madeira Rayon 40 col. 1338
- pale plum rayon machine thread: Madeira Rayon 40 col. 1358
- dark brown stranded thread: Soie d'Alger 4146 *or* DMC 838
- pale gold metallic thread: Madeira Metallic 30 col. 6032
- wine/black metallic thread: Kreinik Cord 208c
- black chenille thread: Au Ver à Soie Chenille à Broder col. Noir
- nylon clear thread: Madeira Monofil 60 col. 1001
- Mill Hill antique glass beads 3036 (wine/bronze)
- Mill Hill petite beads 42014 (black)
- 33 gauge white covered wire (moth wings): four 9 cm (3½ in) lengths (colour wire pale gold if desired, Copic YR24 Pale Sepia)
- 28 gauge brass wire (moth antennae): one 15 cm (6 in) length

The glittering Longhorn Moth, Adela reaumurella, *can frequently be seen clustering over bushes of yellow gorse flowers in summer. Often referred to as fairy moths, and sometimes mistaken for flies, these small insects look dark at first, but when their wings catch the light, they flash bright gold against the black fluffy body. The wings have a feathered edge, the fore wings being metallic gold in colour, the hind wings metallic bronze-plum. The distinguishing feature of these moths is the extraordinarily long antennae of the males—up to six times the length of the body. Female moths have shorter antennae and a less hairy head. The wingspan of these tiny moths ranges from 14 to 18 millimetres.*

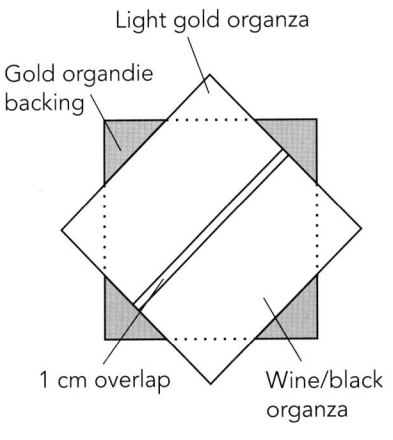

Light gold organza

Gold organdie backing

1 cm overlap

Wine/black organza

Fore Wings and Hind Wings

1. Lay the rectangles of organza side by side, overlapping the long sides 1 cm (3/8 in). Apply fusible web to the resulting 'square' of organzas (use baking parchment to protect the iron and the ironing board). Fuse gold metal organdie to the square of organzas, one layer of fabric rotated 45 degrees to be on the bias grain. Mount the fabrics into the hoop, organza side uppermost.

2. Using tweezers, shape lengths of wire around the wing outline diagrams—a right and a left fore wing and a right and a left hind wing—leaving two tails of wire at the base of each wing. Transfer the shaped wires to the fabric surface, positioning the fore wings over the light gold fabric and the hind wings over the wine/black fabric, holding the wire tails in place with masking tape. Check that the shapes have not been distorted.

3. Using pale gold rayon machine thread in a sharps needle, couch then buttonhole stitch the shaped wire to the background fabrics.

4. With pale gold metallic thread in a milliners needle, work the veins in the fore wings with fly and buttonhole stitches, using the diagram as a guide.

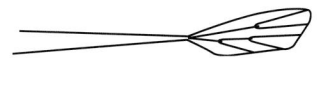

5. With pale plum rayon thread in a sharps needle, work the veins in the hind wings with fly stitches, using the diagram as a guide.

To Complete the Moth

1. Carefully cut out the wings and apply by inserting the wire tails through the upper two dots, using a large yarn darner. Apply the hind wings first, inserting the wire tails through 2, then the fore wings at 1. Bend the wire tails under the wings and secure to the backing fabric with tiny stitches, making sure that the stitches do not protrude outside the wing span. Trim the wire tails when the moth is finished.

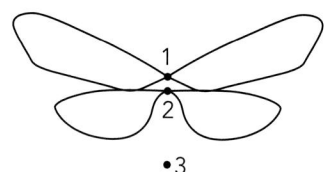

2. The thorax is worked with black chenille thread in the largest yarn darner (to prevent the chenille from shredding). Work one straight stitch across the centre of the wings (from 1 to 2), adjusting the tension of the stitch, thus the fluffiness of the thorax, as desired (it is easier to insert each tail of chenille from the front). Secure the tails of chenille at the back with a few stitches worked in stranded thread.

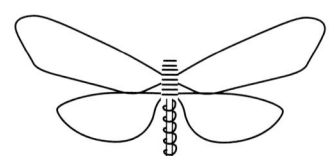

3. The abdomen is worked with a wrapped stitch using seven strands of dark brown thread in a chenille needle. Bring the needle out at 3 and insert at the base of the thorax. Repeat to make a double stitch. Bring the needle out again at 3 and wrap the double stitch back to the thorax (sliding the needle under and around the stitch), adjusting the tension of the wrapping to form the abdomen (this resembles a bullion knot).

4. Using nylon thread in a sharps needle, apply a wine/bronze antique bead at the top of the thorax for the head, working the stitches from side to side through the bead. Stitch a petite black bead on either side of the head for eyes, then take the needle through all three beads and couch between each bead.

5. With one strand of wine/black metallic thread in a milliners needle, work the legs with straight stitches, using the diagram as a guide. Work two straight stitches for each of the two inner segments and one straight stitch for the outer segment of each leg.

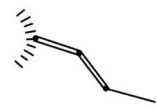

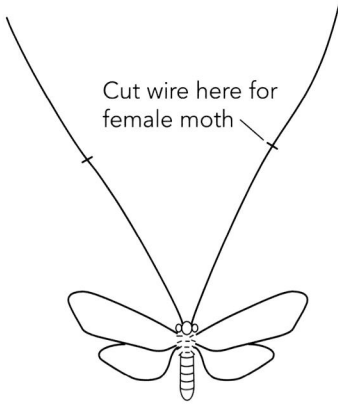

Cut wire here for female moth

6. To form the antennae, fold the length of brass wire in half and insert the folded end through to the back, under the head bead, using a fine yarn darner. Secure the wire end behind the thorax. Shape the wire into smooth, curved antennae by pulling between your fingers. Trim to the desired length, 4–5 cm (2 in) for a male, 2.5 cm (1 in) for a female).

LADYBIRD

Requirements

- red cotton fabric (homespun): 15 cm (6 in) square
- red stranded thread: DMC 349
- black stranded thread: DMC 310
- black metallic thread: Kreinik Cord 005c
- Mill Hill petite beads 42014 (black)
- 33 gauge white covered wire (ladybird): one 12 cm (4³/₄ in) length (colour wire red if desired, Copic R17 Lipstick Orange)

The instructions for embroidering the ladybird are on page 43. Work the abdomen over the embroidered stem segment.

BORDER

This border, inspired by the richly decorated margins in a sixteenth century Book of Hours, is great fun to work; however, it requires precision in the placement of the silk ribbon, the border threads and the beads. Because of the accuracy required, no conversions for the metric measurements are supplied. Before commencing the border, check that the two lines of running stitch (the border lines) are still straight; adjust if necessary. There is no need to remove these stitches.

Requirements

- Hannah bias-cut silk ribbon: 1 cm (7/16 in) wide col. Cabernet
- gilt 3-ply twist
- red thick pearl cotton: DMC Coton Perlé No. 3 col. 349
- red stranded thread: DMC 349
- gold couching thread: Couching Thread 371 col. Dark/ Jacobean gold
- gold metallic thread: Madeira Metallic Art 9803 col. 3007
- fine gold silk thread: YLI Silk Stitch 50 col. 79
- nylon clear thread: Madeira Monofil 60 col. 1001
- gold seed beads: Metallic Delica DBR 31 *or* Mill Hill Magnifica 10076

RIBBON BACKGROUND

The background of the border is a rich magenta bias-cut silk ribbon. The ribbon is optional (the border may be worked very successfully without it).

Cut 75 cm of bias-cut silk ribbon. Using fine silk sewing thread in a sharps needle, stitch the ribbon to the border with large herringbone stitches, following the instructions for the ribbon background for the Bittersweet on page 178.

BORDER EDGES

The border edges consist of couched rows of gilt 3-ply twist and red Coton Perlé No. 3.

1. Following the instructions for the border edges for the Bittersweet, couch the gold twist, with *either* nylon thread in a sharps needle *or* one strand of gold metallic thread in a size 9 milliners needle.

2. Couch the red Coton Perlé with one strand of matching stranded thread (DMC 349) in a Sharps needle.

BEADING

The inside of the border is embellished with gold couching thread, inserted through gold beads in a zig-zag pattern, following the beading instructions for the Bittersweet.

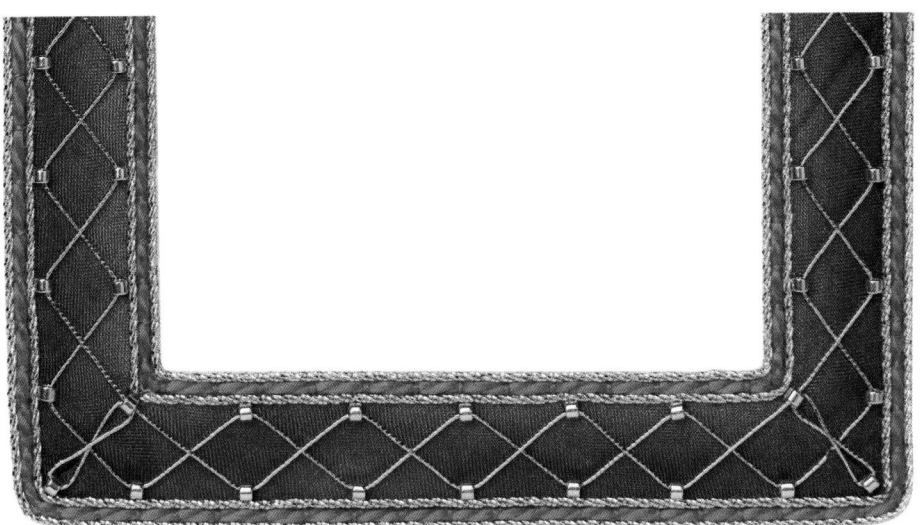

Page of illuminated manuscripts borders, The Grammar of Ornament by Owen Jones,
Plate LXXI, courtesy University of Wisconsin Digital Collections

PART 3:
Techniques, Equipment and Stitch Glossary

This section contains general information about the techniques and equipment that are referred to throughout the book. The bibliography contains a list of specialised reference books which can provide more detailed information if required.

The stitch glossary includes the stitches used.

Techniques

TRANSFERRING A DESIGN TO FABRIC

There are several ways to transfer a design to fabric; choose the most appropriate method for your project.

You Will Need

- tracing paper (I use GLAD Bake/baking parchment)
- sharp HB lead pencil (or a 0.5 mm clutch/mechanical pencil)
- stylus or used ball-point pen (to trace a fine line)
- masking tape (to stop tracing paper from slipping)
- tracing board or small, circular lid (use inside the back of the hoop for support when tracing a design on to the front)

Preparation

1. Mount the main fabric and a backing fabric (quilter's muslin or calico), into a hoop or square frame. The fabrics need to be kept very taut.
2. Trace the design, either on to the front or to the back, *after* the fabrics have been mounted into the hoop to prevent distortion.
3. Do not remove the fabrics from the hoop until all the embroidery is finished, unless instructed otherwise.

Tracing the Design onto the Front

Use this method when the traced lines will be completely covered by the embroidery.

1. Trace a skeleton outline of the design onto tracing paper with a sharp lead pencil. Flip the paper over and draw over the outline on the back (do not make the lines too dark).

2. Attach the tracing, right side up, to the fabric in the hoop, using strips of masking tape on all sides. Check that the design is on the straight grain of the fabric.

3. Place a tracing board (or lid) inside the back of the hoop for support then transfer the design by tracing over the outline with a stylus, used ball-point pen or a pencil.

Tracing the Design onto the Back

Use this method when the embroidery may not cover the traced lines if they were on the front, or when the main fabric is coloured, patterned or textured. To ensure that your design is the 'right way up' on the main fabric, transfer the skeleton outline to the backing fabric as follows:

1. Trace a skeleton outline of the design onto tracing paper with a sharp lead pencil.

2. Tape the tracing, right (pencil) side down, to the muslin backing (check that the design will be on the straight grain of the main fabric).

3. Draw over all the traced lines with a stylus or used ball-point pen, thus transferring a pencil outline onto the backing fabric. *Optional*: draw over the pencil lines with a fine marking pen (Pigma), as they tend to fade over time.

4. Work by referring to the outline on the back as you stitch. The design lines may be thread-traced through to the front with small running stitches, if required.

Thread-tracing the Design

As this method does not permanently mark the fabric, it offers greater flexibility; however, it is difficult to accurately reproduce fine details of a design.

1. Trace the design on to tissue paper with lead pencil. Place the traced tissue paper over the main fabric and attach to the edges of your frame or hoop with masking tape (check that the design is on the straight grain of the fabric).

2. Using fine silk or machine thread, work small running stitches over the traced lines, through the tissue paper and the fabric. Score the lines with a needle then carefully tear the paper away.

3. Remove the tracing threads as you embroider.

Transferring the Design with a Paper Template

Use this method to achieve very accurate outlines or shapes when pencil lines cannot be used, for example, a caterpillar on a leaf (see page 71).

1. Trace the shape onto paper, a removable self-adhesive label or a Post-it note. Cut out the template and hold in place on the front of the fabric with tacking stitches, if necessary.

2. Work around the template to achieve the desired shape or outline, removing the paper when necessary.

Mounting Fabrics into Hoops and Square Frames

Mounting Fabric into an Embroidery Hoop

Good quality embroidery hoops—10 cm, 12 cm, 15 cm, 20 cm and 25 cm (4 in, 5 in, 6 in, 8 in and 10 in)—are essential when working small to medium size designs in stumpwork and goldwork embroidery. Bind the inner ring of wooden hoops with cotton tape to prevent slipping. A small screwdriver is useful to tighten the embroidery hoop. Plastic hoops with a lip on the inner ring are also suitable (because of the lip the inner ring does not need to be bound).

1. Place the main (background) fabric on top of the backing fabric then place both fabrics over the inner ring of the hoop.
2. Loosen the outer ring of the hoop so that it just fits over the inner ring and the fabrics, positioning the tension screw at the top of the hoop (12 o'clock). Ease the outer ring down over the inner ring and fabrics.
3. To tension the fabrics in the hoop, pull the fabrics evenly and tighten the screw, alternately, until both layers of fabric are as tight as a drum in the hoop.

Mounting Fabric into Square or Rectangular Frames

A square or rectangular frame is required for larger designs in stumpwork and goldwork embroidery. An artist's stretcher bar frame, a slate frame or a tapestry frame may be used (I use a slate frame).

To attach the background and backing fabric to a stretcher bar frame

1. Assemble the stretcher bars.

2. Staple or pin (drawing pin/push pin) the background fabric and the calico *together* to the back of one long side of the frame.

3. Stretch and staple or pin the calico *then* the background fabric to the back of the other long side of the frame (fabrics stretched and secured separately).

4. Staple or pin the background fabric and the calico *together* to the back of one short side of the frame.

5. Stretch and staple or pin the calico *then* the background fabric to the back of the remaining short side of the frame.

To attach the background and backing fabrics to a slate frame or tapestry frame

1. Select a frame with internal measurements at least 10–15 cm (4–6 in) larger than the required background fabric.

2. To prepare the backing fabric, cut a piece of firm calico 2 cm (1 in) narrower than the internal width of the frame (the roll bar and webbing) and about 10 cm (4 in) longer than the internal length of the frame. Make sure the fabric is cut on the straight grain.

3. Finish all edges of the calico by first turning under 5 mm (3/16 in) then folding over a 1 cm (3/8 in) hem. Stitch the hem by hand or machine (a length of string may be inserted in the hem of the side edges for extra strength—this is not necessary for smaller embroideries).

4. Mark the centre points of the webbing and calico. With right sides facing and centre points aligned, overcast the top edge of the calico to the webbing edge of one roll bar. Use a double strand of sewing thread and work from the centre point to each end, with the stitches about 5 mm ($3/16$ in) apart. Repeat for the lower roll bar.

5. Assemble the slate frame (or tapestry frame), adjusting the roll bars so that the calico is smooth and taut, but *not* drum tight.

6. Lace the side edges of the calico to the side edges of the frame, using a strong thread (e.g. Cotton Pearl 5 or fine string) still connected to the spool to avoid joins. Make the stitches about 2–3 cm (1 in) apart, leaving a long tail of thread at each end. Adjust the lacing to tighten the calico slightly, but not yet drum tight. Secure the ends of the lacing thread temporarily.

7. Centre the background fabric (e.g. silk) over the calico, taking care to align the grains of both fabrics (a little masking tape can be used to hold the silk in place until secured with stitches). With one strand of sewing thread, sew the background fabric to the calico with herringbone stitch, working one edge of the stitch into the background fabric and the other edge into the calico. Start in the centre of the top edge and work to each corner. Repeat for the lower edge, then the sides. (Do not make the stitches too small or too even!)

8. Tighten the upper and lower bars of the frame, then adjust and secure the lacing on each side so that both layers of fabric are drum tight.

WORKING WITH WIRE

Cake decorator's wire is used to form the detached, wired and embroidered shapes characteristic of stumpwork. I find the following gauges the most useful.

- *30 gauge covered wire* This sturdy wire has a tightly-wrapped, thin paper covering and is available in green and white (which can be coloured). It is a strong wire which maintains a shape well when bent—use it for larger detached shapes, such as large leaves.

- *33 gauge covered wire (flower wire)* A fine wire with a tightly-wrapped, thin white paper covering which can be coloured if desired. This wire is used for small, detailed, detached shapes, such as flower petals and narrow leaves.

- *28 gauge uncovered wire* Uncovered wire (silver in colour) is used when a finer edge is required—use it for small and detailed detached shapes, wings, antennae and tendrils. Select the 28 gauge uncovered wire as the 30 gauge is a little too thin to retain its shape when stitched.

To Stitch Wire to Fabric

- When stitching wire to fabric, either with overcast stitch or buttonhole stitch, make sure that the needle enters the fabric *at right-angles, very close to the wire* (not angled under the wire). The stitches need to be worked very close together, with an up-and-down stabbing motion, using a firm and even tension.

- If you need to renew a thread while stitching wire to fabric, secure the thread tails inside the wired shape (do not use a knot at the edge as it may be cut when cutting out the shape). If you need to renew a thread while stitching wire for a wing, you cannot secure the thread inside the wired shape. Instead, hold the tail of the old thread and the tail of the new thread under the length of wire about

Stitch

Cross section of fabric, wire and stitch

Wire

Fabric

to be stitched. Catch both tails of thread in with the new overcast stitches.

- When working veins inside wings with metallic thread, it is safer to keep the tails of thread at the front of the wing until it has been cut out, then stitch the tails through the corner of the wing to the back. The tails of metallic thread are secured *after* the wing has been applied to the main fabric.

- Using very sharp scissors with fine points, cut out the wired shape as close to the stitching as possible (stroke the cut edge with your fingernail to reveal any stray threads). If you happen to cut a stitch, use the point of a pin to apply a minute amount of PVA glue to the cut thread. This will dry matt and clear.

To Colour Wire

White paper-covered wire may be coloured with a waterproof ink or paint if desired. *This is optional.* When I colour wires I use Copic markers, which are available from art supply stores. These markers are fast-drying and refillable and come in a huge range of colours.

To Attach Wired Shapes to a Background Fabric

Detached wire shapes are applied to a background fabric by inserting the wire tails through a 'tunnel' formed by the eye of a large (size 14) yarn darner needle.

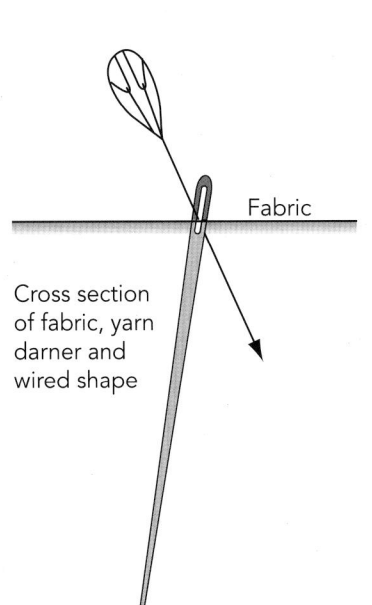

Fabric

Cross section of fabric, yarn darner and wired shape

1. Pierce the background fabric at the required point with the yarn darner and push it through until the *eye* of the needle is halfway through the fabric (this forms a 'tunnel' through to the back of the fabric).

2. Insert the wire tails into the tunnel formed by the eye of the darner, through to the *back of the fabric*. Thread tails can also be taken through at the same time.

3. Gently pull the darner all the way through, leaving the wire tails in the hole.

4. Stitch the wire tails to the backing fabric with small stitches, preferably behind an embroidered area (make sure the securing stitches will be hidden behind embroidery or underneath a detached shape).

5. Use tweezers to bend the wired shape as required then trim the wire tails. I do not cut any wire tails until the subject is finished (just in case I need to unpick and re-do). Do not let any wire protrude into an unembroidered area as the tails may show when the piece is framed.

Working with Paper-backed Fusible Web

Paper-backed fusible web (also known as Vliesofix, Bondaweb and other brand names) is used to fuse or bond one material to another by applying heat with an iron. I also use paper-backed fusible web to obtain a precise design outline on felt—it is very difficult to trace a small shape onto felt and to cut it out accurately.

To Fuse a Design Outline to Felt

1. Trace the outline on to the paper side of the fusible web then fuse to the felt (fusible web/glue side down) with a medium-hot dry iron.

2. Cut out the shape along the outlines. Remove the paper before stitching the felt shape to the background fabric (e.g. flower padding).

To Fuse Sheer Fabrics for Wings

Gauzy, wired, detached wings are a delightful feature of stumpwork bees and dragonflies. Almost any sheer, organza-like fabric or ribbon—plain, shot, variegated, metallic or pearlised—can be used for the upper layer of the wings. Use similar fabrics for the lower layer, or more opaque pearl, gold or copper metal organdie, to provide a lovely sheen under the sheer organzas. Use a layer of baking parchment (GLAD Bake) on either side of the fabrics to be fused to protect your iron and the ironing board.

A 'wing sandwich' is made by fusing the upper and lower layers of fabric together with paper-backed fusible web as follows:

1. Fuse paper-backed fusible web to the upper layer of fabric (both cut the same size). If using ribbon as the upper layer, remove the selvedges, cut the fusible web to the same width and fuse together. Remove the backing paper.

2. Place the lower layer of fabric on the ironing board (over baking parchment). Place the upper layer of fabric, fusible web side down, over the lower layer—rotating the upper layer 45 degrees (bias grain) for a pretty effect (this also provides a more stable fabric to stitch and cut out).

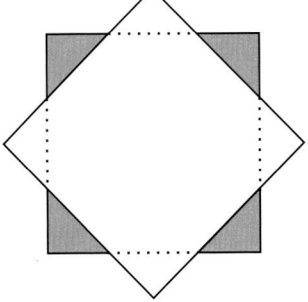

3. Cover the sandwich with baking parchment and press firmly with an iron (on about nylon setting). The temperature needs to be hot enough to fuse the fabrics but not so hot as to cause bubbling. Mount the wing sandwich into a hoop while still warm for best results—the fabric needs to be kept very taut.

To Fuse Wing Fabric to the Main (Background) Fabric

Some projects require the background wings to be fused to the main fabric before applying the detached wings. Use a layer of baking parchment to protect the item to be fused, your iron and the ironing board. Fuse background wings to the main fabric as follows:

1. Prepare the wing sandwich as for the detached wings *or* use a single layer of fabric (as directed).

2. Trace the wing outlines onto the paper side of paper-backed fusible web. (Note: the outlines need to be a mirror image of the required shape.) Fuse to the *back* of the wing sandwich.

3. Carefully cut out the wing shapes, remove the paper backing and position the wings on the main fabric. With a board underneath the main fabric for support (and using baking parchment), fuse the wings to the main fabric.

WORKING WITH LEATHER

Leather is available in a wide range of colours, thicknesses and finishes—fine kid, thicker leather, suede and snakeskin—and is used in stumpwork, goldwork and other areas of embroidery to provide a contrast in texture and colour.

To Cut a Leather Shape

Trace an outline of the required shape onto paper, a removable self-adhesive label or a Post-it note (make sure the sticky section is underneath the traced outline). Cut out the paper shape and apply to the leather to use as a template. Using small, sharp scissors cut the leather around the paper template with a long cutting motion (short cuts can cause an uneven edge or damage to the fine metallic coating of some leathers). If the leather is thick, it may be necessary to bevel the edges at the back. Do this with a sharp craft knife or scissors.

To Pad a Leather Shape

Leather is usually applied over a padding of one or more layers of felt. If more than one layer of felt is required to pad a shape, cut one piece of felt the actual size, and one or more successively smaller shapes. Applying the smallest shape first, attach each layer of felt with small stab stitches (coming out of the background fabric and stabbing into the felt), ending with the largest layer on top.

To Stitch Leather

Using a size 12 sharps needle and clear nylon thread (or fine silk thread in a matching colour), apply the leather with small stab stitches, bringing the needle out just under the edge of the leather, and stitching into the leather about 1–1.5 mm ($^1/_{16}$ in) from the edge (not too close to the edge or the leather may tear). The stitches should be worked fairly close together (1.5–2 mm apart) to avoid bulges between them, and need to be fairly firm to pull the sides of the leather down to hide the cut edge. Tweezers or a nailfile can be used to smooth and ease the edges of the leather into shape after it has been applied.

Equipment

The Embroiderer's Workbox

The well-equipped workbox will contain:

- Good quality embroidery hoops—10 cm, 12 cm, 15 cm, 20 cm and 25 cm (4 in, 5 in, 6 in, 8 in and 10 in), either wooden, with the inner ring bound with cotton tape, or plastic with a lip on the inner ring.
- A small screwdriver to tighten embroidery hoops
- Slate frames in various sizes for larger embroideries and goldwork
- Wooden tracing boards of various sizes to place under hoops of fabric when tracing
- Needles (see below for detailed information)
- Thimble
- Beeswax
- Fine glass-headed pins
- Embroidery scissors (small, with fine sharp points), goldwork scissors (small and strong with sharp points) and paper scissors
- Small wire cutters or old scissors for cutting wire
- Mellor or old metal nailfile (for easing threads or leather into place)
- Assortment of tweezers (from surgical suppliers)
- Eyebrow comb (for Turkey knots)
- Tracing paper (I use GLAD Bake/baking parchment)

- Fine (0.5 mm) HB lead pencil (mechanical)
- Stylus or used ball-point pen (for tracing)
- Masking tape (for tracing and to hold threads and wire tails to the back of the fabric)
- Post-it notes or removable self-adhesive labels (for templates)
- Rulers—15 cm and 30 cm (6 in and 12 in). *Hint:* Photocopy a small ruler and cut it out. This paper ruler is very useful for goldwork and, when used on its side around a curve, for accurately positioning beads in a border.

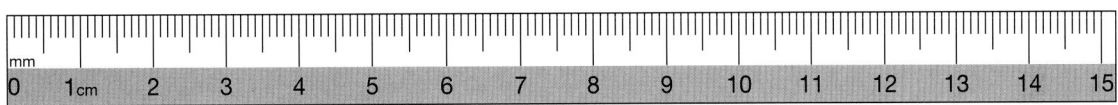

Needles

An assortment of needles is required. When selecting a needle, make sure that it is the appropriate type to suit the purpose. The thread should pass easily through the eye, and the needle should make a hole in the fabric large enough for the double thickness of the thread to pass through easily (without damaging the thread).

- *Crewel/embroidery sizes 3-10* Crewel needles are used with embroidery silks and cottons. They have a sharp point and long eye to take one or more strands of thread. Use a size 10 needle for one strand of thread, a size 9 for two strands (the more strands of thread, the larger the needle required).
- *Milliners/straw sizes 3-9* Milliners needles have a round eye and a long shaft that does not vary in diameter from its eye until it tapers at the point. They are ideal for working French and bullion knots, and for stitching with metallic embroidery threads (make sure the needle is thicker than the thread). A size 9 is used with one strand of fine metallic thread.

- *Tapestry sizes 24–28* Tapestry needles have an elongated eye and a blunt point which makes them ideal for working raised stem stitch and needle-weaving.

- *Sharps sizes 8–12* These are sharp needles with a round eye. Size 12 is ideal for stitching with fine machine threads, silk and nylon monofilament, and to apply leather and beads. Use the larger sizes when stitching with metallic thread— the thicker the thread the larger the needle.

- *Beading sizes 10–13* These are very fine sharp needles with a long eye. Use to stitch beads with a very small hole.

- *Chenille sizes 18–24* Chenille needles are thick and sharp and have an elongated eye. Use when stitching with thick thread (e.g. soft cotton), and for sinking some metallic threads through to the back.

- *Yarn darners sizes 14–18* Yarn darners are sharp and thick with a long eye. Use to insert detached wired shapes (e.g. petals and wings), for sinking the tails of metal threads through to the back and for stitching very thick threads and chenille.

GLOSSARY OF PRODUCT NAMES

This list gives equivalent names for products used in this book which may not be available under the same name in every country.

biro	ball-point pen
calico	muslin
clutch pencil	mechanical pencil
GLAD Bake	baking parchment
quilter's muslin	finely woven calico or cotton homespun
Vliesofix	paper-backed fusible web, Bondaweb

Stitch Glossary

This glossary contains most of the stitches used in this book, in alphabetical order.

For ease of explanation, some of the stitches have been illustrated with the needle entering and leaving the fabric in the same movement. When working in a hoop this is difficult (or *should* be if your fabric is tight enough), so the stitches have to be worked with a stabbing motion, in several stages.

Back Stitch

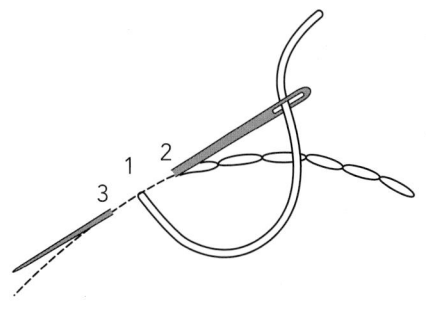

This is a useful stitch for outlining a shape. Bring the needle out at 1, insert at 2 (sharing the hole made by the preceding stitch) and out again at 3. Keep the stitches small and even.

Back Stitch, Split

See Split back stitch

Bullion Knot

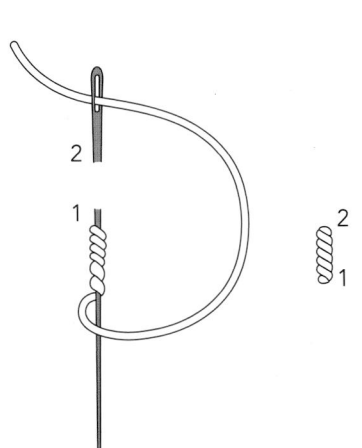

Bullion knots require some practice to work in a hoop. Use a milliners/straw needle of the appropriate size, with the number of wraps depending on the length of the knot required. Bring the needle out at 1, insert at 2 leaving a long loop. Emerge at 1 again (not pulling the needle through yet) and wrap the thread around the needle the required number of times. Hold the wraps gently between the thumb and index finger of the left hand while pulling the needle through with the right hand. Pull quite firmly and insert again at 2, stroking the wraps into place.

BUTTONHOLE STITCH

These stitches can be worked close together or slightly apart. Working from left to right, bring the needle out on the line to be worked at 1 and insert at 2, holding the loop of thread with the left thumb. Bring the needle up on the line to be worked at 3 (directly below 2), *over* the thread loop, and pull through to form a looped edge. If the stitch is shortened and worked close together over wire, it forms a secure edge for cut shapes, for example, detached petals.

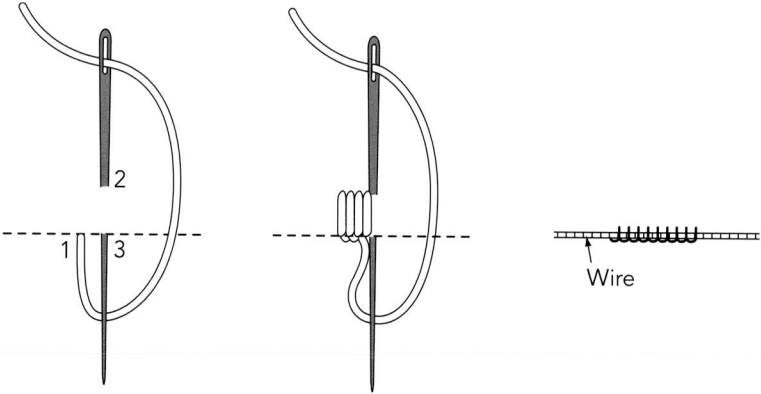

BUTTONHOLE STITCH, LONG AND SHORT

In long and short buttonhole stitch, each alternate stitch is shorter. Bring the needle out at 1, insert at 2 and up again at 3 (like an open detached chain stitch). When embroidering a shape like a petal, angle the stitches towards the centre of the flower.

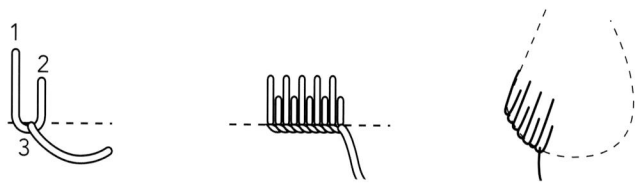

Chain Band, Raised (Raised Chain Stitch)

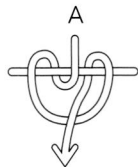

Raised chain band (stitch) is worked with a tapestry needle over a grid of evenly spaced straight stitches worked 1.5–3 mm apart (depending on the thickness of the thread), for example, couching stitches across the abdomen of an insect.

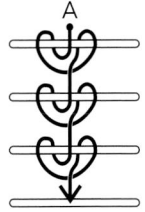

First work the grid of straight stitches then bring the needle out at A, just above the first straight stitch. Slide the needle over then under the first straight stitch, coming out to the left of A. Take the needle over then under the first straight stitch again, to the right of A (like a buttonhole stitch), bringing the needle through the resulting loop. Pull the thread to form a chain stitch over the first straight stitch.

Take the needle over then under the second straight stitch, coming out to the left of the previous stitch. Take the needle over then under the second straight stitch again, to the right of the previous stitch, bringing the needle through the resulting loop as before. Repeat these two movements to work a row of chain stitches over the grid of straight stitches.

Chain Stitch

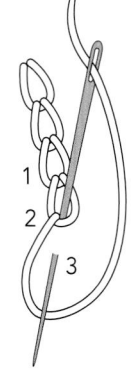

Bring the needle out at 1 and insert it again through the same hole, holding the loop of thread with the left thumb. Bring the needle up a short distance away at 2, through the loop, and pull the thread through. Insert the needle into the same hole at 2 (inside the loop) and make a second loop, hold, and come up at 3. Repeat to work a row of chain stitch, securing the final loop with a small straight stitch.

Chain Stitch, Detached (Lazy Daisy Stitch)

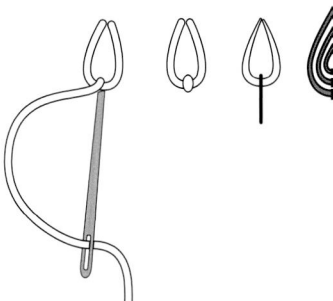

Detached chain stitch or lazy daisy stitch is worked in the same way as chain stitch except that each loop is secured individually with a small straight stitch. The securing stitch can be made longer if desired, for example, in a butterfly's antennae. Several detached chain stitches can be worked inside each other to pad a small shape.

Chain Stitch, Whipped

This is a useful method for working a raised line. Work a row of chain stitch then bring the needle out slightly to one side of the final securing stitch. Using either the eye of the needle or a tapestry needle, whip the chain stitches by passing the needle under each chain loop from right to left, working back to the beginning of the row. When whipped chain stitch is used for stems, the thickness of the outline can be varied by the number of threads used.

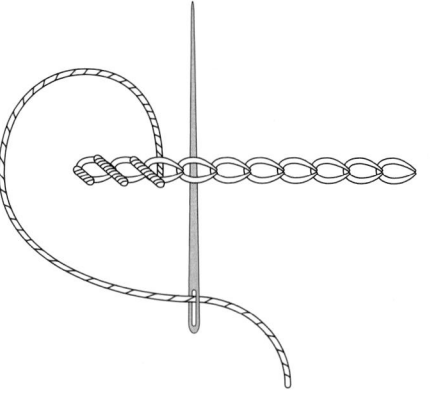

Couching

Couching is used to attach a thread, or bundle of threads, to a background fabric by means of small, vertical stitches worked at regular intervals. The laid thread is often thicker or more fragile (e.g. gold metallic or chenille) than the one used for stitching. Couching stitches are also used for attaching wire to the base fabric before embroidering detached shapes.

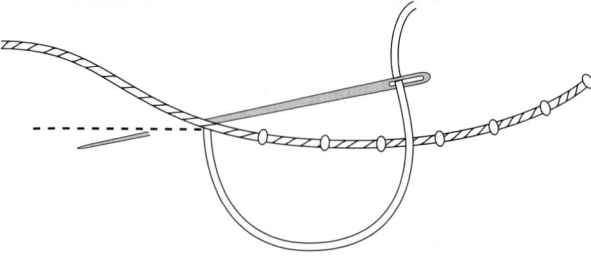

Couching, Lattice

Lattice couching is one of the endless variations of couched fillings. The design area is filled with a network of laid, parallel, evenly spaced threads. Where two threads cross, they are secured to the background with a small straight stitch.

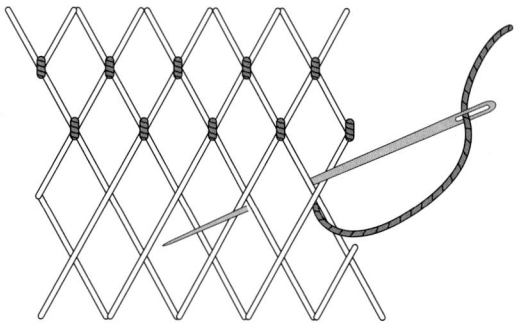

Detached Chain Stitch

See Chain stitch, detached

Encroaching Satin Stitch

See Satin stitch, encroaching

Feather Stitch

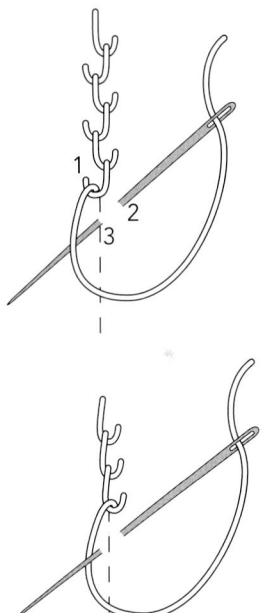

This stitch is made up of a series of loops, stitched alternately to the right and to the left, each one holding the previous loop in place. Come up on the line to be followed at 1. Insert the needle to the right at 2 and come up on the line again at 3, holding the thread under the needle with the left thumb. Repeat on the left side of the line, reversing the needle direction.

Feather Stitch, Single

Work the feather stitch loops in one direction only, either to the right or to the left. This variation is useful for working the veins in dragonfly wings.

Fly Stitch

Fly stitch is actually an open detached chain stitch. Bring the needle out at 1 and insert at 2, holding the working thread with the left thumb. Bring up again at 3 and pull through over the loop. Secure the loop with either a short anchoring stitch, as for antennae, or a longer anchoring stitch as, for example, the veins in butterfly wings.

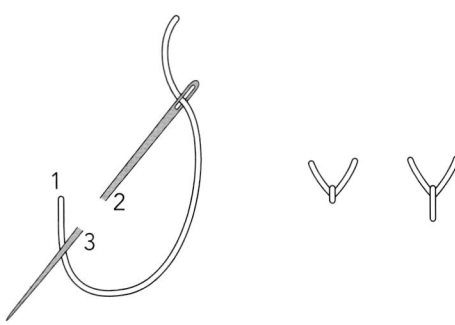

French Knot

Using a milliners/straw needle, bring the thread through at the desired place, wrap the thread once around the point of the needle and re-insert the needle. Tighten the thread and *hold taut* while pulling the needle through. To increase the size of the knot use more strands of thread, although more wraps can be made if desired.

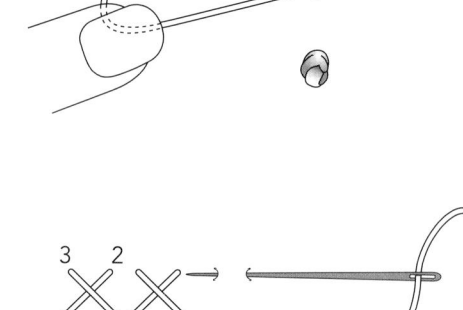

Herringbone Stitch

This stitch is worked from left to right, along an imaginary double line (or within the borders of a ribbon). Bring the needle out on the lower line at 1. Insert the needle a little to the right on the upper line at 2, and bring out to the left at 3. Insert the needle on the lower line again, to the right at 4, and bring it out to the left at 5, from which point the stitch is repeated.

Lattice Couching

See Couching, lattice

Lazy Daisy Stitch

See Chain stitch, detached

Long and Short Stitch

This stitch can be used to fill areas too large or irregular for satin stitch, or where shading is required. The first row, worked around the outline, consists of alternating long and short satin stitches (or long and short buttonhole stitch may be used). In the subsequent rows, the stitches are all of similar length, and fit into the spaces left by the preceding row. For a more realistic result when working petals, direct the stitches towards the centre of the flower. The surface will look smoother if the needle either pierces the stitches of the preceding row or enters at an angle between the stitches.

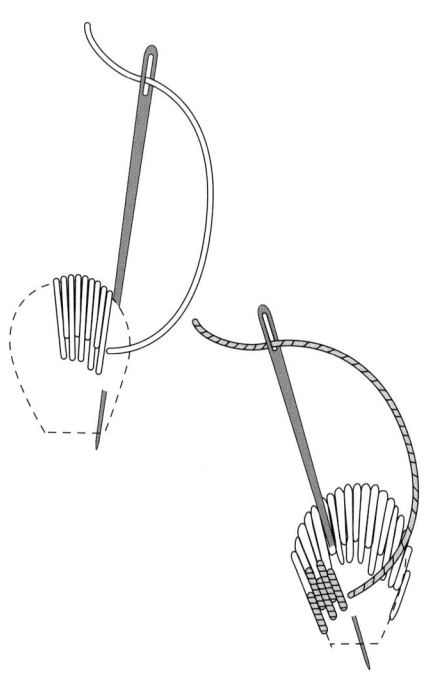

Long and Short Buttonhole Stitch

See Buttonhole stitch, long and short

Needle-weaving

Needle-weaving is a form of embroidery where thread in a tapestry needle is woven in and out over two or more threads attached to the background fabric. Work needle-weaving over a loop to form sepals as, for example, in the Star of Bethlehem. Use a length of scrap thread to keep the loop taut while weaving.

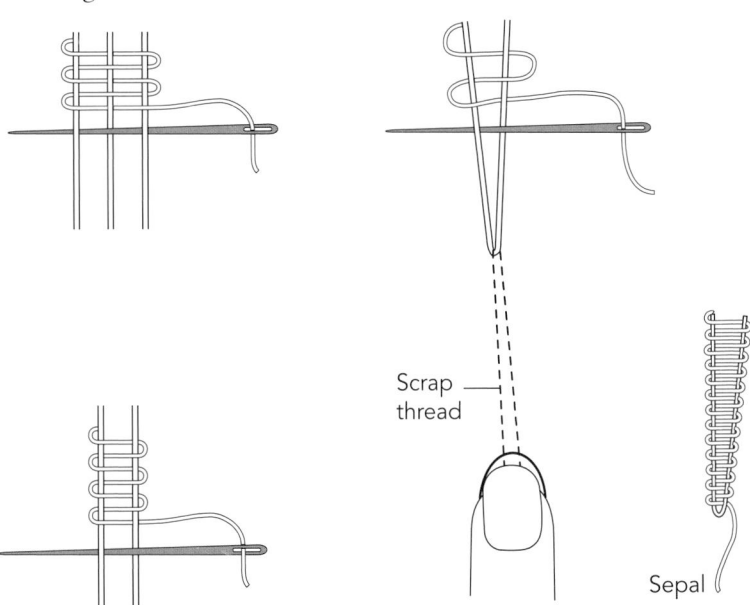

Scrap thread

Sepal

Outline Stitch

Worked from left to right, this stitch is perfect for working both simple and complicated outlines. Worked in the same way as stem stitch, the only difference is that the working thread is kept to the left of the line being worked. To start, bring the needle out at 1 on the line to be worked. Go down at 2, come up at 3 (to the right of the stitch) and pull the thread through. Insert the needle at 4, holding the thread above the line with the left thumb, and come up again at 2 (in the same hole made by the previous stitch), then pull the thread through. Go down at 5, hold the loop and come up again at 4, then pull the thread through. Repeat to work a narrow line.

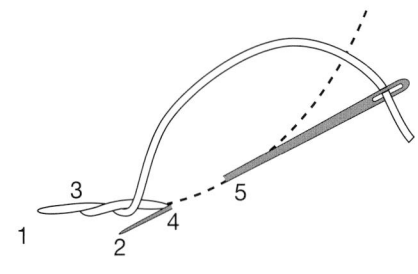

OVERCAST STITCH

This stitch is made up of tiny, vertical satin stitches, worked
very close together over a laid thread or wire, resulting in a
firm raised line. When worked over wire it gives a smooth,
secure edge for cut shapes (e.g. dragonfly wings). Place the
wire along the line to be covered. Working from left to right
with a stabbing motion, cover the wire with small straight
stitches, pulling the thread firmly so that there are no loose
stitches which could be cut when the shape is cut out.

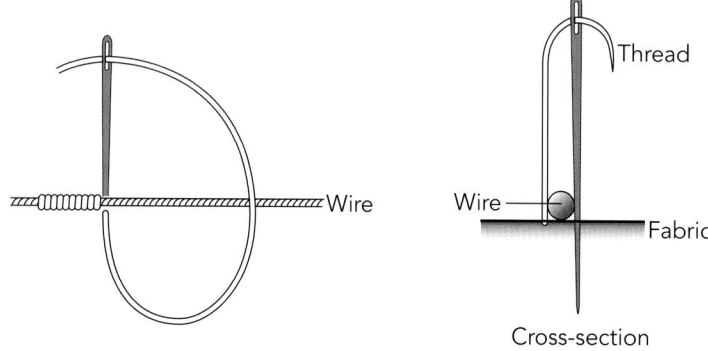

PAD STITCH

Pad stitch is used as a foundation under satin stitch when a
smooth but slightly raised surface is required. Padding stitches
can be either straight stitches or chain stitches, worked in the
opposite direction to the satin stitches. Felt can replace pad
stitch for a more raised effect.

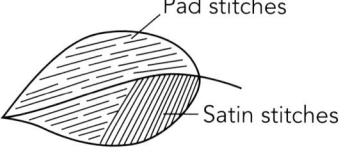

RAISED CHAIN STITCH

See Chain band, raised

SATIN STITCH

Satin stitch is used to fill shapes such as petals or leaves. It
consists of horizontal or vertical straight stitches, worked
close enough together so that no fabric shows through, yet
not overlapping each other. Satin stitch can be worked over
a padding of felt or pad stitches. Smooth edges are easier to
achieve if the shape is first outlined with split stitch (or split
back stitch).

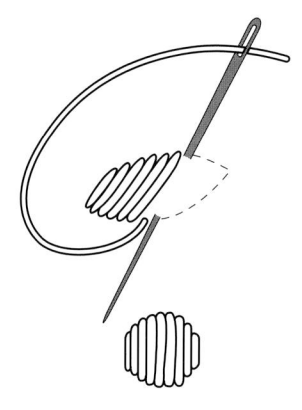

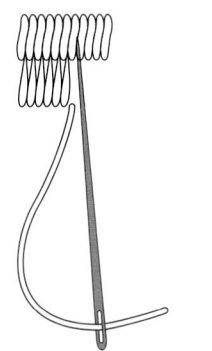

SATIN STITCH, ENCROACHING

Encroaching satin stitch is a useful method of shading. First work a row of regular satin stitch. In the second, and all subsequent rows, the head of each satin stitch is taken *between* the bases of two stitches in the row above, so that the rows blend softly into each other—see, for example, the Blue Butterfly. Vary the length of the stitches to achieve more subtle shading.

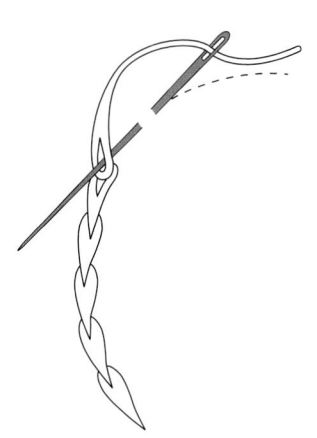

SPLIT STITCH

Split stitch can be used either as an outline stitch or for smooth, solid fillings. In the Middle Ages, split stitch was used to work most of the silk-embroidered faces, hands and feet of human figures on ecclesiastical vestments. Split stitch is worked in a similar way to stem stitch; however, the point of the needle splits the preceding stitch as it is brought out of the fabric. To start, make a straight stitch along the line to be worked. Bring the needle through to the front, splitting the straight stitch with the point of the needle. Insert the needle along the line, then bring through to the front again to pierce the preceding stitch. Repeat to work a narrow line of stitching, resembling fine chain stitch.

SPLIT BACK STITCH

An easier version of split stitch, especially when using one strand of thread. Commence with a back stitch. Bring the needle out at 1, insert at 2 (splitting the preceding stitch) and out again at 3. This results in a fine, smooth line, ideal for stitching intricate curves.

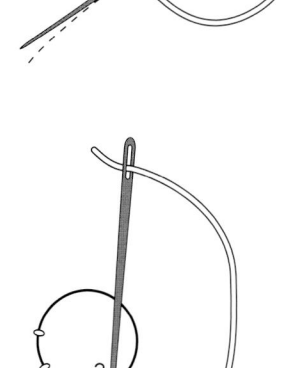

STAB STITCH

Stab stitch is used to apply leather or felt shapes to a background fabric. It consists of small straight stitches made from the background fabric over the edge of the applied shape, such as a leather shape over felt padding. Bring the needle out at 1, and insert at 2, catching in the edge of the applied piece.

STEM STITCH

Worked from left to right, the stitches in stem stitch overlap each other to form a fine line suitable for outlines and stems. A straight (not slanted) form of stem stitch, in a stabbing motion, is ideal for stumpwork. To start, bring the needle out at 1 on the line to be worked. Go down at 2, come up at 3 and pull the thread through. Insert the needle at 4, holding the thread underneath the line with the left thumb, and come up again at 2 (sharing the hole made by the previous stitch) then pull the thread through. Go down at 5, hold the loop and come up again at 4, then pull the thread through. Repeat to work a narrow line.

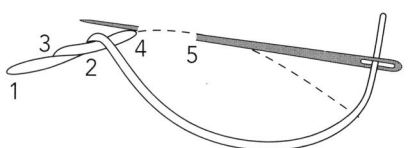

STEM STITCH BAND, RAISED

Stem stitch can be worked over a foundation of couched padding thread to produce a raised, smooth, stem stitch band, ideal for insect bodies. Lay a preliminary foundation of padding stitches worked with soft cotton or stranded thread. Across this padding, at fairly regular intervals, work straight (couching) stitches at right angles to the padding thread (do not make these stitches too tight). Then proceed to cover the padding by working rows of stem stitch over these straight stitches, using a tapestry needle so as not to pierce the padding thread. All the rows of stem stitch are worked in the same direction, starting and ending either at the one point (1) or as in satin stitch (2).

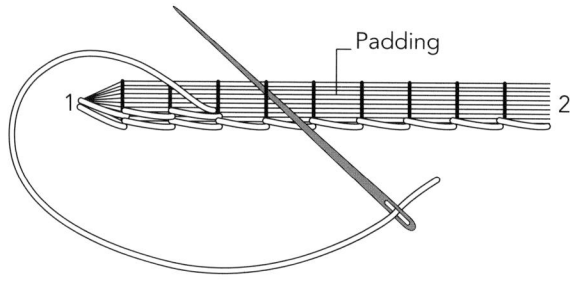

Turkey Knot

Turkey knots are worked then cut to produce a soft velvety pile. Although there are several ways to work Turkey knots, the following method works well for small areas. Use two strands of thread in a size 9 crewel or sharps needle.

Insert the needle into the fabric at 1, holding the tail of thread with the left thumb. Come out at 2 and go down at 3 to make a *small* securing stitch. Bring the needle out again at 1 (piercing the securing stitch), pull the thread down and also hold with the left thumb.

For the next Turkey knot, insert the needle to the right at 4 (still holding the tails of thread). Come out at 5 and go down at 2 to make a small securing stitch. Bring the needle out again at 4 (piercing the securing stitch), pull the thread down and hold with the left thumb as before. Repeat to work a row.

Work each successive row directly *above* the previous row, holding all the resulting tails with the left thumb. To complete, cut all the loops, comb with an eyebrow comb, and cut the pile to the desired length. The more the pile is combed the fluffier it becomes.

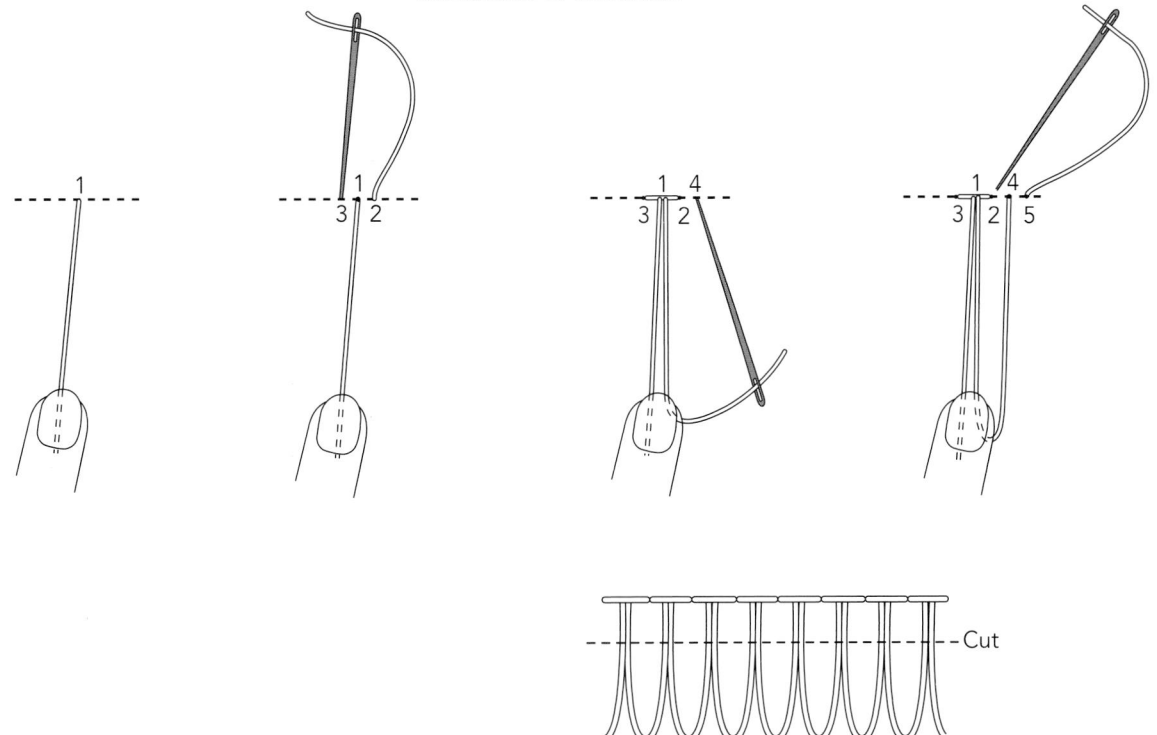

Grapes and snail illumination from Grandes Heures d'Anne de Bretagne, *Ms Latin 9474, Folio 156, Bibliothèque nationale de France.*

Bibliography

I gain an immense amount of pleasure from my books and can always justify the addition of another volume to the collection! I have referred to the following for information and inspiration.

MEDIEVAL FLORA

Bahouth, Candace. *Medieval Needlepoint*. Conran Octopus, London, 1993.

Bilimoff, Michèle. *Promenade dans des Jardins Disparus*. Éditions Ouest-France, Rennes, 2001.

Bologna, Guilia. *Illuminated Manuscripts*. Thames & Hudson, London, 1988.

Cowley, Des & Williamson, Clare. *The World of the Book*. The Miegunyah Press, Melbourne, 2007.

Fisher, Celia. *Flowers in Medieval Manuscripts*. The British Library, London, 2004.

Fisher, Celia. *The Medieval Flower Book*. The British Library, London, 2007.

Gordon, Lesley. *A Country Herbal*. Webb & Bower, Exeter, Devon, 1980.

Hobhouse, Penelope. *Plants in Garden History*. Pavilion Books, London, 1992.

Innes, Miranda & Perry, Clay. *Medieval Flowers*. Kyle Cathie Ltd, London, 1997.

Jones, Owen. *Decorative Ornament*. Tess Press, New York, 2006.

Johnston, Ann. *The Mediæval Folk in Painting*. Sally Milner Publishing, Australia, 1994.

Kingsbury, Noël. *The Wild Flower Garden*. Conran Octopus, London, 1994.

Landsberg, Sylvia. *The Medieval Garden*. British Museum Press, London, 1995.

Martin, W. Keble. *The Concise British Flora in Colour*. Ebury Press, London, 1965.

Tymms, W. & Wyatt, M. *The Art of Illuminating*. Wordsworth Editions, London, 1987.

Urquhart, F.A. *Introducing the Insect*. F. Warne & Co., London, 1965.

Vickery, Roy. *Oxford Dictionary of Plant-Lore*. Oxford University Press, Oxford, 1995.

Voronova, T. & Sterligov, A. *Western European Illuminated Manuscripts*. Chrysalis Books, London, 2003.

Zahradnik, Jiri. *The Illustrated Book of Insects*. Treasure Press, London, 1991.

Embroidery

Christie, Grace. *Samplers and Stitches*. Batsford, London, 1920.

Enthoven, Jacqueline. *The Stitches of Creative Embroidery*. Schiffer, USA, 1987.

Thomas, Mary. *Dictionary of Embroidery Stitches*, Hodder & Stoughton, London, 1934.

Stumpwork

Nicholas, Jane. *Stumpwork Embroidery: A Collection of Fruits, Flowers, Insects*. Sally Milner Publishing, Australia, 1995.

Nicholas, Jane. *Stumpwork Embroidery: Designs and Projects*. Sally Milner Publishing, Australia, 1998.

Nicholas, Jane. *Stumpwork Dragonflies*. Sally Milner Publishing, Australia, 2000.

Nicholas, Jane. *Stumpwork, Goldwork & Surface Embroidery Beetle Collection*. Sally Milner Publishing, Australia, 2004.

Nicholas, Jane. *The Complete Book of Stumpwork Embroidery*. Sally Milner Publishing, Australia, 2005.

Picture Credits

Page 8. Pomegranates illumination from *Grandes Heures d'Anne de Bretagne*, Ms Latin 9474, Folio 120, Bibliothèque nationale de France.

Page 11. Roses and Lilies illumination from *Grandes Heures d'Anne de Bretagne*, Ms Latin 9474, Folio 27, Bibliothèque nationale de France.

Page 14. Star of Bethlehem illumination from *Grandes Heures d'Anne de Bretagne*, Ms Latin 9474, Folio 128, Bibliothèque nationale de France.

Page 15. Grapes and snail illumination detail from *Grandes Heures d'Anne de Bretagne*, Ms Latin 9474, Folio 156, Bibliothèque nationale de France.

Page 20. Image of corncockle courtesy of Dr Chris Gibson.

Page 24. Cornockle illumination detail from *Grandes Heures d'Anne de Bretagne*, Ms Latin 9474, Folio 38, Bibliothèque nationale de France.

Page 36. Photo Broad bodied dragonfly, http://commons. wikimedia.org/wiki/File: Yellow_Dragonfly_bgiu.jpg available under the terms of the GNU Free Documentation License, Version 1.2.

Page 41. Photo Blue beetle courtesy http://www.entomart.be/

Page 43. Photo Ladybird, Hamed Saber, Wikimedia Commons.

Page 47. Photo courtesy of sannse, http://en.wikipedia.org/ wiki/User:Sannse

Page 50. Herb Robert illumination detail from *Grandes Heures d'Anne de Bretagne*, Ms Latin 9474, Folio 44, Bibliothèque nationale de France.

Page 67. Photo Blue butterfly courtesy http://www.entomart. be/

Page 71. Photo green caterpillar, http://commons.wikimedia. org/wiki/File:Lagarta2.jpg available under the terms of the GNU Free Documentation License, Version 1.2

Page 75. Photo Star of Bethlehem, Onderwijsgek, licensed under the Creative Commons Attribution-ShareAlike 2.5 Netherlands License.

Page 78. Star of Bethlehem illumination detail from *Grandes Heures d'Anne de Bretagne*, Ms Latin 9474, Folio 128, Bibliothèque nationale de France.

Page 91. Photo Mining bee, Fritz Geller-Grimm, licensed under the Creative Commons Attribution ShareAlike 3.0 License.

Page 94. Photo Great green grasshopper, http://commons. wikimedia.org/wiki/File: Tettigonia_viridissima3.jpg available under the terms of the GNU Free Documentation License, Version 1.2

Page 101. Tansy illumination from *Grandes Heures d'Anne de Bretagne*, Ms Latin 9474, Folio 60v, Bibliothèque nationale de France.

Page 102. Photo Tansy, Georg Slickers, licensed under the Creative Commons Attribution ShareAlike 2.5 License.

Page 106. Tansy illumination detail from *Grandes Heures d'Anne de Bretagne*, Ms Latin 9474, Folio 60v, Bibliothèque nationale de France.

Page 115. Photo Striped bug, Luis Miguel Bugallo Sánchez, licensed under the terms of the GNU Free Documentation license, Version 1.2.

Page 120. Photo Azure damselfly, Soebe, licensed under the terms of the GNU Free Documentation license, Version 1.2.

Page 125. Photo Venus' Looking Glass, Thomas Meyer, Günzburg, licensed under the terms of the GNU Free Documentation license, Version 1.2.

Page 128. Venus' Looking Glass illumination detail from *Grandes Heures d'Anne de Bretagne*, Ms Latin 9474, Folio 89, Bibliothèque nationale de France.

Page 143. Photo Buff-tailed bumblebee, Alvesgaspar, licensed under the terms of the GNU Free Documentation license, Version 1.2.

Page 146. Photo Large copper butterfly, Jeffdelonge, licensed under the terms of the GNU Free Documentation license, Version 1.2.

Page 152. *The Grammar of Ornament* by Owen Jones, Plate LXXIII, courtesy University of Wisconsin Digital Collections.

Page 153. *The Grammar of Ornament* by Owen Jones, detail from Plate LXXI, courtesy University of Wisconsin Digital Collections.

Page 154. *The Grammar of Ornament* by Owen Jones, Plate LXVII*, courtesy University of Wisconsin Digital Collections.

Page 155. Photo Bittersweet, http://en.wikipedia.org/wiki/File:SolanumDulcamara-flower-sm.jpg#file , licensed under the terms of the GNU Free Documentation license, Version 1.2.

Page 157. Bittersweet and butterflies illumination from *Grandes Heures d'Anne de Bretagne*, Ms Latin 9474, Folio 59, Bibliothèque nationale de France.

Page 170. Photo Hoverfly, Alvesgaspar, licensed under the terms of the GNU Free Documentation license, Version 1.2.

Page 174. Photo Scarce copper butterfly, Geiserich77, licensed under the terms of the GNU Free Documentation license, Version 1.2.

Page 183. Photo Snowdrops, Tocekas, licensed under the terms of the GNU Free Documentation license, Version 1.2.

Page 185. Snowdrop illumination from *Grandes Heures d'Anne de Bretagne*, Ms Latin 9474, Folio 22, Bibliothèque nationale de France.

Page 193. Photo Snowdrop, André Karwath, licensed under the Creative Commons Attribution ShareAlike 2.5 License.

Page 214. Photo Cranefly, Alvesgaspar, licensed under the terms of the GNU Free Documentation license, Version 1.2.

Page 218. Photo Scarlet tiger moth, Konrad Lackerbeck, licensed under the Creative Commons Attribution 3.0 Unported.

Page 225. Photo Wild pea, Hans Hillewaert, licensed under the Creative Commons Attribution ShareAlike 3.0 License.

Page 227. Wild pea illumination from *Grandes Heures d'Anne de Bretagne*, Ms Latin 9474, Folio 48, Bibliothèque nationale de France.

Page 231. Photo *Lathyrus sylvestris*, Kristian Peters, licensed under the terms of the GNU Free Documentation license, Version 1.2.

Page 246. Photo Longhorn moth, Luc Viatour, licensed under the terms of the GNU Free Documentation license, Version 1.2.

Page 252. *The Grammar of Ornament* by Owen Jones, Plate LXXI, courtesy University of Wisconsin Digital Collections.

Page 253. *The Grammar of Ornament* by Owen Jones, detail from Plate LXXIII, courtesy University of Wisconsin Digital Collections.

Page 280. Grapes and snail illumination from *Grandes Heures d'Anne de Bretagne*, Ms Latin 9474, Folio 156, Bibliothèque nationale de France.

Acknowledgements

I would like to extend my gratitude to all those people who continue to share their passion for stumpwork with me. Whether by correspondence or in class, your enthusiasm continues to be an inspiration.

Researching the material for this book has been a long and fascinating journey. A big thank you to Gay Eaton and Helen Packer for introducing me to Michèle Bilimoff's delightful and informative book, *Promenade dans des JardinsDisparus*. I am indebted to Victoria Bouchard for her assistance in translating large sections of *Promenade* (very challenging for my schoolgirl French!).

Along the way I have received unfailing encouragement and support from my family—John, Katie, David, Joanna and Lynn. Special thanks to John for his patience and attention to detail when making all those kits!

Sincere thanks to my dear 'sewing friends' for their companionship and the opportunity to share ideas and cherished stitching time.

Finally, to all those involved in the production of this book at Sally Milner Publishing—your expertise, and belief in my work, is sincerely appreciated.

JANE NICHOLAS 2009

Stumpwork Supplies and Kit Information

The threads, beads and needlework products referred to in this book are available from *Jane Nicholas Embroidery* and specialist needlework shops.

A mail order service is offered by *Jane Nicholas Embroidery*. Visit the website and view the entire range of stumpwork kits, books and embroidery supplies including wires, fabrics, leather, beads, hoops, needles and scissors. Thread ranges include Au Ver à Soie, Cifonda, chenille, DMC, Kreinik, Madeira and YLI, and goldwork supplies. Framecraft brooches, boxes and paper-weights are stocked for finishing. A mail order catalogue is available on request.

Jane Nicholas Embroidery
PO Box 300
Bowral NSW 2576
AUSTRALIA
Telephone: +61 2 4861 1175
Email: jane@janenicholas.com
Web: www.janenicholas.com

TANACETUM
VULGARE

SPECULARIA
HYBRIDA

RO